W9-AQC-799

Czechoslovakia
The Party
and the People

Czechoslovakia
The Party and the People

Andrew Oxley
Alex Pravda
Andrew Ritchie

St. Martin's Press New York

Library of Congress Catalog Card Number: 72-93032

First published in the United States of America in 1973

Printed in Great Britain

AFFILIATED PUBLISHERS: Macmillan & Company, Limited,
London – also at Bombay, Calcutta, Madras and Melbourne – The
Macmillan Company of Canada, Limited, Toronto

Contents

Preface

The selection of articles and statements which we have included in *The Party and the People* does not pretend to be a history of the Czechoslovak revival process, but a journey, in the words of the people involved, through the process. There have been a great many books about the Prague Spring and the occupation of Czechoslovakia, but none so far has attempted to give a representative selection of the ideas put forward during the internal development in Czechoslovakia. We have preferred to let the writers, journalists, politicians and workers of the revival period speak for themselves.

We have arranged the articles and speeches into a thematic order. This meant dividing up some of the more important longer articles, although we have avoided splitting or abbreviating the articles too much, since that would distort their meaning.

We have concentrated on making our translations as readable as we could rather than making them as literal as possible. If some of the Communist Party statements read in a dry way, it is because they are like that in the original.

For reasons which we have explained elsewhere, the period we cover is limited to January to August 1968, with a few exceptions. We have not therefore covered the international situation in detail, and we have avoided covering in any great depth the questions of the economy and of the Slovak nation. The rest is an attempt to trace the development of a period of great social and political flux, and to outline the main forces and conflicts and the polarization of opinion created by the revival process.

Andrew Oxley
Alex Pravda
Andrew Ritchie

September 1972

Introduction

A lot has been written *about* 1968. The implications of the revival process have been systematically analysed in the world's press. This selection of articles, speeches and ideas is intended to give an idea of what was said, what happened and what was important in Czechoslovakia in 1968 until 21 August, the day of the invasion. The ideas and events which made the Soviet Union consider a Warsaw Pact invasion necessary have inevitably become distorted by this spectacular reaction to them.

The Czechoslovak 'experiment' to create something the world had never seen, to realize a 'socialism with a human face', 'a quiet revolution without tanks or barricades', these and other clichéd descriptions filled the world's press in 1968, and countless books since. The 'experiment' is talked about as though all that needed to be done was to apply the magic formula. If the 'experiment' had succeeded, it is sometimes suggested, the whole world might have felt the impact of its new interpretation of Marxism–Leninism, and Czechoslovakia might have become a prototype for the future development of both socialist and capitalist countries. The New Left in western Europe was enthusiastic and optimistic, hoping that the old oppressive, bureaucratic socialism might be liquidated and a new model developed which might validate their own critique of capitalist society. And 'reactionary' journalistic circles greeted this new socialist direction with the appropriate anti-communist noises.

On March 25 1968, one could read in the *Guardian* that:

> Czechoslovakia's peaceful revolution not only marks a new stage in the development of Communism, but it may alter the political shape of the world, if the powers in both East and West see their opportunity and take it.

The actual process inside Czechoslovakia was far more complex. As will be seen from the documents themselves and the introductions, the whole period was still dominated by *Realpolitik*, the discussion was free and wide-ranging, but the concrete administrative realization of actual changes in society was far more limited. And it is this discussion, this 'unfinished dialogue', that we are concerned with and which is important to us. It survives tanks and power politics. The Czechoslovak contribution to the intriguing development of socialism was the surprisingly rational atmosphere which made possible a comparatively calm discussion between the official Party leadership and the people, and between the communist and non-communist intelligentsia. Issues could be thrashed out on paper, and the freedom of the discussion was one of the most exciting and characteristic features of the whole process. Nor was 1968 primarily motivated by the need for economic changes, though these were very strongly present, and delved far deeper than for instance the revolt in Poland in December 1970. The moral and national crisis, which we talk about more fully in the introductions to the sections on 'Our Present Crisis' and 'The Past Re-examined', was the impulse behind 1968, the sense of not having 'gained a place on the world's stage' (Vaculík).

The short historical summary of Czechoslovakia which is usually given at this stage can be left out, since the speeches which Vaculík and Kundera delivered at the Fourth Congress of Czechoslovak Writers probably can't be bettered (see 'Our Present Crisis'). Yet there are several vital features of the beginnings of the revival process which should be noted.

The long-oppressed Czechs and Slovaks had always valued their intellectual leaders very highly, and these intellectuals participated actively in politics, the best among them considering themselves to be the 'conscience of the nation', a role which a few of them did their best to fulfil in the dark twenty years between 1948 and 1968. A second essential fact is that the pre-war Republic had been highly industrialized, and, with all the faults endemic to bourgeois democracy, was a democratic, parliamentary system, which managed to resist the central European tendencies towards dictatorship. The Communist Party of Czechoslovakia in 1946 won one third of the votes in the last free election to be held, and when it manoeuvred its way into power in 1948, helped by the international 'carve up', by its own organizational abilities and the opposition's lack of ability, a very large part of the population supported the new government.

Ludvík Vaculík's verdict on the twenty years of Party rule is in no way an exaggeration of the reality: 'In twenty years in our country not one human problem has been solved . . .' Once the old excuses about the tension of the international situation and the necessity of constant vigil against imperialist subversion had disappeared, once it had been admitted that the state of affairs was 'normal', the full inefficiency of the ludicrously over-centralized, bureaucratized system was revealed. Since 1956, when the Twentieth Congress of the Communist Party of the Soviet Union had caused a wave of revolt throughout the communist satellites, Novotný had resisted the successive waves of criticism from the writers on a broad front of civil liberties, intellectual freedom and democracy. From the late fifties, the increasingly disastrous state of the economy, for which the leadership was hard-pressed to find favourable comparisons in the pre-war figures, and which culminated in an unprecedented crisis in 1963, had given rise to decentralizing proposals. These ideas, following Soviet leads, culminated in the elaboration of the New Economic System, or Model, by a team led by Professor Ota Šik. The System was accepted officially in 1965, and introduced at the beginning of 1967.

The basic ideas of the New Economic System were to make efficiency, and economic and market criteria, and not the whim of the central planners, the determining factor in the economy. The plan combined the market economy and a decentralization of economic decision-making with a retention of a good deal of central planning. Even if it was still restricted to the micro-economic sphere, the direction of the New Economic System was towards the breaking-up of the centralist conception of organization, towards the dismantling of the Stalinist monopoly control in which only the orders of the Party leadership counted, and in which economic criteria, consumer production and actual demand were subordinate to extensive, heavy industrial growth. What was important about the introduction of the New Economic System, even if the measures which were actually taken were not up to the original intentions of Šik and his team, was that it made an ideological and practical breach in the wall of Novotný's neo-Stalinist model.

Novotný hoped that changes in the economic sphere, the admission in just one sector that the iron, centralized system had failed, could be isolated from the all-important political sphere. Work was begun in 1967, however, by a team of the Czechoslovak Academy of Sciences on an analysis of the best future political system. Led by Zdeněk Mlynář, they came to the conclusion that some variation of a pluralist system must inevitably be introduced which would correspond to the differentiation of interests which existed in a socialist society.[1] The constitution of 1960 had declared that Czechoslovakia had reached a stage where the conflicts between class interests were no longer dominant, and the Thirteenth Party Congress (1966) had announced that the years since the Twelfth Congress in 1962 had seen the 'liquidation of class antagonism', though both these statements contrasted strangely with the fact that whenever a pretext was needed, the class threat was always introduced to keep either the workers or the intellectuals in order.

The ideas which emerged during 1968 from the official line about political reform were those which had been formulated in the last years of Novotný's rule. All that prevented them being put into action at that time was the increasingly intensive alternation of 'relaxation' and subsequent 'reaction'.

The 'crisis' of 1967 was in many respects only a more extreme expression of the outbursts of the intellectuals, in 1956 and 1963 in particular, against the moral, political and economic bankruptcy of the outdated régime. Articles demanding the rectification of the 'deformations', the rehabilitation of the victims and of history in general managed to slip through the spasmodic, but tough, net of censorship and control of the mass media. The demands made by the writers at the Fourth Congress were not new: they had appeared since 1956 in various shapes and forms, and were the traditional themes of any protest against a totalitarian régime, socialist or fascist. What made this 'crisis' different was that it coincided with another severe 'crisis' within the Party and in the economy; without this fact, the protests of the writers would

1. See Mlynář, 'Towards a democratic political organization of society' in 'On the Theme of Opposition'.

probably have not had any great impact on Novotný's position of power.

Opposition within the Party itself had always existed; after 1963, the methods of dealing with it had become less drastic, and Novotný's tactics had become increasingly inconsistent. Barák, the Minister of the Interior and a close friend of the First Secretary and President (Novotný had held this office also since 1957), had been arrested in 1962 on trumped-up charges and given a fifteen-year sentence because he had represented a threat to Novotný's dictatorship. And more significantly, in the Slovak crisis of 1963, Bacílek and Široký[2] had both been sacrificed in order to appease the critics of the régime. During these years there had been an influx of younger men, more susceptible to progressive ideas, who had been appointed to high position. Dubček, despite Novotný's efforts, became and remained first secretary of the Slovak Communist Party; Lenárt became prime minister instead of Široký. Many people hoped that these new post-Stalinist men, together with the rehabilitated politicians who were slowly returning to prominence and the slowly emerging victims of the 'deformations' (as all the purges and the measures connected with the cult of the personality and the early fifties were euphemistically called), could form the kernel of a progressive faction within the Party. Even though they did show signs of more moderation and humanity than the old guard, without the constantly degenerating state of the Party itself and the clumsy mishandling and wrong tactics of Novotný, these 'new men' would not by themselves have overthrown the old leader. This observation is vital for a proper understanding of the sort of political reformer that Dubček was, filling a platform created for him more by the weakness of the old leadership than by the strength and conviction of his own attitudes.

It was Novotný himself who contributed to his own downfall more than anyone else. 1967 was a particularly hard year, especially in contrast to the relaxation of late 1966 and early 1967, when many people regarded Czechoslovakia as 'the most liberal country of the socialist camp'. The outbursts of the writers at their Congress

2. Karol Bacílek: Minister of National Security 1953, First Secretary of the Slovak Communist Party 1953–63, replaced by Dubček. Viliam Široký, another Slovak, Prime Minister 1953–63, replaced by Lenárt.

were rewarded by the expulsion from the Party of the most outspoken, Vaculík, Liehm and Klíma; the elections of the Writers' Union were reorganized by the Party, and their weekly newspaper, *Literární Noviny*, was forcibly taken over by the Ministry of Culture. At the October plenum of the Central Committee of the Communist Party, Dubček's reasoned criticisms of the Party's position and his tempered recommendations were countered not with arguments, but with accusations of 'bourgeois nationalism'. Novotný had not learned the lesson of 1963: he still persisted in aligning the powerful nationalism of the Slovaks against himself, and even such conservative apparatchiks as Bil'ak were provoked into attacking the person of the First Secretary. Wild and rather desperate talk about using Polish methods of clearing out the opposition frightened the stolid and cautious conservative majority in the Central Committee, and it was the vote of Jiří Hendrych, Novotný's right hand man, which divided the Praesidium five–five on the issue of the separation of the functions of first secretary and president. Fears of being turned into another Barák are alleged finally to have made up Hendrych's mind.

The victory for the anti-Novotný faction was not a victory based on any solid programme of reform. The main unifying bond was dislike of Novotný himself together with the growing awareness that the Party's position really was disastrous. Its position had been serious for many years; the novelty was that now reports were made to the Central Committee which showed how serious it was, and people such as Šik, Smrkovský, Špaček and Dubček sat in the Central Committee and felt strongly enough to get up and draw the obvious conclusions from the reports about low attendance at Party meetings, passivity and the demand for change.

Novotný's withdrawal from the more enlightened policies and outlook of the Thirteenth Party Congress alienated the more progressive members of the *apparat*, while his past concessions to the decentralizing concepts of the New Economic System, with their emphasis on efficiency and real qualifications, frightened those unqualified, inefficient functionaries who still occupied the best jobs in the country. The Soviet support which Novotný had commanded while Khrushchev had been in power had disappeared with him, and Brezhnev showed that he would not exert any pressure on the Czechoslovak Party to save Novotný.

He did come to Prague at Novotný's request on 8 December, but merely declared: 'Comrades, it is your own affair' (as reported by Smrkovský at the Congress Palace, 20 March 1968).

Dubček's election to the post of first secretary was indicative of the fragile nature of the victory. No one had any strong protest against the Slovak leader, whereas men like Smrkovský or Šik would have been wholly unacceptable. Šik's analysis at the December plenum was coolly received. Dubček seems to have been elected as much for his moderation and lack of militancy as for the fact that he was acceptable to all factions. His Slovak and Soviet loyalty, however, was in no doubt. His election might have been taken as an example of the levelling of personality which critics of the old political system complained so strongly about. The communiqué issued after the 5 January changeover betrayed almost no indication of impending reform or even of any immediate changes. Continuity with the line of the Thirteenth Party Congress was emphasized. The public had not expected the end of Novotný's long rule to come so suddenly, although there had been rumours of a rift in the Praesidium and the Central Committee circulating for some time in better-informed Prague circles.

Once again, it was Novotný himself who was the direct cause of the opposition success. In December an attempt had been made to prevent Novotný's overthrow, engineered mainly by Mamula, the head of the notorious Eighth department of the Central Committee, in charge of the Army and of Security, with the help of General Šejna. Their aim was to use the moral and physical force of the Army and arrest the leaders of the 'opposition' group. This abortive plot put the victors of January on their guard against attempts by the defeated faction to persuade the workers that the changes were in fact a conspiracy of the wicked economists, nationalist Slovaks and pernicious intellectuals against the working class.

To refute the idea that the change was just a coup in the highest Party echelons, Smrkovský, Šik, Špaček, Borůvka and others fed interviews and information to the press, radio and television, which clarified the whole situation for the general public. The division of the offices of the first secretary of the Communist Party and the presidency was to be the beginning of a strict implementation of a division between Party and state throughout the administration.

Encouraged by this outspokenness from the Party, journalists began to write more openly, and to ask questions about subjects which had previously been regarded as taboo. Censorship was applied much less stringently from mid February onwards, and by the time the official declaration about the Central Publications Board was made in early March, public discussion, particularly on the radio and television and in the press, had caught up with the anti-Novotný group.

Alexander Dubček gave his first public speech indicating a change of tone on the anniversary of the February Communist takeover:

> We cannot preserve past values by constantly defending them, but above all by looking new problems straight in the face, by solving them in a new creative way, and in a way demanded by the present situation. I am not oversimplifying if I say that today, more than ever before, it is a matter not of basing our policy on 'the struggle against' but on 'the struggle for . . .'

And the following day he appealed in an unusually warm and genuine way to all the people, and not, as was customary, just to Party members, leaving out the citizens as second best.

Great hopes were expressed at the beginning of March. The writers' chairman, Eduard Goldstücker, hoped that all shared his 'blissful awareness' of the unique chance given to them by history 'to attempt for the first time to join socialism and freedom, which belong inextricably together, in a real marriage'.

The new leadership concentrated on the problem of clearing the conservative domination of the *apparat*, and encouraged the lower Party organizations to follow the example set by the plenum itself and start to change their working methods. From now on, the old artificial unity in the Party was to be a thing of the past, the power organs were to play a far more important role in the making of Party policy than before, the dictatorship of the Praesidium or of an internal group in the highest Party organs was to end, and the Party was to be a truly democratic one. The practical manifestation of this intra-Party democracy was the removal of those functionaries who were closely linked with the old command system and who could not reform their ways. In many ways, the progressives 'used' the pressure of public opinion to force these people out of their positions, and at last the campaign which had the President as its ultimate target succeeded in making Novotný abdicate on 22 March.

It was during March that the most spontaneous activity of the whole period occurred. In the process of attacking the worst of the old bosses, criticism of the whole system which they represented began to appear. With the relaxation of the controls, and the melting away of the official condemnation, which had continued for twenty years, of all views which did not coincide with the current Party line, all the pent-up grievances emerged. Ideas which had been forming in previous years were now openly expressed. It was admitted that there was a state of crisis not just in the Party but in Czechoslovak society as a whole, if not within socialist society throughout the Soviet bloc. Inevitably, analysis of Czechoslovakia's past began to absorb perhaps too much time and energy. What had brought about and maintained the neo-Stalinist concept, what had caused Czechoslovakia to experience the longest and most brutal political trials in post-war Europe: such questions were posed insistently. But the slate had to be wiped clean for moral as well as for practical reasons. (See the Introduction to 'The Past Re-examined' and Hamšík's article in that section.)

Mass meetings were organized at which panels of Party and extra-Party reformers and 'new men' answered the questions put to them by predominantly student audiences. Party speakers warned everybody about being responsible, and held over them the often-repeated argument that no pretext should be given to the conservatives to demand that controls and censorship should be reimposed. Nothing remained taboo at these communal psychotherapy sessions, which one Czech journalist described as 'a national binge'. The people were drunk with their new-found freedom, but the situation was very fluid: no definite policies had been announced. The one achievement, and it remained the most spectacular achievement of the whole of 1968, was the free discussion which had been encouraged by the Party. The old structure was laid open to attack.

The chairman of the Trade Unions, for instance, was dismissed, the old habits of merely carrying out instructions from the Party were condemned, and promises were made that in the future only the interests of the workers would be taken into consideration. This was all well and good, but what guarantees were there? And to make it worse, Karel Poláček, who was first and foremost a Party yes-man, was foisted on the unprotesting conservative Central Council of Trade Unions. The protests that followed from Prague workers were proof enough that a new situation had come into existence, but they were politely side-stepped.

A similar kind of 'half-way democracy', which was perfectly expressed in the term 'democratization' which was always being used in 1968 and had often been heard before, was shown by the appointment of a new government which contained the usual predominance of Party members, most of them holding important Party positions in addition to their state functions. Smrkovský was chairman of the National Assembly and a member of the Party Praesidium, Černík was the prime minister and also in the Praesidium; Kriegel was chairman of the National Front and a member of the Party Praesidium. Some people began to point out that in the light of the new principles the fact that the candidate of the Central Committee for the post of president was the only real candidate was undemocratic, and that the other people who had been proposed by other bodies outside the Party had given over their places to the official choice, General Svoboda.

In the midst of all the elation, doubts quickly appeared and grew about the permanence of these democratic ideas, about the likelihood of their ever really being effective and real. There were no guarantees, a complaint that can frequently be heard in our section on the workers. People began to realize that it was all very well talking about democracy, but it had to be guaranteed by legal and institutional reform. Dubček's encouraging words in mid March, at the height of the alliance against the Novotnýites, about the impossibilities of going on working in the same old ways and the generally praiseworthy quality of people's activity, were accompanied even at this early stage by cautionary remarks about the dangers of extremism.

Such apprehension was only reinforced by the April plenum, which laid down the policy that enough had been said and that it was time 'to pass from words to deeds'. Some people interpreted the use of this slogan as meaning that the Party was telling them to stop analyzing and questioning and to get to work, which made them suspicious of the Party's protecting itself, since they did not think at that stage that the analysis had yet gone deep enough. 'What the society that is being asked to pass from words to deeds is really being told is that from the moment laid down by the Party, words are unnecessary and harmful,' wrote one political commentator. They saw the process slowing down, and the fading of all the promises of early March, when, with the Šejna scandal and the golden opportunity to get rid of the conservatives, there had been no desire to regulate or control developments.

The long-heralded April Action Programme came as a disappointment, not because of what it contained, but because of what it omitted. Events had in fact developed much faster than the theories of men like Mlynář and the 'establishment reformers'; concern increased within the ranks of the new leadership about the possible uncontrolled nature of the 'revival', concern which grew as foreign pressure mounted, especially after the early May visit to Moscow. Internally their position was not successfully secured by attempts to persuade the compromised 'conservative' members of the Central Committee to see the light and to resign voluntarily. At the April plenum, Novotný tried to whitewash himself, and no counter-attack was made against him. At the May plenum, only a handful of conservatives acknowledged their own redundancy, and so Dubček finally had to accede to the demands voiced in April for the convening of an Extraordinary Congress of the Party at an early date. Only a Congress could elect a new Central Committee; one was set for September 1968. At the same plenum the increasingly authoritarian tone of the 'men of January' was expressed in harsher terms than at any time since January by Dubček, in his speech to the Central Committee. '... Anti-communist tendencies have intensified and there are certain elements which are trying to adopt more intense forms of activity,' said Dubček, warning that they constituted 'the main threat to the further development of the democratization process ...' At the same time he expressed his fears about the right-wing danger, consisting in 'conventional ways of thinking which survive, and in the persistence of bureaucratic methods and habits'. The balance, the attempt to please all sides at home and abroad, was typical of Dubček, but the stress he gave to the dangers of anti-socialist forces, and the hard line he took in support, for instance, of the People's Militia, the Party's 'private army', provoked a series of appeals and protests. It produced a polarization of opinion and the confrontation between the different viewpoints which culminated in the Two Thousand Words affair (see 'Two Thousand Words').

The Two Thousand Words, written by Ludvík Vaculík and signed by a whole host of leading Czechoslovak writers and intellectuals, is probably the most important single document of the revival process, more for the impact it had than for its actual profundity or originality. It was a provocative polemical call to action. It restated more forcefully many of the points about which the progressives had been expressing their concern since the March 'honeymoon'. It made the basic statement that the Communist Party deserved no thanks for having started the revival, since it was only they who had the organizational means to do it. It further stated that this 'initiative' of theirs was merely the beginning of the repayment of the immense debt that the Party owed the nation, and did not constitute a *carte blanche* for its policies over the next years or immunity from criticism calling for new methods and solutions.

The Two Thousand Words was a call to the whole of society to activate itself, and to make sure that no vestige of the old system should remain to disturb the progress of the revival. Many people had said that the conservatives, who still made up the mass of the Party hierarchy, should have been thrown out immediately after Dubček came to power, by means of strikes and personal demonstrations. By calling for their removal, in a calm, controlled and reasonable manner, which in fact showed the Party hierarchy's ineffectiveness, the Two Thousand Words made a direct challenge to the authority of the Party to control the revival at a pace which suited it. There was no longer any doubt that some sections of society were moving much faster and farther than others.

What was more, some Party organizations dared to contradict the official Praesidium condemnation of the Two Thousand Words, and the whole affair showed that the confidence which the new leadership had won for itself earlier on had drastically decreased. It was definitely on the defensive. Only the complaints and the pressure tactics of the Soviet Union quickly restored faith, this time on a national basis. The solidarity of the Czechs and Slovaks after the invasion has sometimes been assumed to indicate that society was moving forward with equal solidarity before the invasion, but the Two Thousand Words shows what immense rifts there were between communist and non-communist, between the Party and the people. Once the immediate danger following the Warsaw Pact letter had passed, the natural differentiation of opinion reappeared. After the huge patriotic display at the time of the Čierna talks (29 July–1 August), discontent was voiced about the dismissal of General Prchlík, who had spoken out against the inequalities in the countries of the Warsaw Pact. Official reaction to the continuation of a petition movement, which had been sanctioned when it had supported the Czechoslovak delegation at Čierna, but was attacked by the government when it tried to get the People's Militia abolished, showed the ever-present differences between Party leadership and the nation.

The invasion, with which this book is not concerned, obliterated these differences and put a halt to the revival process. It stopped the free development and resolution of the conflicts which were going on in Czechoslovakia. Nothing was the same after the invasion; the nature of socialism, the case for the 'Czechoslovak road to socialism' was discussed in the light of a traumatically different reality. The history of post-invasion Czechoslovakia needs another book. Only Vaculík's Semily rejoinder, which we have included as a post-script, hints here at the 'consolidation process' which followed the invasion. The normal course of the Extraordinary Congress was interrupted, and a clandestine one held under siege conditions in a large factory in Prague[3] – a significant indication of exactly how much trust the Communist Party was able to put in its workers under this kind of international pressure. The new candidates to the Central Committee comprised only 25 per cent of the old complement, and the conservatives would have surely been excluded altogether if the revival had not been interrupted. Even the 'new men' of January, including Dubček himself, might have had to give way at the top of the

3. For a documentary record of the Congress see *The Secret Vysočany Congress*, ed. Jiří Pelikán, Allen Lane, 1971.

Party, and in a newly constituted National Front, to other politicians and other parties.

Intervention created unity between leaders and people as at a time of war, and disputes were forgotten in the face of the common enemy. A monologue, such as had existed for a certain time in the March days, was reintroduced for a time. Everybody rallied to the principles of the Action Programme, which had failed to capture the people's imagination before, but were now at least a basis on which to agree. Nationalism adopted democracy.

Such an adoption had dominated the situation in Slovakia throughout the pre-invasion period. Here democratization had already been in 1963 primarily a nationalist motivated movement. Quite early, long before the Prague Spring, the demand for a Federation, for independence from the centralist, exploiting and stifling control of Prague, came to dominate Slovak politics. It was generally agreed that the Federation should come first, and should only be subordinated to democratization if a choice had to be made between them: but some Slovak writers declared that there was no point in talking about which should take priority since a Slovak-centred bureaucratic government would be no better than one in Prague.

In spite of this, the most popular politicians in Slovakia were men like Husák and Novomeský, who stressed the importance of the demand for the Federation, and did not exactly show themselves to be the most ardent of democrats. The attitude of the Czechs to the whole problem of Slovak autonomy and the Federation was rather patronizing, as it had always been to the younger, smaller, not so well-educated and poorer sister nation, which only spurred the Slovaks on to consider that the Czechs were unrepentant for their 'oppression' in the past. Because of this situation, the most interesting and advanced ideas on the reform did not appear in Slovakia in 1968 as they had done in 1963 and after, and that is why they do not appear in this selection of documents.

Even within the Czech lands, that is Bohemia and Moravia, the situation varied a great deal. The degree of progressiveness seemed to decrease with the distance away from Prague. Most of the regional towns held their revival meetings, like the one that Vaculík describes, on the lines of those held in Prague in March,

April or even May. Often they were largely preoccupied with criticism, usually of a detailed and personal nature, and not concerned directly with the larger issues. After twenty years of enforced silence, dominated by the rule of all the 'little Novotnýs', it was obvious that it would take much longer than the few months available to relieve the provincial people particularly of all their grievances. Vaculík's 'Semily' shows the reality of the revival, the unspectacular nature of the transition in Czechoslovakia. It illustrates the good and the bad of the revival, the organized resentment, the pettiness, hesitancy and stupidity, as well as the patience and reasonableness. It took most of 1968, before the invasion, to remove the old leading Party secretaries, as the majority of them refused to admit their conservatism and professed their support for the new policies if possible before and more insistently than their new opponents. The opposition in the regions was often too frightened to air its views in an open forum; that, they thought, was all very well for fashionable Prague, and they restricted their protests to Semily-like meetings and slogans on the walls.

If the outlines of the fluctuations in the relationship between the Party leadership and the people seem to leave nothing very favourable to say about the Dubček team, then this has not been our intention. The difficulties which beset the new leadership from the moment of their first victory up until the invasion, on the domestic and particularly on the foreign front, do go a long way to explaining and excusing their hesitation and their reluctance to allow the development of the revival to get out of control. Dubček, the man and the politician, was cautious, orthodox, conventional and not very imaginative; unluckily for Czechoslovakia, a Party member first and a statesman second. But only such a personality could have emerged in the difficult December and January days; to have expected sudden new vision and a penetrating social and political imagination would be to demand the impossible from the Czechoslovak situation. The nature of Czechoslovakia's debasement as a nation and a people demanded that any analysis started from the most elementary realities, whether the analyst was a politician or a writer. One of the realities was the position of the Communist Party and the necessity of recognizing it. Beautiful theory did not attract the Czechs; they had had enough of it.

Because personalities play an all-important part in communist systems, paradoxically a more important one than in western democracies, we must examine the character of Dubček. His role in the long and difficult negotiations with the Russians after the invasion does not concern us here,[4] but his character was an equally vital factor even before 21 August.

The accounts of Dubček from western newspapers and books have nearly all over-idolized a man who never idolized or vaunted himself. The capitalist press loves a hero, and it made Dubček into one. In fact, he exhibited both the best and the worst of the revival process. His speech of acceptance showed the hesitancy, the essential modesty, of the new first secretary, characteristics which were in themselves refreshingly different from Novotný's. He never had any desire to impose his own personality on the Party, or indeed on anything. Although he had always been devoted to the Party, and remained devoted to it throughout, his ideas were influenced very profoundly by its failure to fulfil its true role, its failure to win the people's trust, to be a Party of the people, and not a political élite which used all the means available to modern dictatorship to enforce a 'dictatorship of the proletariat'. Dubček genuinely wanted to do what the people wanted, what the rank and file Party members wanted, and instead of starting to make speeches and immediate reorganizations, he spent an alleged sixteen hours a day in early February studying reports from all the various organizations.

Dubček's natural inclination was to try to see everybody's point of view: he tried to reconcile the differences within the leadership, and his middle-of-the-road speeches were aimed at uniting the widest possible front in support of the democratization process, at ensuring a course in which the process would be allowed to run its natural course without external interference. The threatening presence of the Soviet Union should always be taken into account whenever a criticism is made of Dubček's

4. For the best comment on Dubček in the 1968–9 period see the excellent book by Pavel Tigrid: *La chute irrésistible d'Alexander Dubček*, Calmann Levy, 1969; and especially for his pre-1968 life see William Shawcross, *Dubček*, Weidenfeld & Nicolson, 1970.

vacillation or willingness to compromise. And his behaviour after the invasion, as indeed the behaviour of the entire Czechoslovak people, was conditioned by this dread of moving to too extreme a position, the dread of a colonial nation. It is on this point that the New Left critique of Dubček's 'betrayal of the interests of the Czechoslovak working people' when he agreed to negotiate in Moscow, break down completely.[5]

Perhaps Dubček should have called the Extraordinary Congress earlier; perhaps he should have acted with more firmness when faced with the Soviet threat, for instance, by briskly moving all Czechoslovak troops from the western to the eastern frontiers of his country; perhaps he should have taken the people of Czechoslovakia into his confidence more and have been more open with them right from the start about the difficulties he could expect from their Soviet allies. But if Dubček had done all this, if he had not defended the 'thousands of honest and hard-working communist functionaries' from what were sometimes called indiscriminate attacks, and tried to be reasonable and patient in his arguments against the unreasonable demands of the Soviet Union, he would no longer have been Dubček, just as a more decisive, resolute and extreme revival would have had little to do either with the character of the Czechoslovak people or with the reality of their political and historical position. There was no alternative course of action which he could have taken which might definitely have prevented the Soviet intervention; it was always a possibility, and would have been so under any other leader, whoever he had been.

Dubček may have been a poor judge of people: he supported Švestka, the editor-in-chief of *Rudé Právo*, against the protests of his staff, and even allowed him to be promoted to the Praesidium; he is said to have thought a lot of Šalgovič, who was put in charge of the secret police and promptly prepared the ground for the invasion. He was too ready to believe in people's good qualities. On the other hand, this belief in people was in stark contrast to the distrust of the Soviet leaders and of the old Czech leader towards the masses. Dubček's humanity was a vital part of the moral regeneration which Czechoslovakia so badly needed. He

5. See Hans Jurgen Krahl: 'Czechoslovakia, the Dialectic of the Reforms', *New Left Review*, No. 53, January–February 1969.

refused early on to sack the old guard from their positions, because this would have been too reminiscent of the old methods. His sincerity and the subordination of his own survival in power to the principles in which he believed established a set of values unique among Communist Party secretaries.

Smrkovský, on the other hand, stood out as the epitome of the old, honest but tough Party leader. Along with Husák he represented the strong war-time communist who placed discipline above democracy if that choice ever arose. Smrkovský gained an enormous following among the people, but this was threatened when he began to toughen his internal policy. Dubček stayed a far more consistent leader in the popularity stakes published in the numerous public opinion surveys, a typical feature of the reasonable, scientific way in which politics were regarded during 1968. Smrkovský, even if he believed firmly that he knew what was good for the people, and believed that only the Party could lead the nation to this general bliss, did constantly defend the journalists against conservative attacks, and he had a kind of faith that they would anyhow support the Party policy because it was the only solution to the country's problems. He did appear to be slightly less attractive because he emphasized action rather than words all the time, and a lot of people interpreted this in the context of 1968 as an attempt to dictate once again to them what they should do and think, and an unwillingness to allow them to think for themselves and act accordingly.

Words, however, emerged as the most valuable legacy of 1968; the Czechoslovak people were also able to gain the conviction that they finally knew who their friends were, and could no longer have any lingering doubts about the system which they had been trying to change. A great melting pot, a vast discussion group had been held, and a willingness to change society had been apparent. A common sense of dissatisfaction had been aired and shared in public. Moral indignation had become too strong to be contained. There were comparatively few positive achievements. August was to catch most administrative measures in the planning stage. Preliminary censorship was abolished; a law was passed to speed up the rehabilitation of the victims of all the 'deformations', and bodies were established to find out who was to blame for them. The powers of the Security Police, the Action Programme declared, were to be severely restricted, tapping and buggings were to be stopped, but in practice neither of these measures were carried out thoroughly, despite the great efforts of the Minister of the Interior, Josef Pavel. Measures were taken to make travelling abroad easier, and although a great deal was said about revising the laws of assembly and association, nothing was put on the statute book before the invasion. Little was achieved in the best-prepared field, the economy: the ministries were reorganized, an economic council erected, and long and frequent speeches made about the need to complete the introduction of the New Economic System, but the political system was so unstable most of the time, and the wage-demands of the workers threatened to place such a strain on the economy, that no unpopular or unstabilizing reforms, such as the closing down of inefficient plants, or drastic de-centralizing action, were attempted. Workers' councils were set up 'from above' on an experimental basis, while workers' committees for the defence of the press arose from the factories.

Nevertheless, the need for action on a decisive scale grew very urgent, and paradoxically a movement which had started out partially motivated by the need to bring political conditions into line with the economy, in order to make it possible to carry out economic reforms, ended up in a situation where the political reforms needed the reassuring prospect of economic prosperity and stability. Workers' councils were set up – but had not worked out any detailed organizational plans, other than those suggested by Šik, before the invasion. They were planned to operate on the basis of the co-management of workers and the technical intelligentsia in the running of the enterprises. The acceleration of reform was the intention of the workers' committees for the defence of the freedom of the press, ultra-progressive groups in the context of 1968 and the general hesitancy of workers. These might have become the basis for separate workers' interest groups, or become absorbed into the workers' councils (see 'What About the Workers?').

The greatest changes in 1968 were negative ones. The old centralized institutions began to disintegrate; what was called 'anarchy' after the invasion began to offer the basis for a new social order. The Czechoslovak Union of Youth fell apart early on, and a new organization was set up by the students. In the trade union movement there was the usual tendency to try to reduce the control of the central bodies over the whole movement: many amalgamated unions demanded and got their own separate unions; the basic organizations took far more active decision-making roles into their own hands; and the engine-drivers went so far as to defy the prohibitions of their union and Party oligarchy and form their own break-away independent union. New clubs and organizations sprang up, of which K231 and KAN, the clubs for former political prisoners and for 'committed non-Party people' respectively, were by far the most important.[6]

In the rest of the organization-ridden structure of society, concern was centred on replacing the old team with the new men, on getting rid of the rigid bonds of the centralized hierarchy. Every society or organization, from the trade unions to the Society of Puppeteers, wanted to undergo its own revival process.

The non-communist parties changed their leaders and grew in size and strength. The churches made an attempt to assert their rights, but in general these formally established front organizations, which had served for so long as withered fig-leaves for the dictatorship of the Communist Party, were slow in gaining the confidence of their former and potential new members.

All this 'de-organization' of society was free from the disruption and the feeling of upheaval which had characterized the events of 1956 in Poland and Hungary. In the countryside there was not one instance of the dissolution of a cooperative farm, although the methods which had been used to create these farms would have justified more than the mildly voiced demand for compensation; and the agricultural workers made little protest when their new 'social interest organization' was given to them from above, in a way which did not coincide with their wishes.

No organized anti-socialist or even anti-communist force appeared in Czechoslovakia, in contrast to the events of 1956. The Czechoslovaks were quite justified when they pleaded this cause to the unbelieving Soviet Politburo. KAN and K231 were the only potentially solid platforms for such an opposition, and

6. For the role of these two clubs see the introductory section to 'On the Theme of Opposition'.

the Social Democrats were still embryonic at the time of the invasion. Even if these might have become the starting point for the formation of a socialist faction, disagreeing with the Party on the issue of its 'leading role', hardly anyone in Czechoslovakia envisaged a return to the capitalist system. Almost everybody wanted democracy, keeping the fundamental principles of the common ownership of the means of production.

Democracy and socialism were the central points, the magic combination behind the whole process. It was a movement to establish what has come to be known as 'socialism with a human face', or as it was called much more often in the pre-invasion period, democratic socialism. The reintroduction of such 'bourgeois' values as humanism and freedom of the individual was certainly a revolution in terms of Novotnýite neo-Stalinist ideas. Sviták wrote in February 1967, in a speech which he did not deliver but which was published in *Student*, 20 March 1968, that, 'Democracy without socialism and humanism is as absurd as socialism without democracy and humanism. And humanism without both of these parts is an empty idealistic phrase.'

In spite of the fact that the 'experiment' failed, there is no reason to reject the significance of the events. The Party's 'decision' to allow freedom of speech, free discussion and criticism, to stipulate that no other means except argument and persuasion with better ideas and better examples should be used against political opponents, and the Party's near adherence to its new principles in the pre-invasion period: these were a unique advance in the thinking and, above all, practice of a Communist Party in power. The change in the concept and especially practice of the Party's leading role – 'The Party cannot impose its authority, but this must be won again and again by Party activity. It cannot enforce its line by means of directives but by the work of its members, by the truthfulness of its ideals' (The Action Programme) – was a revolutionary one, which underlay the ideas of the whole of the revival.

Here lies the real heart of the reform of 1968. Freedom of speech was a remarkable phenomenon for a country in the Soviet bloc, but only the means to an end. As was often repeated during 1968, there was no guarantee, unless guarantees were introduced, that the democratization would last. There had to be some new legal authorization for the platforms of those who disagreed with the Party.

What remain of the revival process are the ideas and conflicts of 1968. Many of these ideas sound rather elementary to westerners, but they should realize that the Czechoslovaks had to start from the beginning, basic positions had to be established and common ground laid out, and the backlog of the past had to be dealt with. Just how original and important these ideas and controversies were, and still are, can be judged from the selections which follow.

Alex Pravda
Andrew Ritchie

Notes on authors

The following notes give information on the more prominent authors in this book.

Writers and journalists

Eduard Goldstücker. A pre-war communist who was ambassador to Israel and Sweden after February 1948. He was sentenced to life imprisonment in 1953 for being a 'Jewish bourgeois nationalist', released in 1956, and resumed work at Charles University where he was professor of German literature. Responsible for the rehabilitation of Kafka in 1963. In 1967 he came out strongly against the attempts to silence the writers, although as an 'old communist' he could have been less outspoken. Chairman of the Writers' Union in 1968 and politically active throughout the period. He now lives in England.

Dušan Hamšík. A historian and journalist; editor-in-chief of *Literární Listy* in 1968 (until June). In his views he belonged to the centre of the *Literární Listy* writers. 'The trials' shows his historian's approach to be on a broader front than most of the writing of 1968.

Václav Havel. A dramatist, whose best-known plays are *The Garden Party* and *The Memorandum*. Very active in politics, although one of the few leading writers not in the Communist Party. He attacked censorship in his speech to the Fourth Congress, and continued to contribute to the discussions throughout the period, not only on paper, but at meetings and by organizing, with others, the Circle of Independent Writers (for the non-communist writers) of which he became chairman.

Ivan Klíma. A dramatist and novelist. An editor of *Literární Listy*; was one of the three expelled from the Party after the Fourth Congress, and reinstated in March 1968.

Notes on authors

Karel Kosík. A philosopher at Charles University. His outstanding work is *The Dialectic of the Concrete* (1965). On the editorial board of *Literární Listy*, he was also active at meetings in 1968. Was elected to the Central Committee in August 1968 and expelled from it the next year.

Milan Kundera. A novelist from Moravia, whose best-known work is *The Joke* which appeared in Czechoslovakia in 1967 and in English, in Penguins, 1970 (see extract at the beginning of the introduction to 'The Past Re-examined'). His speech to the Congress was the point of departure for the whole proceedings, although it was far less direct and new in tone than Vaculík's.

Petr Pithart. A young lawyer and political theorist, who was secretary of the Mlynář team. He took a more radical position on the need for political 'opposition' than his superior. He wrote extensively throughout the period.

Radoslav Selucký. An economist and journalist, one of the first to attack the 'cult of the Plan' in 1963. He commented widely on events in 1968, and now lives in the United States. See his analysis of the old system, and his outline of the new, in *The Plan that Failed*, Nelson, 1970.

Ivan Sviták. The most outspoken critic of 1968. A philosopher whose unorthodox views as early as 1956 (on the personality cult) brought suspension from the Academy of Sciences. In 1964 he was expelled from the Academy and from the Party and worked in the Film Institute, where he was still officially employed for a part of 1968. His litanic style is a sign of the somewhat affected nature of his writing, but what he said, however inclined to showmanship, is still the most direct of the comments produced in 1968. Sviták was active in KAN, even though he denied being one of its founders, and in improving relations between the workers and the intellectuals, by taking an interest in their point of view and not only by 'preaching' the need for democracy (see the Doubrava exchange). He was viciously attacked by Kolder, and later by the Soviets in the 'White Book', their version of what had happened in 1968. Sviták now lives in the United States.

Ludvík Vaculík. A novelist from Moravia, *The Axe* being his best known work. It appeared in Czech in 1966. He was expelled from the Party for his unique speech to the Congress (see the speech in 'Our Present Crisis'), which is outstanding not only for what it said, but particularly for its directness and lack of compromise. Vaculík was the best journalist of 1968, as he was able to speak in language unmarred by ambiguity (see the introduction to 'Semily').

Politicians

Alexander Dubček (b. 1921). Lived with his family in the Soviet Union 1925–38 and studied at the Party College in Moscow 1955–58. He rose through the Party apparatus in Slovakia. In 1958 became a member of the Central Committee of the CPCz (Communist Party of Czechoslovakia), and a secretary in 1960. In 1963 he replaced Bacílek as First Secretary of the Slovak Communist Party, and in January replaced Novotný as First Secretary of the CPCz. Remained in this post until April 1969; lost his place in the Praesidium of the CPCz in September 1969, and was 'exiled' as ambassador to Turkey (from January to June 1970), and expelled from the Party in June. Is now thought to be working as a forestry worker. For a comment on the part his character played in the pre-invasion period see Introduction.

Gustav Husák (b. 1913). A Slovak like Dubček, but here all resemblance ends. A pre-war Slovak communist leader, one of the organizers of the Slovak uprising of 1944. Sentenced for Slovak 'bourgeois nationalism' in 1954, released in 1960, and rehabilitated in 1963. Became Deputy prime minister in April 1968. Very popular in Slovakia as he placed primary importance on the need to realize federalization, if need be before thorough democratization. As a former victim of Novotný, he was a leader of the efforts to force him to admit his responsibility for the past. Always a hard-line, orthodox and discipline-inclined member of the post-January régime, he was suited for the post of First Secretary in April 1969, as he commanded far more popularity than the other conservative candidates.

Zdeněk Mlynář (b. 1930). Studied law in Moscow 1951–4. In the Prosecutor General's office 1955–6. At the Institute of State and Law of the Czechoslovak Academy of Sciences 1958–63, and head of the department of the Political Leadership of Society 1962–8. From late 1966 head of the team investigating the development of the political system in socialist society (see his ideas on this in 'On the Theme of Opposition'). In the Central Committee of the CPCz from late 1967. Secretary of the Central Committee of the CPCz June to November 1968, and head of the Central Committee law commission April to November 1968. From September until his resignation in November in the Praesidium of the CPCz. Then worked in the Prague National Museum. Essentially a very pragmatic reformer 'from within'.

Ota Šik (b. 1919). Economist, author of the New Economic Model (see *The Plan and Market under Socialism*, 1967), the driving force behind the New Economic System (for an outline see Introduction). One of the most 'progressive' of the new leadership who was therefore unacceptable to Moscow and to the conservatives. He was not elected to the Praesidium in 1968, and was only given a Deputy premiership. Concerned himself largely with economic matters, but was kept from being chairman of the Economic Council which was set up in 1968. Professor Šik remained in Switzerland where he was at the time of the invasion.

Josef Smrkovský (b. 1911). The 'strong' man of the new leadership. A pre-war communist who took a leading part in the Prague uprising of 1945. Imprisoned in 1951 and sentenced for life, released in 1955, and rehabilitated in 1963. Minister of Forestry and Water Conservation (January 1967–April 1968). In April 1968 became a member of the Praesidium of the CPCz and the chairman of the National Assembly. Dismissed from all posts in 1969, and later expelled from the Party. An 'old' communist, a far more progressive and courageous man than Husák, outspoken in the negotiations after the invasion (see Introduction for a comment on Smrkovský).

Oldřich Švestka (b. 1922). Editor-in-chief of *Rudé Právo* from 1958, and not dismissed from this post despite opposition to him from the staff (see Introduction). Member of the Central Committee of the CPCz (1962) and of its Ideological Commission from 1963. Member of the Praesidium, a surprising appointment, from the May plenum 1968. One of the conservative group in the Praesidium, who has shown his ability to stay in power since the invasion.

One
The Revival Process in Semily

A second basic illusion consists in the assumption that the exceptional atmosphere in Prague also affects the towns and villages in the countryside, whereas the conservatives know very well that this is not true. The political structure of power in the towns and villages has been left virtually unaltered by the recent changes, so that the reader who wrote from a provincial town near Prague, 'If we didn't have the press and the radio and television, no one would know here that some kind of revival process was going on at all', was quite right.

Ivan Sviták, 'Forbidden Horizons',
Literární Listy, 14 May 1968

Semily is a small Czech town near Liberec, with a population of about 10,000. Vaculík's 'The revival process in Semily' appeared in *Literární Listy* on the same day as the Two Thousand Words, and is an account of a visit that Vaculík made to the town as journalist and observer. These two essays in *Literární Listy* are the apex of Vaculík's very important contribution to the revival process.

In 'The revival process in Semily' we see Vaculík as an observer rather than as a polemicist, but the article's light style and irony do not conceal its biting political message. Vaculík brings the political generalizations, the slogan-mongering of central government politics down to a grass-roots level. The very title of the piece has a gentle mocking quality, rather like saying 'The great revolution in Tunbridge Wells'.

Vaculík puts the people of one 'warm and weary little town' under a microscope. His satire is reminiscent of a Miloš Forman film. Forman too, in '*A Blonde in Love*' and '*The Fireman's Ball*', for instance, is interested in small-town mentality. Vaculík is simply trying to show the people as they reacted and behaved during the meeting he describes, and to suggest that it is not very easy to get the revival process going. People know in an emotional way what they want, he suggests, but haven't much idea how to go about it. Even the two people who are the instigators of the meeting don't know that it is impossible to read out a resolution as part of an introductory speech, and that they can hardly include in the statutes of a Youth Club that it will be open to everybody 'regardless of age or political affiliation'. It is just these subtle observations which make the piece so funny and so indicative of political realities in 1968. The impact of the past and of provincial jealousies is heavy in Semily. Not every town is as sophisticated as Prague.

Vaculík illustrates very well the dangers into which the revival process was falling. It became the opportunity for the settling of old scores, and gave the extremists the possibility of speaking out again. And it shows the frustrations of this little town, where so many people feel that something needs doing, and yet everyone is waiting for the initiative to come from Prague. The Semily article and the Two Thousand Words are saying basically the same thing: that the conservative forces in society are tremendously strong and can't be expected to melt away without struggling. Vaculík understands that a kind of vacuum has been created by the discrepancy between the surprising and sudden emergence of a reformist Central Committee and the still solidly conservative Regional and District Party bodies, and that it is into this vacuum of hesitation that the revival process has to be injected. 'If the officials in all the Districts had quickly carried out as decent a putsch as the Central Committee of the Party did,' remarks Vaculík, 'this democratization movement would never have got off the ground.'

What the Semily article shows best of all – and this is why it is very significant for our understanding of the revival process – is the range of emotions, intentions and sympathies which were involved in the process. Here is a combination of practical politics, misinformed enthusiasm, naïve optimism, clumsy manoeuvring, provincial prejudice, Utopian day-dreaming and genuine concern which is the substance of any movement of social change. What it shows is something the Communist Party itself had perhaps never allowed itself to understand, that beautiful theories are all very well, but they always come face to face with human beings.

The theme of the revival process in this one small town had such an impact on the readers of *Literární Listy* that Vaculík was continually being asked after the invasion, 'What happened in Semily?' And on 6 March 1969 a second report called simply 'The process in Semily' appeared in *Literární Listy*, just two months before it was closed down.(By dropping the word 'revival' from the second report from Semily Vaculík creates a pun in Czech, as 'proces' means both a 'process' and a 'trial', the title of Kafka's book.)

Ludvík Vaculík
The revival process in Semily

Literární Listy, 27 June 1968

A thin young man came to see me and asked if I would go to Semily to speak at a meeting of the Youth Club. I told him I didn't go to meetings. He objected by suggesting that this time I should make an exception, because Semily was the most backward district, where the revival process had not penetrated at all. I told him that that was what everybody said. Litoměřice is also the most backward district, so is Ústí on the Orlice and many other places. Everywhere they're waiting for someone to come over from Prague to put things right for them. But let them see to it themselves, we're only a newspaper, we should be writing about it so as to encourage others as well.

The young man told me that they wanted to put things right, but that if I spoke to people, it would stir them into action more quickly. I told him I intended to do nothing of the sort and asked him what sort of meeting it was supposed to be. The pale, thin, young man told me that there would probably be about nine hundred people there who would put questions to the chief officials of the district and if need be ask them to resign. I was surprised at this, and said that as a journalist and observer it would interest me. When the young man went away, he left me his visiting card: Kája Hádek, commercial photographer, Semily.

On 15 May 1968 I discovered that Semily is a warm and weary little town, where everyone goes slowly about his business. On the asphalt of the square the strident slogans were strangely out of place: 'Dubček ano, Loskot ne!', 'Svoboda projevu, Svoboda president!', 'Národ sobě!'[1] I didn't know what it wanted for itself.

Mr Kája Hádek, after welcoming me, announced that the district officials, shamefully, had sent their apologies, but the meeting would be held all the same! I laughed. I asked whether Loskot was

1. 'Dubček yes, Loskot no!' 'Freedom of speech, Svoboda for president!' 'The nation for itself!' Svoboda also means freedom.

the leading secretary of the District Committee of the Communist Party.[2] Yes, Mr Hádek affirmed, and he added that as late as the previous day Loskot had personally promised that either he or his representative would take part in the meeting, but today he had left a message for Mr Hádek with the foreman, saying that a conference of secretaries had decided that no one should go to the meeting. The VB[3] had also sent a letter of apology, signed by Major Špáta:

> Members of the National Security Corps of the Semily District fully support the revival process, as they have already expressed in a resolution sent to the Central Commitee of the Communist Party of Czechoslovakia . . . (laughter in the hall later) . . . Members of the VB are not afraid to appear in public to defend the results of their work . . . (laughter in the hall) . . .

The members of the VB would, however, appear when they received a proper and official invitation from some organization of the National Front. I asked Mr Hádek how they had been invited, and he replied that he had invited them quite officially, that is, personally, on behalf of the Youth Club, and it only remained for me to ask whether the Youth Club existed.

'And does that Youth Club of yours exist then?' I asked.

'We've constituted it and asked the local Council for permission.'

'Did you get it?'

He showed me the Council's reply. It said in effect that the Youth Club should send a transcript of the constituent meeting, state the composition of its representative body, and submit its statutes within fifteen days.

'Have you got the statutes?' I wanted to know.

'No, we haven't, that's exactly what we thought you might help us to write down.'

I laughed and said that I couldn't and possibly wasn't allowed to

2. The organizational hierarchy consists of: the Central Committee headed by its Praesidium (which until 1968 took all the important decisions and merely had them approved by the Central Committee), the Regional and City committees, the District committees, and committees in primary organizations, factories and places of residence.

3. VB and STB. Veřejná Bezpečnost, and Státní Bezpečnost, i.e., the ordinary police force and the State Security, the 'secret police'.

go around the Republic founding Youth Clubs. Mr Hádek said that the Club had been founded, it just didn't have any statutes. I would only have to advise them.

Deep in thought, I went over to the window, hands folded behind my back. I turned it over in my mind. Yes, as far as I remember, communists always used to do that, and they were only too glad to when the people asked them. And so should I. But who is Hádek? And what people has he got behind him?

'How old are you?' I asked.

'Twenty-two.'

'And how many people do you think will come today?'

'About eight hundred.'

'How do you know?'

'Because not long ago the Czechoslovak Union of Youth arranged a meeting like this here. It was packed out.'

'Why are you having another meeting then?'

'Because theirs didn't get us anywhere. At every ticklish question Loskot said the same thing, that it was an internal Party matter.'

'Is that really what he said? But surely the only internal matters today are Party membership dues!'

'Anyway people laughed at him.'

Mr Hádek brought me an apple and some coffee. I sat down at a table. Of course I hadn't read any statutes in my life except the statutes of the Communist Party. And so I wrote: 'The Youth Club is an ideological bond . . .' No, I'm just making fun! I've also read the statutes of the Club of Kindred Souls of the Semafor Theatre. I tried to make the Youth Club sound something like that kind of cultural association, catering for different interests, cultural activities, discussions, lectures . . . Mr Hádek wanted the Youth Club to be open to everybody regardless of age or political affiliation. I worked this into the statutes. But I did refuse to work into them any statement that the Club would put up its own candidates in the elections. I said, 'Yes, they can try it, if they have the support, but this has no place in the statutes.' I wrote down how the Club Committee was elected, where the Club would get its funds from. And I wrote that it would be dissolved by resolution of a members' meeting.

'How many members do you have?' I asked. He answered

that members would actually be recruited at today's meeting, where application forms would be given out.

'Why isn't there anybody here from the preparatory committee?' I wanted to know.

'Pepík Dohnal is coming any moment,' Mr Hádek replied.

Again I went over to the window and looked down onto the square. 'The nation for itself'.

'What does the nation want for itself?' I asked.

'The nation has to give something to itself as well, and not to somebody else all the time,' Mr Hádek explained to me.

'What did they say to that?' I asked.

Laughing, he told me that the mechanical road-sweeper had appeared straight away the day after and tried to scrub off the inscription 'Dubček yes, Loskot no!'

'What does your dad think about all this?' I asked.

'Nothing now. We've got this rebelliousness in our family. He's a communist, and that's what he fought for . . .'

At that moment Comrade Hádek came in through the door. We greeted each other.

'What do you think of what your son's doing?' I asked him.

'Well, what should I say? I think we've got this rebelliousness in the family!'

Comrade Hádek, originally a workman, in the fifties employed by the Council, today a workman again, remembers the hard times when he had to carry out such irksome tasks as moving the kulaks from the village. The whole village looked on, the kulak's family cried, the VB man who was helping refused to do a thing, and so Comrade Hádek had to take his jacket off himself and carry the things out of the house.

'Father is partly to blame for what went on, and so he can't say anything to me now that I'm trying to put it right,' Mr Hádek said.

'Well, yes, what can I say to him now?' said Comrade Hádek.

After that Pepík Dohnal arrived, because the hour was getting near. He is also twenty-two, an electrical maintenance worker. I asked who was opening the meeting.

'I'll say something there to start off, and then people will be off on their own,' Mr Hádek answered.

I felt no desire at all to be at such a meeting. 'What conclusions do you intend to reach?' I wanted to know.

'Pepík and I were just thinking that you'd help us to put a resolution together. You're such a literary sort of bloke!'

'I can't possibly do your resolutions for you! You must know yourselves what you want!'

'We know what we want, but we can't express it.'

I went and stood at the window and read the slogans on the square.

'And what is it you want?'

'We want Loskot and Putůrek to go.'

'You can't dislodge Loskot, that's an internal Party affair.'

'But we can ask Putůrek, can't we? He's the chairman of the local council and he's not popular with anybody.'

'You can only do it in a case where there are serious grounds against him. You can only take your cue from the meeting itself.'

'Of course, that's understood,' Messrs Hádek and Dohnal said.

'What are people likely to be demanding?' I asked.

'People will mainly be furious that none of those gentlemen has come.'

'Then the first point of the resolution ought to be something like this: "We condemn the attitude of the officials whom we invited and who have not come . . ."' I wrote it down. In the next point they wanted to ask the District Committee of the Party publicly to declare itself in favour of the Dubček line so that the old mistakes and wrongs would begin to be put right in the district. I found them the right words. In addition, they wanted a legal investigation into the activities of Comrade Putůrek and for him to resign his position. I emphasized to these lads that this point could be read out only if voices were raised to that effect at the village hall. The last point of the declaration was that the assembled citizens would not take part in any elections if such people as – (to be filled in according to the decisions of the meeting) should figure in them.

'You can only demand from the platform things that are put forward by the body of the meeting,' I told them again, and then I told them very seriously that they should never tell anyone about my share in preparing the resolution; I'm curious as to whether they kept their promise or not.

When the sun was going down in a blaze of gold, cars arrived at the hall, which filled up with about eight hundred people. Workers and the local intelligentsia; men and women, old and young;

parents with adolescent children; inquisitive people; guests from the neighbourhood. I had to remind myself that this was none of my doing, that I had come along as an observer. The lads got up on the platform where at a long table only two out of the whole gamut of officials called to account were sitting: the District Prosecutor and the STB chief. Yes, they knew their duty! Mr Hádek, in a white sweater, stepped up to the microphone, and the revival process in Semily had begun.

I was witness to a unique scene, for which history only provides the opportunity once in twenty years. I don't know if it wasn't rather a meeting in a Chinese commune or a happening. At moments I was so excruciatingly embarrassed that I wanted to crawl under a chair, but then I would laugh it all off.

Mr Hádek opened by inviting all those present to join the Youth Club, 'those who wished Semily well'. If there would be a lot of them, the officials wouldn't be able to afford not to come next time and they would have to pay their respects here, 'even though perhaps it isn't very pleasant for them'. As for those who hadn't turned up, he expressed the hope that 'we won't miss them. We shall try to answer your questions ourselves.' But before this promise began to be carried out in an informal way, his comrade-in-arms Pepík Dohnal spoke, and as an opening to the whole discussion read the draft of the resolution in which there was a demand for the District Committee of the Party to declare itself immediately in favour of Dubček, for Putůrek to resign and for an investigation into his activities to be initiated, because the assembled citizens would not go to any elections in which people like Putůrek would figure. The meeting was then supposed to vote on the draft resolution, but it didn't feel like it.

Just then Comrade Jíně, an employee of the military administration and candidate for the District Committee of the Communist Party, got up and protested that the resolution was being submitted before the discussion. He expressed the view that those invited should certainly have come, but naturally they had excused themselves in some way. At that Mr Hádek related how he had been to see Loskot, who had promised to attend, but who had let him know today, through the foreman, that neither he nor anyone else would come. He then read out the letter of apology from the chief of the local VB, while people kept on laughing.

The written questions from the floor were answered by Mr Hádek. For instance: 'Why is the Communist Party in Semily at the tail end of the revival process, while in Prague it is at its head?' – 'Because in Semily someone else must do it.' To the question as to how it was possible that Putůrek had still been around to officiate at the May Day Rally, Mr Hádek answered that he probably thought that as we seemed to have democracy now he could get away with it. Someone else asked how many plain-clothes policemen there were in the hall: Mr Hádek said that none had been invited, and STB chief Major Stříbrný confirmed from the platform that he was the only one there. 'Well, that's excellent then,' said Mr Hádek, 'we can have a good old natter,' and we all laughed. To the letter from the worker Františka Valentová asking why there were unqualified people in the leading posts in the Kolora enterprise, Mr Hádek replied that he had also invited the director of Kolora, who, however, felt that there were no problems and that was why he hadn't come, and he went on to say that every dictatorship is filthy and that it now depended on us whether we were to be a socialist or a bourgeois state. He personally inclined towards our remaining a socialist state, now that we already were one, but that it was no longer possible for it to be under the leadership of the Communist Party of Czechoslovakia, because that could be seen very easily in Semily. And so it was necessary to found an opposition party.

And thus the evening wore on, and I was asked to speak twice. Me? Not likely! This way it was immensely more valuable. Several times I went out to convince myself that the crowd was standing listening in all the adjoining rooms. From the back of the packed crowd I heard somebody's comment on the investigation methods of Captain Tůma of the local STB.

'My goodness!' Mr Hádek laughed into the microphone, 'and he looks as if he wouldn't hurt a chicken. It seems to me he'll be hearing more about this. And he was so sheepish when we invited him. He must have suspected something!'

Citizen Naděje, a member of K 231 addressed a complaint to the STB chief present about how he was treated after the amnesty. The chief replied at length that he too had been surprised by the revelations being made by the mass media, and said how shocked he was by the brutalities, which they had known nothing about in the district. He was reminded from the floor to keep to the point. It occurred to me what horrible uncertainty all these people up and down the Republic must be living in, what a peculiar paralysis had been spreading over them from Prague, when this STB chief said: 'There are also many cases, *and our friends here* from the K 231 could confirm this, where there were real spies, terrorists and saboteurs among them.' In the struggle against them about three hundred Security members had laid down their lives. 'They too can't be brought back to life,' said Comrade Stříbrný, but he was interrupted by the audience, tried to carry on, and then was again interrupted by Mr Hádek. 'Just as you wish,' the STB chief said, 'have it your own way.' And he said that under his term of office there had not been any illegal dealings by the STB in Semily. Again he was interrupted and laughed at when he proclaimed that letters had not even been read, nor telephones tapped. Whatever he said, it had no effect. Some people can say anything, but it just doesn't have any effect at all. But this time, and I wondered for how long, it was somebody else's turn to be defenceless.

Citizen Chalabala, a worker, got up, and related how after being amnestied he had been terrorized and soon put in prison again on the evidence of dishonest witnesses. He named them: Novotný and Váňa. To a question from the hall as to which Novotný, he answered, old Novotný from Podmoklice. And he got a total of twenty-seven years . . . (astonishment in the hall) . . . and cannot understand how Miss Hendrych and Miss Kosař could give evidence against him, but he wasn't surprised that photographer Hilgr gave evidence against him, that professional informer! . . .

While such speeches were going on, people watched the STB chief, but the whole evening the person I watched most was the District Prosecutor, a small dark man, who all the time grinned into his sleeve as he enjoyed himself and thought about something.

A former prisoner stepped out onto the village green – for at certain moments it reminded me of a tribal court – and related how after he had been let out of prison, a clerk of the local Council, Mrs Stehlík, had made it impossible for him to find work. And lo, she was in the crowd as well, and she came out to defend herself spiritedly. A sharp confrontation, in which both stuck to their guns. The people around them maintained an objective silence. Someone observed that Daníček, the schoolteacher, should also be rehabilitated: he had formerly been thrown out of the secondary school that time, the one where Comrade Tichánková is now headmistress, and transferred to a remote school.

Citizen Křapka, a private farmer, gave a vivid picture of how, one winter, he had wanted to go to the quarry on brigade work. 'I couldn't afford to pay the fines which Petr Putůrek gave me, the scoundrel . . . (a stir in the hall) . . . just because I didn't want to join the United Agricultural Cooperative . . . So in order to be able to pay the fines I go to Mrs Stehlík and she says: "No! You're only going on drainage work!" "No," says I, "no, madam, I can't do that, I've got rheumatism, I can't go near water." So I wasn't allowed to go to the quarry either, do you hear? And Poláček, Petr Putůrek and Kratochvíl, they're a fine lot . . . (loud laughter) . . . I'll say it in public: I've been inside prison twice, and I'll get put there a third time now, and then the whole lot of them scoundrels'll go there too!'

Now the lads were supposed to come forward with their resolution! But Comrade Zelinka came forward, an employee of the District Committee of the Communist Party. The Committee too were in the hall. They tried to defend the Party about four times. Although they did it absolutely inadequately, the people in the hall were somehow not too prejudiced against them. The fact that they had come at all was, on the contrary, appreciated. The community somehow didn't particularly let itself be provoked into anti-communist outpourings. The community only shouted them down when in that sadly hackneyed, perfunctory way they attacked the First Republic and Masaryk. I would say that the majority of people didn't invariably associate compromised officials with the Communist Party, and if in such a mood and situation as then (I don't know what the mood and situation is in Semily today), some 'organ' of the Party had gone there himself and dismissed the unloved dignitaries, the Party would have won a new authority in almost the same primitive fashion as it did in 1945. Fortunately they have nowhere understood this at the District Secretariats, fortunately they're defiant and resist, so that people are forced to reflect more deeply on how to make do with the Communist Party. If the officials in all the Districts had quickly carried out as decent a putsch as the Central Committee of the Party did, this democratization movement would never have got off the ground. Now Comrade Zelinka, a Secretary of the District Committee of the Party, claimed that 'it's already some time since our Central Committee passed down the instructions it did, now it's almost a year since this has been under way'. Amid laughter, he rejected the assertion that the Party was to blame for the decline in the economy, and he ended with a piece of folk wisdom, 'He who doesn't stick his neck out, doesn't risk losing it.' People slowly began to leave the meeting.

But I must mention the memorable speech by Comrade Nyklíček, chairman of the local organization of the Union of Youth. It appears strange to him that that same generation which has been teaching him for twenty years who is a traitor and who is a villain should now begin giving instructions to the contrary. He refuses to change his scale of values so quickly. He's annoyed that in all the discussions he hardly hears any communists speaking. He doesn't recognize this Youth Club, because he has no confidence in Mr Hádek. After all, who is Mr Hádek? We all know that he's got a record for robbing a chemist's shop and for pushing an old man into the Jizera that time. People like Mr Hádek can't stand at the head of any organization . . . (Applause).

First of all Mr Hádek rejected the assertion that this assembly had ever taught Comrade Nyklíček anything for twenty years. It was the Communist Party which had taught him, and it had made a proper example of itself. He should appeal to the Party in his predicament, let them explain it to him there, and let them leave us non-Party members in peace. For everything that's happened only the Party's to blame, because it had everybody who spoke up against it locked up . . . (also applause) . . . Calmly and almost trustingly the community heard out the following explanation of Mr Hádek's: 'Yes, I did steal from the chemist's, but I was younger then and was just a fool. Believe me, I wouldn't do it today! Because I'm more sensible. And as for that man I threw into the river, Comrade Nyklíček here didn't say why I threw him in, and that I had my own good reasons for doing it. If I was a yob once, then I've founded this club because I don't want to be a yob any more.'

From the floor schoolmaster Daníček spoke in great detail in order to explain the fate of his family after he was thrown out of the school where Comrade Tichánková is now headmistress. He gave us a glimpse of the school life which we all know about: jealousy, malice, envy, cowardice, servility.

The highlight of the evening for me came from Citizen Tomíček, a young worker, who in those cursed times hadn't got to university. His speech was a perfect rabble-rouser as I remember them from pre-February times. Allow me to quote from it:

'Dear friends, dear fellow citizens! We had martyrs among us, we have torturers among us. These days we often learn of the lives of outstanding people who have suffered a great deal. The lists of martyrs grow, their torturers remain unknown. The dearest people have gone from us, murderers live among us. As if the central authorities knew nothing about them! And those who are known about are being dealt with in an unbelievably slapdash way. We most certainly can't rely on the Security, which for us means insecurity . . . (applause) . . .' His masterly speech was often interrupted by applause, during which at some moments I trembled from old memories and seriously expected him to be shouted down. I looked round at the people. 'The Communist Party of Czechoslovakia must be seen as the criminal organization it really has been, and it must be excluded from public life, howevery prettily its present representatives get themselves up. Of course the communists must be held responsible for ruining the economy . . .' I looked at the Prosecutor. He was completely enthralled. Besides the Communist Party, Citizen Tomíček condemned the other Parties as well, which had compromised themselves under the communist rule of terror. He expressed the view that the next elections too would be a farce, but a less brazen one. But he who considers all communists bad or all communists good was making a great mistake. 'He who is really good will be recognized as such when the Communist Party has been deprived of its privileged position in a democratic way.' Loud applause, and the Prosecutor stood up. Allow me to quote from his speech:

'Dear friends, I considered it not only my official, but also my civic duty to come here in order to adopt a standpoint and to answer questions, if there should be any. A person who puts his head in the sand in the face of such a meeting as this is definitely not choosing the correct way . . . The present democratization process is truly in embryo. We must not be too sensitive to what is taking place here. I think that any shouting down of democracy when it is still in an embryonic form will probably do no good. Also we shall probably not be able to be too sensitive to some of the harsh words which have been heard here. Yes, in the heat of rhetoric things are said for which it would be neither democratic nor just to hold a citizen responsible . . .' Jiří Kuník, the Prosecutor, went on to express the conviction that young people in particular had the right to hear, to know, to demand an explanation from those who were witnesses. 'Everyone will have to learn democracy. The revolution also brings the dregs to the surface, and it is this which breeds the cases of violent treatment and careerism such as for instance schoolmaster Daníček has revealed here. A régime which was built on mediocrity had to lead to the removal of the capable. Capable equals inconvenient . . .' (Applause) . . . Not even the class war may use bad means, however. 'I think', the Prosecutor said, 'that at the present time members should learn during their Party training what the Charter of Human Rights is, which our Republic also wants to associate itself with . . . (applause) . . .' The Prosecutor answered a few questions, and of those he couldn't answer, he said that he was taking a note.

An old man stepped up to the microphone. Grey, careworn; it was Mr Tichánek, the father of the headmistress of the school. In sad detail he began to explain quietly what his daughter had done, what conditions had been like at the school, his daughter this and that . . . what was required . . . his daughter this and that . . . what the regulations were . . . that his daughter hadn't done anything wrong . . . why schoolmaster Daníček had really had to leave and that not even his salary had been affected; sadly he named the basic rates of pay and the supplements for additional hours. People slowly began to leave the hall. 'It doesn't interest any of you,' Mr Tichánek went on into the tired microphone, 'but I must explain that my daughter . . .' he carried on quietly and all the more alone. For even the platform began to empty.

And when at last Mr Hádek again put the resolution to the vote, out of eight hundred there were about seventeen citizens left, so that it was embarrassing all over again. And so ended the meeting, which someone had to convene.

(According to the latest information, Mr Tomíček was assaulted in the park and Comrade Putůrek is suing Mr Hádek.)

Two
Our Present Crisis

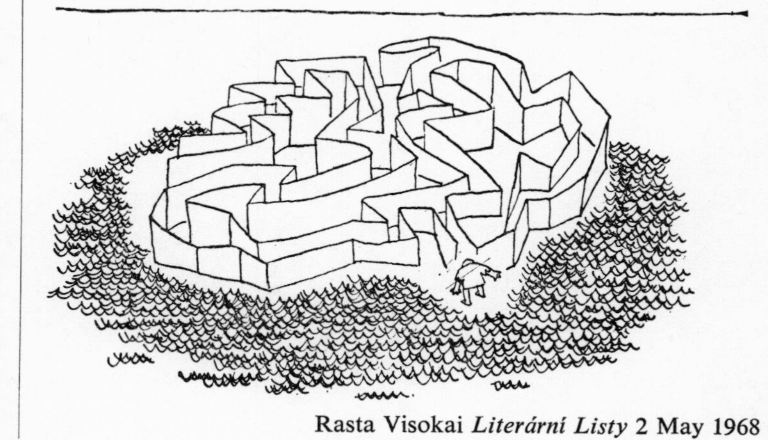

Rasta Visokai *Literární Listy* 2 May 1968

In twenty years not one human problem has been solved in our country, from the primary needs like flats, schools, and the health of the economy, to the more subtle needs, which the non-democratic systems of the world cannot provide a solution to, such as the feeling of fully fulfilling oneself in society, of subordinating political decision-making to ethical criteria, the belief that even insignificant work is important, the need for people to trust each other, and the development of education. And I'm afraid that we haven't even gained a place on the world's stage; I feel that the name of our Republic has lost its good reputation. I see that we haven't given mankind any original or good ideas.

Ludvík Vaculík, from the speech
to the 1967 Writers' Congress

Our present crisis represents not just the collapse of everything old, obsolete and inefficient, but at the same time an opportunity to create something new. Either it will become a transition point to a new indifference and routine, or it will be understood by revolutionary social and political forces as a rare moment of history when it was possible to create a new policy, new social relations, a new way of thinking and new forms of political alignment.

Karel Kosík, 'Our Present Crisis',
Literární Listy, 11 April–16 May 1968

As soon as the taboo preventing an open discussion of their own situation had relaxed, following the gradual loosening of the restrictions on the press in the early part of 1968, the Czechoslovaks, both inside and outside the Party, had no hesitation in admitting quite openly that the country was in a state of crisis. Karel Kosík's 'Our Present Crisis' appeared in *Literární Listy* over a period of six weeks, and Ivan Sviták replied with his 'Your Present Crisis', while the Action Programme headed one of its sections 'Surmounting the causes of profound social crisis'.

In fact it had been acknowledged for years within the Party and in society at large that Czechoslovakia was in a state of crisis. The economic crisis was just the outward sign of a crisis which went far deeper than inefficient management and production. It was this more profound political and, above all, moral crisis which was laid bare at the Fourth Writers' Congress in June 1967.[1] In place of the customary discussions on cultural life, with a few 'daring' departures from the strict lines laid down by the Party's ideological department, Vaculík, Kosík, Kundera and others spoke out clearly and bravely about matters which were the concern of the whole nation, and indeed of the whole socialist world.

These writers defined the moral nature of the crisis and thus of the revival for which they were calling. The question of revival was not merely to find a more efficient political system, but also a more humane one. They explained how Novotný's recipe for socialism did not work and cannot work. Deeply immersed in Czechoslovak history, they realized that the political, economic and social revival was, and still is, a matter of national, cultural and linguistic survival. Unless something happens soon, they warn, there won't be anything left to rescue.

In exposing the crisis in this way, Vaculík and Kundera particularly take on themselves the role of 'the conscience of the nation', comparing the real problems of society, the problems of continuity and of coming to terms with history, with the fragmentary ideological interpretation of the communists. They do not prophesy or idealize; they state the truth as they see it, with a humanism and a sense of responsibility which is the very essence of their contribution to the revival process.

Halfheartedness, compromise, caution and tact were thrown aside. Kosík's denunciation of the specifically Czech vice of compromise typified the attitude of the writers. In his allegory based on the trial of Jan Hus and the Council of Constance, he warns that compromise on principle was fatal, and the disregarding of both reason and conscience in favour of tactics led to disaster:

1. For events surrounding the Congress see Dušan Hamšík, *Writers Against Rulers*, Hutchinson, 1971.

The man who has replaced reason with his own calculations and suppressed his conscience in such a way that he has changed it into a bad conscience, is a man without reason or conscience. Such a man has lost everything and gained nothing.

Vaculík refused to heed any considerations of what the Party's anger might bring, and in direct and simple language exposed the situation of socialist Czechoslovakia. Power had corrupted socialist rule, just as it could and would corrupt any government. It was finally necessary to talk as adults, and therefore such taboo subjects as the nature of power, the past failures of the régime and the nature of socialism could not be avoided yet again. His criticism of Czechoslovak society was not directed at socialism as such, but only at the particular kind of socialism which Czechoslovakia had lived through during the previous twenty years, and this was what had to go, in order that people's self-respect could be recovered.

Milan Kundera sets the crisis in this mould in a more wide and abstruse way. For him it is a crisis of security and identity, the crisis of 'a nation which cannot take itself for granted', but which has to keep on reaffirming its identity and its commitment, and which has suffered a great deal in the past. His speech was undoubtedly not as much to the point as Vaculík's had been, was not as direct, and bears some of the marks of the circuitous route of thinking which was usually taken by the writers to avoid being completely silenced. It was published, even if in a castrated form, while there would never have been any possibility of Vaculík's even being considered for publication at the time. Kundera suggests that a new revival is needed if people are not going to start repeating the question that was asked in the nineteenth century during the revival of the Czech language and literature, that of whether it had been worth reviving the nation in the first place. A great opportunity existed for this vital regeneration, and the nation had to realize its chance. Culture, which had always played a role of first importance in the history of the Czech nation, had to be freed from the ridiculous bonds of censorship and control. Voltaire's 'I don't agree with what you say, but I will fight to the death to defend your right to say it,' was used as a rebuke against the Party's refusal to allow any freedom of speech and criticism.

The Party's reaction to such an open challenge from the writers, who had indeed revealed themselves as the 'conscience of the nation', was unusually, but not surprisingly, harsh: Vaculík, Liehm and Klíma were expelled from the Party, others were disciplined, and the writer's organ, *Literární Noviny*, was taken over by the Ministry of Culture. But this reaction did nothing to dispose of the crisis which the writers had declared existed: no prohibitions or force could solve that problem.

The reaction of President Novotný was to go back to pre-Thirteenth Congress terms, such as the emphasis on the 'class antagonisms' still left in society. He gave away nothing in his own assessments of the past, but tried to reply by counter-attacking. 'All our political measures', he said, 'were correct and necessary, because they were in accordance with class principles, which governed and continue to govern the Communist Party.' Czechoslovakia is a 'class democracy' and freedom 'a class freedom'.

> There are some people who seem to think that they are predestined, goodness knows by whom, to defend or conduct some kind of revival process in our society and in our Communist Party. And yet many of them have a long way to go before they could participate in any progressive process . . . Only the Communist Party, and not this or that group which thinks itself able to, can be allowed to watch over and direct a social process, and if the need arises, remedy the shortcomings and errors which may occur in the evolution of society.[2]

Desperation seems to have caused him, in another speech on 5 September, to talk of using old methods of the forcible cleansing of all the opposition, but his stand on this matter did show that Vaculík was not exaggerating when he generalized about the state of the country, and the power-hungry motives of its rulers.

The crisis appeared in a far more dangerous form within the Central Committee itself and within the Praesidium. Šik's speech of 19 December 1967 to the Central Committee, during which he demanded the resignation of Novotný, was the most penetrating given at the December–January plenum of the Party, and set the scene for Novotný's dismissal in the context of a crisis of society and the Party.

> We must admit, comrades, that the people's political discontent, discontent with the present development of our society, is growing.

2. Speech to graduates of the Military Academy, reported in *Rudé Právo*, 2 September 1967.

The situation is critical, he continues, and solutions must be found; it is not possible just to brush the problems aside. His speech is full of urgency, aware of the nature of the crisis which he had been trying to come to terms with in the economy for several years: 'The Party', he says, 'has to adapt itself and carry out a new mission in new conditions,' and moreover it has not really given a proper explanation of the Personality Cult:

> Policies which have gone on for years . . . are having a ruinous effect on morale and on relationships between people . . . If the Party is not to lose its authority and its leading role entirely, if economic developments are not going to deteriorate still further, if the social tensions are not to become extremely acute and put the future of socialism in danger, we must, comrades, determine to carry out certain severe measures . . .

The crisis situation was relieved by the statements from the Action Programme, the Party's new programme adopted on 5 April 1968, which were a fundamental break with the hard line of Novotnýism. It was admitted that bureaucratic methods had persisted, that these had been responsible for the failures in every field of activity. A completely black picture was of course avoided in such an official statement, but concern for the human aspects of socialism which seemed to have been missing from the past was expressed. Sviták, the most extreme of the political commentators of the revival period, a philosopher who had been dismissed from the Academy because of his disagreement with the Party line, had no compunction in using such expressions as totalitarian dictatorship to describe the twenty years of Party rule, and never ceased to hit very hard in this manner throughout the revival process. If he is a little obvious and theatrical in his intellectual performances, Sviták is also extremely perceptive and a very shrewd political commentator.

Karel Kosík is a philosopher whose writing has a logic and simplicity which hides the complexity of the issues he discusses. What he says sometimes sounds obvious, but it is important to remember that he is discussing issues which have not been talked about for years. 'Our present crisis is not just a political crisis,' he declares in his wide-ranging analysis of the whole of Czechoslovak society, 'but a crisis of politics.'

Karel Kosík
Reason and conscience

Literární Listy, 1 March 1968, a speech given to the Fourth Congress of Czechoslovak Writers in June 1967

On 18 June 1415, a great Czech intellectual[3] wrote from prison: 'A certain theologian said to me that for me everything is good and permitted, if only I submit to the Council, and he added, "If the Council declared that you have only one eye, although in fact you have two, it would be your duty to agree with the Council that it was so." I answered him, "And if the whole world told me the same, I, possessing reason, would not be able to acknowledge it without my conscience being repelled."'

This letter is unique in world literature and is among those immortal thoughts in which the fundamental truths about man and the world are expressed. That is why we have to read this text carefully in order to understand exactly what it means, and, in particular, we must examine with the greatest care wherein lies its significance as a fundamental truth.

To be fundamental means above all to create a base, and only on the strength of this base does an idea have its existence, its justification. As soon as this base is destroyed or dismissed or forgotten or deformed, the idea in question loses its base, and everything without a base becomes weak, shallow, and empty. But the basic truth which the Czech intellectual of the fifteenth century expresses does not concern ideas but man, which means that man without this fundamental truth loses his base, he loses the ground under his feet and becomes a man uprooted, a man without a base.

Who is a man uprooted and without a base? He who has lost his

3. Jan Hus (1369–1415), the leader of the Bohemian Reformation, was condemned to death as a heretic by the Council of Constance in 1415 for the dissenting views he had been preaching in Bohemia. After spending several months in prison, Hus was allowed to appear before the Council to expound his views, and the letter from which Kosík quotes was written from prison after he had been sentenced to death.

reason and conscience, answers the Czech intellectual of the fifteenth century. Let us take good note: reason and conscience exist together, they form a unity and only in this unity do they become the basis of human existence. Later times and our time too consider reason and conscience merely as quantities which are independent of each other, which are indifferent or hostile to each other. And for modern times any connection, and above all any substantial connection, between reason and conscience is even something suspicious. But suspicion and suspiciousness are bad counsellors where truth and its problems are concerned. We must ask on the contrary what consequences this separation of reason and conscience, which already seems to be natural and time-honoured, has had and still has for man and for his world.

Let us return to the text which we quoted: we are such prisoners of historical facts, from which we know how the Council's quarrel with a man who did not want to lose his reason and conscience ended, that we completely ignore the possible alternative variation of the result, which is indicated by the text. In the name of the Council and representing the Council, the theologian offers the intellectual the following alternative: if you agree with the Council that you only have one eye, even though you know that you have two, not only will you be forgiven everything, but also everything will be permitted to you. This second alternative is not without its attraction: in it the man is offered the choice of gaining everything – everything will be permitted to him – if he renounces one thing. And who, in a dispute between everything and something, would not choose the everything and refuse the mere something? But above all who, in a dispute between 'real' prospects and 'illusory' prospects, would not prefer the first to the second and would not criticize from this realistic standpoint the intellectual who chose the second alternative for being a headstrong radical, an arrogant extremist, or an incorrigible eccentric? For realism reflects as follows: if he asks me to admit that I have only one eye, although I know that I have two eyes, surely he is asking something necessary, beneficial and useful of me, in short something intelligent? What can the voice of conscience do against the voice of this insistent reason? In comparison with the authoritative and public reason, which asks me to admit that I have only one eye, although I know that I have two eyes, the voice of my conscience appears not only as a private affair, but above all as a small and futile nonentity. As this is a clash between an important and a futile authority, I can suppress the voice of conscience in good faith as something futile. In the realist reason always triumphs over conscience.

But such reason, which in the reasoning of the realist triumphs over conscience, has only its name in common with true reason: that which in the considerations of the realist battles against the 'revulsion of conscience' is not reason but personal calculation, petty haggling over one's own personal prospects, the pursuit of private interests. The realist has suppressed the 'revulsion of conscience' in order to gain everything, but in this consideration of private interest he has in reality lost everything, he has lost both his conscience and his reason.

The Czech intellectual of the fifteenth century, in contrast to the realist, defends the unity of reason and conscience, but by doing so he asserts a certain conception of conscience. Unity is so important for the character of reason and the nature of conscience, that if this unity is lost, reason loses substantiality and conscience reality. Reason without conscience becomes the utilitarian and mechanical reason of computation and calculation, and a civilization founded on it is a civilization without reason, in which man is subordinate to things and their mechanical logic. Conscience divorced from reason sinks to an impotent inner voice, or the vanity of good intentions.

According to the Czech intellectual of the fifteenth century reason and conscience form a unity and only in this unity can reason be what it is: reason must be understood in its original and not in its derived sense, as to think and to understand, to have a comprehension of the meaning of things, the meaning of man, the meaning of reality. Only in this unity can conscience be what it is: the backbone and strength, the inviolable and inalienable property of man. He who suppresses the 'revulsion of conscience' in order to admit to the Council that two times two is ten does not lose his conscience but transforms his conscience into a suppressed conscience. And every suppressed conscience is a bad conscience, displayed and realized in the form of malice, suspiciousness, and deep-rooted resentment. And explosions of resentment occur in history, as is well known, in the form of entrenched hatred, savage fanaticism and bestial violence.

The Czech intellectual of the fifteenth century defended the unity of reason and conscience and refused the offer of the Council as the wrong alternative, for a man who agrees with the Council that he has only one eye although he knows full well that he has two gains nothing and loses everything, for to lose reason and conscience means to lose the basis of his humanity. The man who has replaced reason with his own calculations and suppressed his conscience in such a way that he has changed it into a bad conscience is a man without reason or conscience. Such a man has lost everything and gained nothing. He has become a futile man, a man ruled by futility. And if we know that nothing means nihil, a man without reason and conscience is a true nihilist.

Hence the Czech intellectual of the fifteenth century was making a choice between conscience and reason on the one hand and nihilism on the other. And because the difference between truth and futility is a radical one, it seems that his choice too could only be a radical one.

Comrades! Ludvík Vaculík

Literární Listy, 28 March 1968, a speech given to the Fourth Congress of Czechoslovak Writers in June 1967

Comrades!

The Draft Resolution of the Union of Czechoslovak Writers states that the purpose of a socialist society is to lead to man's reintegration and to guarantee his status as a citizen. The word 'citizen' was once a glorious revolutionary word. It used to express the idea of a person who wouldn't allow himself to be dominated, and if he was ruled, then it was only in a subtle way, by being given the impression that he was in fact ruling himself. It was the aim of politics – a specialized and demanding profession – to create this impression among the governed. Of course, in reality the idea of a citizen who would govern himself has always been and always will be a myth.

The Marxist critique of power threw light on the connections, which had not been analysed before Marx, between political power and the ownership of the means of production. This innovation, together with the interpretation of the history of man as a history of class struggle, laid the foundations of a socialist revolution in which we hoped to be able to provide a new solution to the age-old problems of power. Although the revolution has succeeded in Czechoslovakia, the problem of power still remains. We may have caught the bull by the horns, but someone keeps on kicking us in the behind at the same time. Power, it seems, is subject to its own unalterable laws of development and behaviour, no matter who is exercising it. Power is a peculiar human phenomenon which is based on the fact that someone has to give the orders in any group of people, that even in a society made up exclusively of noble-minded people, someone has to glean knowledge from discussion and formulate the necessary conclusions. Power encompasses both the rulers and the ruled and is unhealthy for both.

Comrades!

Thousands of years of experiencing power have led men to try to elaborate various kinds of political rules, such as formal democracy, with its control mechanisms and the limitations which it places on the periods of power of each ruler. . . . The maintenance of such a system of formal democracy doesn't create very decisive government, it just allows the conviction to develop that the next government can be better. The government may fall, but the citizen is renewed. If, on the other hand, a government stays in power for a long time, then the citizen falls. And where does he fall to? I shan't oblige my enemies by saying that he falls into a place of execution. That is a fate reserved for just a small number of citizens.

But this small number has a big impact, because as a result the whole nation declines into a state of fear and political apathy; it becomes resigned, concerns itself with its futile daily worries and petty wishes, depends more and more on its insignificant rulers, in short, it falls into a state of subjection of such a new and unprecedented sort that here in Czechoslovakia you can't even explain it to a visitor from a foreign country. I don't think there are any longer any citizens left in Czechoslovakia. I have my own reasons for thinking this, which I have developed during many years working for newspapers and for the radio. I won't look very far afield for other reasons. This Congress didn't convene when the members of our organization decided it should, but when the boss kindly gave his consent after having taken all things into consideration. And, as he's been in the habit of doing for the past few centuries, he expects us in return to pay homage to his dynasty. I propose that we don't pay this homage any longer. I suggest that we analyse the text of the resolution, and erase everything there which smacks of a servile mentality. In nations which have developed their cultures in the process of criticizing the ruling power, it is the writers, least of all, who should abandon this good old popular tradition.

May I suggest that everybody who has still to address us here gives an outline of his solutions to the problems that are on his mind. We shouldn't agree to this game of playing at being citizens, just because we've got permission to do it in this playground. We should behave for the rest of the time we still have as if we were grown-up adults. I am speaking here as a citizen of a country which I shall never want to leave, but in which I can never live happily. I'm thinking of my rights as a citizen, but I find myself in a sticky position. I'm also a member of the Communist Party and so I'm not supposed to talk about internal Party matters, and in fact I don't want to. It turns out, however, that there's practically nothing which doesn't turn out at some point in the debate to be a Party matter. What should I do when both my Party and my government have done their best to merge their programmes? Personally I think that both of them are now at a disadvantage. And a difficult situation is also created for us citizens assembled here. Party members are not supposed to talk about crucial issues in front of non-Party members, who themselves have no way of getting into the assemblies where the really crucial decisions are made. So both of these groups have their basic individual freedom – the right to negotiate as equals – curtailed.

I want to come back now to my analysis of the character of power . . . Power of course, prefers people whose inner disposition is similar to its own. But because there is a shortage of them, it must also use other people whom it adapts for its needs. People who are useful to power are quite naturally those who themselves long for power, as well as those people who are naturally obedient, people with bad consciences and people whose Utopian yearnings, whose longing for success or profit, are not restrained by moral considerations. It is also possible to adapt people who are frightened or have lots of children, people who have been humiliated in the past, and who trustingly accept an offer of a new pride and status, and then also people who are naturally just stupid. For a certain time, under certain conditions, and for certain purposes, various kinds of moral absolutists and unselfish but badly informed enthusiasts, such as myself, may also be made use of temporarily. People are won over by the use of a few old and basic methods: physical and mental temptation; the threat of suffering; getting people into compromising situations; using informers; unjustifyingly suspecting a person, who then, in defending himself, shows where his loyalties actually lie; allowing people to fall into difficult situations and then hypocritically saving them from them. By sowing general mistrust. Confidence is categorized into first, second and third class confidence – which presupposes a mass of people who are not trusted at all. In the same way, information has various degrees of quality, on pink paper, on green, on yellow and on just ordinary newspaper . . .

In Czechoslovakia, too, people were chosen according to how power was able to make use of them. The people who were trusted were the obedient ones, those who didn't cause any trouble, who didn't ask questions which weren't first asked by the régime itself. In all these choices, it was the mediocre man who came off best, and the more complicated people, people with personal charm and especially people whose qualities were a silent and inconspicuous standard of general decency, a yardstick of the public conscience, disappeared from public life. In particular, humorous and original personalities disappeared from political life . . . The fabric of the non-material structure and individual culture of communities like the villages, factories and workshops was torn to shreds. Nothing was allowed to bear the distinctive mark of somebody's individuality, and only rarely was the idea of a workshop preserved. Headmasters were sacked from their schools, heads of cement works who were critical about the environment around their factories were dismissed, well-established cultural and sports clubs and associations were disbanded, although for certain social groups they were the essence of continuity in their villages, regions and in the country as a whole.

In *Wild Jaja* Benjamin Klička wrote: 'Remember that ability is impudent. You can offend your superior with it, and so you have to be thicker than a doornail, so that you can live a long while and have a nice time.' I don't have to read this; I can recite it by heart, I've repeated it to myself so many times. It's forty years old, and was directed at society before the social revolution had taken place. But I think it's only after it that it acquired its real meaning for Czechoslovakia, and that everybody could see how true it really was. Have you noticed that all of us, Czechs and Slovaks, have the feeling that at our various places of work we are all directed by a man who is less capable than we are ourselves? And we all, when we meet each other, just whimper. This is horrible, because as well as those who perhaps have good cause to complain, incapable, lazy people are also making angry complaints, complete time-wasters and feeble people, who say that they're not allowed to do this, that and the other. In other words, an artificial and harmful connection is established between people who obviously are not of the same sort. We're all bound together by the most miserable links that anybody could ever conceive – there is a common disgust, but the motives for it are different.

People who were practical found that they were able to compensate in various ways, but the impractical ones put on a martyr's halo. In literature there is a fashion for depression, and nihilism. An orgy of snobbery. Even a clever man can become stupid, and show an impulsive need to protect himself, to hit out right and left . . . And let us bear in mind that for twenty years now, the most successful people have been those who have least resisted all these demoralizing influences produced by power. We should bear in mind that people with sensitive consciences are not supported by the ruling power, and do not have recourse to laws, which according to the Constitution they should have . . .

Recently, I've been reading the Constitution quite a lot, and I've come to the conclusion that it is a badly composed work, and that is perhaps why it has lost its authority among citizens and administrators. Stylistically, it is verbose and also, in many important instances, very vague. I shall quote an example which is very relevant to the work of our Union. Article 16 reads as follows: 'Cultural policy in Czechoslovakia and the development of education, upbringing and teaching, are conducted in the spirit of the scientific world-view of Marxism–Leninism, and in close collaboration with the life and work of the people.' It's not quite clear to me what organ and perhaps which court is able to decide how scientific a certain viewpoint is, when the movement and modification of viewpoints in accordance with the progress of knowledge is contained in the very idea of science, and when this flexibility is a living rejection of the definitiveness and immutability of concepts demanded by every legal formulation. Of course, it wouldn't be a good idea if this expression 'the scientific world-view' were more exactly defined, for in that case the question would arise whether our state wasn't a doctrinaire one rather than the scientifically directed one which the legislature presumably had in mind.

And here's another example which illustrates what I'm talking about. Article 28 states: 'In harmony with the interests of the working people, all citizens are guaranteed freedom of expression in every aspect of the life of society, and especially freedom of speech and of the press.' In my opinion, the freedoms mentioned are obviously in the interest of the working people, and that's why I think the turn of phrase here is not only redundant, but also positively confusing, because the interpretation of what exactly is in the interest of the working people is thus left to anybody . . . The vagueness of the language and the flaccidity of the ideas in the Constitution make it impossible to apply in practice. Our supreme legal norm becomes therefore a programme of good intentions rather than a legal guarantee of the rights of the citizen . . .

I have expressed my point of view about the character, the development and the behaviour of power and tried to show that the mechanisms of control, designed to keep a check on it, have broken down in our country, with the result that the citizen has lost his self-respect, and also his status as a citizen. When this state of affairs lasts for as long as it has lasted in Czechoslovakia, it's understandable that it makes an impression on a lot of people's minds, especially on those of the younger generation and on their philosophy of life. They have not learnt, either through study or experience, that there is any continuity in human efforts to achieve a more perfect form of democracy. And if this state of affairs continues much longer, and at the same time natural human defence mechanisms do not counter it, the very character of our nations will in fact change in the next generation. In place of a cultural community with a certain power of resistance we would turn into an anonymous mass, easily dominated, and it would be child's play for foreigners to govern us. If we were to allow this to happen, our thousand-year-old struggle would have been in vain.

Assuming that none of us was born to be governed easily, I suggest that the Union of Writers, with perhaps the cooperation of the Union of Journalists and other Unions whose work is related, takes the initiative of demanding the Czechoslovak Academy of Sciences for its expert advice on the Constitution. And if it turns out to be necessary, the Union should launch a movement for the revision of the Constitution . . .

As I stand here, I have not at all got that feeling of freedom which a man should have when he says what he wants to say. I have rather the feeling that I am in the process of exploiting, in a rather cowardly manner, a kind of truce between the citizen and the régime, that I am sinning by breaking it, disturbing this summer holiday which has graciously been allowed writers and artists. How long it will last, I don't know – perhaps until the winter or perhaps until tomorrow. Just as I don't think that the citizen and power can ever agree, or the governed and the governor sing together in the same choir, so I don't believe that art and power can ever feel comfortable in each other's presence. They never will do, they never can do, they are different, they don't go together. What is possible, and what gives some hope for the success of our efforts, is that these two partners will both take note of the existing situation and work out some reasonable rules to regulate their mutual contact. Writers are human beings, and the ruling circles are also composed of human beings. Writers don't want anarchy, because they also would like to live in pleasant towns, to have decent flats and to hope for them for other people. They hope that industry will prosper and commerce flourish. And this is impossible without the organized activities of the government.

Art cannot be indifferent to government because to govern means to be continually making direct or indirect decisions, through the administration, about people's lives, their well-being, their hopes and disappointments, and what they are thinking about, things which you can't make direct decisions about. Power makes contact with art wherever there is no real answer to a problem, but where nevertheless answers have to be found in one way or another. It is for this reason that art cannot abandon its criticism of government, because governments are products of the culture of the nations to which they belong.

All that our cultural life has achieved, all the beautiful things that people have created in Czechoslovakia, all the good products, the fine buildings, the creative ideas coming from our laboratories, studies and institutions, all these have been achieved in spite of how our ruling circles have behaved for many years. All has been done quite literally in spite of them . . .

It is years and years now since I've thought to myself while reading a lecture by one of our leaders, 'What a splendid idea. Why didn't somebody think of that before?' On the contrary, I've often thought gloomily, 'So what? Everybody's known that for a long time.' . . .

I see now that power only retreats when it meets with very strong opposition. Arguments can't beat it. Only failure, repeated failure, when it is always trying to do things in the same old way. A failure which is costing us all a lot of money and shattering our nerves. I see a permanent danger that the bad old days may return. For what sense is there in saying that we have got a union, a literary fund, a publishing house and a newspaper? People threaten us with their confiscation if we don't behave ourselves. But are they really the masters of everything? And what do they leave to other people's judgement? Nothing? Then we might as well not exist. Then it would be perfectly clear that fundamentally just a handful of people want to decide about the existence or the non-existence of all this, of all that has to be done, thought and felt. This is the situation of culture in our state . . .

Recently we have often had the occasion to hear that the ruling circles recognize that culture has a certain amount of autonomy in its own field. But culture should not feel annoyed, they say, if it is castigated when it sallies into the political arena. Then they accuse us of stepping outside our own field of activity: every activity should be carried out by specialists. Perhaps it's true that politics should be conducted by specialists, but who are the specialists? I don't know . . . Autonomy of art and culture? That's nothing more than a slogan and a tactic which is frequently used. One thing today, another tomorrow, they seem to change.

But you don't have to be a great expert to see that it's all pouring out of the same barrel, except that there are two different taps. Just as I don't feel very secure in a political-cultural situation which the ruling power can turn into a field of conflict, so I don't feel secure as a citizen outside the walls of this room, outside this playing field. Nothing is happening to me now, and nothing has happened to me yet. Am I supposed to be grateful? I don't think so; I'm afraid. I don't see any certain guarantees. It's true that justice is now much better carried out by the courts, but do the judges themselves have any guarantee, and do they feel secure? If they like, I would be happy to interview several of them for the newspaper. But do you think it would be published? I wouldn't be afraid to interview the Chief Prosecutor himself and to ask him why people who have been unjustly condemned and then rehabilitated don't get all their original rights back again, and how it is that the National Committees don't want to give them back their flats or their houses – but that wouldn't be published. Why doesn't somebody offer a decent apology to these people? Why have they not received all the same advantages that those who were political prisoners have received; why do we haggle with them over a little bit of money? Why can't we live where we want to? Why can't tailors go to Vienna for three years and painters to Paris for thirty years without being considered criminals when they come home?

One legal principle is well known: *nullum crimen sine lege*, there is no crime without law. It is applied here in such a way that the state produces as many criminals as it needs. Why can't people who definitely don't like it in this country take themselves off to the devil? And why don't people who don't want to see the democratic measures completed just go away?

It's true that several new and better laws have been passed. It's true that others are being prepared. It's also true that the new press law is good. And an amendment to the law on the other civil liberties, freedom of assembly and association, is also being prepared. A draft is being prepared by the Ministry of the Interior – but an article on it which was already type-set for *Literární Noviny* was withdrawn. I see no guarantees. What are they? I don't know. Here I pause, because I've arrived at the last point, that one great doubt: whether the ruling circles themselves, the government and its individual members, have any guarantees of their own civil liberties, without which nothing creative, not even politics, can be produced. And here my analysis of the inner laws of power comes to its conclusion, and I can only just hint at a well known saying about the mill that sometimes grinds those who used to turn it . . .

On the way to achieving this dream to which our nations have been aspiring from their earliest history, we have had certain periods of partial success. One of these was the period of the rise of an independent Czechoslovakia . . . After all, this was how there arose a state which, in spite of all its imperfections, achieved a high level of democracy during its day . . . The continuity of the idea of a socialist state after the war turned directly into a programme for socialism. The peculiar conditions in which this programme was put into practice . . . caused the deformations in Czechoslovakia, and events followed which are neither explicable just in terms of local conditions, nor the result of the nature of our people or our history. When this period is talked about, when people look for an explanation of the fact that we lost so much moral and material power, of why we are so backward economically, the ruling circles say that it was necessary. I think that it wasn't at all necessary to any of us, but that it was only necessary for the spiritual development of the organs of power, which forced all the other advocates of socialism to go through this development with them.

In twenty years not one human problem has been solved in our country, from the primary needs like flats, schools, the health of the economy, to the more subtle needs, which the non-democratic systems of the world cannot provide a solution to, such as the feeling of fully fulfilling oneself in society, of subordinating political decision-making to ethical criteria, the belief that even insignificant work is important, the need for people to trust each other, and the development of education. And I'm afraid that we haven't even gained a place on the world's stage; I feel that the name of our Republic has lost its good reputation. I see that we haven't given mankind any original or good ideas . . . that so far we have been dully following the dehumanized American type of civilization, that we are just repeating the mistakes of East and West, that nobody would look at our society for a possible alternative to the noisy and smoky Western way of life.

I'm not trying to say that we've lived for nothing, that it's all completely pointless. But the question is whether our experience serves as a warning. If it could serve that purpose, the whole knowledge of mankind would have benefited; but all the same this object lesson needn't have been provided by a country which was already aware of the dangers . . .

To sum up, I would like to state explicitly, perhaps unnecessarily, what surely follows from the whole of my speech: I'm not blaming socialism when I criticize power in Czechoslovakia, because I'm not sure that such a development of socialism was necessary here, and because I don't identify this power with the idea of socialism, as those in power themselves want to do. And if the people who are in positions of power – just for the time being I'm supposing they are somehow conjured away from their responsibilities, and I'm referring to them as individuals with their own thoughts and feeling – if they came here and asked us all one question, whether this dream of socialism is realizable, they would have to take it as an expression of our good will and at the same time of our supreme sense of social responsibility, if our answer was, 'We don't know.'

Milan Kundera
A nation which cannot take itself for granted

Literární Listy, 21 March 1968,
speech at the 1967 Writers' Congress

In spite of the fact that no nation has existed for ever, and the very idea of the nation is a relatively recent one, most nations nevertheless take their existence for granted as a gift from God, from nature, from time immemorial. Nations feel their culture, their political system and their frontiers as their own personal affairs, as questions and problems. But national existence itself is for them something that they never think to question. The unhappy, uneven history of the Czech nation, which has even come perilously close to death's door, has made it impossible for us to allow ourselves to be lulled into this false sense of security. The existence of the Czech nation has never been a matter to be taken for granted, and it is this fact which is its central predicament.

It is seen most clearly at the beginning of the nineteenth century, when a handful of intellectuals made an attempt to resurrect the half-forgotten Czech language, and, in the next generation, an almost extinct nation as well. This resurrection was the result of deliberate intention, and every choice is a matter of deciding between the pros and the cons. The intellectuals of the Czech Revival, although they made a positive decision, also knew the weight of the arguments against them. . . .

For the great European nations, with their so-called classical history, the European context is something natural. But the Czechs have been through periods of wakefulness and periods of sleep, and several vital phases in the evolution of the European spirit have passed them by. They have had to appropriate, acquire and create the European context for themselves over and over again. For the Czechs have never been able to take anything for granted, neither their language nor their being a part of Europe.

And the nature of their Europeanness is their eternal conundrum: either leave the Czech language to stultify and become a mere European dialect and Czech culture a mere European folklore, or the Czechs must become one of the European nations with all that this entails.

Only the second choice can guarantee real life for the Czechs, but it is an extraordinarily difficult choice for a nation which all through the nineteenth century had to devote most of its energy to building its foundations, from secondary education to an encyclopedia. Yet as early as the beginning of the twentieth century, and especially in the period between the two world wars, a cultural flowering occurs which is without any doubt the greatest in Czech history. In the short space of twenty years there grew up a whole pleiad of men of genius, who in a bewilderingly short space of time raised Czech culture for the first time since the days of Comenius on to a European level, as a self-sufficient entity.

This great period, which was so brief and so intense, and which we still feel nostalgia for today, was quite naturally a period of adolescence rather than of maturity. Czech letters were still in a predominantly lyrical style, at an early stage of development, which needed nothing more than a long, peaceful and uninterrupted period of time. For such a fragile culture to be interrupted for almost a quarter of a century first by occupation and then by Stalinism, for it to be isolated from the rest of the world, to destroy its many rich internal traditions and to lower it to the level of fruitless propaganda, all this was a tragedy which threatened to thrust the Czech nation once more, and this time decisively, back into the suburbs of European culture. If in the last few years Czech culture has again been developing, if today it is without any doubt the most successful of our national activities, if many outstanding works of art have been created and certain cultural activities, such as the Czech cinema, are experiencing the greatest flowering in the whole of their history, then this is the most important national event in the past few years.

But is the nation, as a community, aware of what is happening? Is it aware of the fact that an opportunity has presented itself of carrying on from the point at which inter-war literature was interrupted, during its promising adolescence? And that this is a chance that will not be repeated? Is it aware that the fate of its culture is the fate of the nation? Or has the Revivalists'[4] view that without strong cultural values our national existence cannot be guaranteed lost its validity today?

The position of culture in national life has certainly changed since the time of the Revival, and the danger of our being suppressed as a nation hardly threatens us today. But nevertheless, I don't think even today that our culture has completely lost its meaning for us as a means of protecting the nation and justifying its existence. In the second half of the twentieth century great prospects of integration have been opened up. Mankind's evolution has for the first time been united in a single world history. Small units blend with larger ones. International cultural efforts are being concentrated and united. Mass travelling is developing. All this makes a few world languages all the more important, and the whole of life becomes more and more international, and the influence of the languages of small nations all the more limited . . .

It is a priority for the whole community to become fully aware of the importance of our culture and literature. Czech literature, and this is yet another of its oddities, is not at all aristocratic; it is a plebeian literature addressing itself to a broad section of the public. Its strength and its weakness can be found in this fact. It is strong in that it has a well-established hinterland in which its words echo powerfully, but weak in that it is not emancipated enough and too dependent on the public, on their receptivity and education, and it seems all the time to doubt the strength of its own convictions, its own cultural level. Sometimes today I become very frightened when I think that our civilization is losing that European character which was so close to the hearts of the Czech Humanists and Revivalists. Greek and Roman and antiquity and Christianity, the two basic sources of the European spirit which created the conditions for the development of Czech culture, have almost vanished from the consciousness of the young Czech intellectual, and this is a loss which can never be replaced. It has to be remembered that an

4. The Revivalists were poets, writers, thinkers and politicians who, from the beginning of the nineteenth century, supported and encouraged the separation of the Czech lands from German influence. They wrote in Czech, on Czech themes, rather than in German, in order to bring about a renaissance of the Czech language. This had survived as a spoken language, but was hardly written in the eighteenth century. The leading writers of the Revival were Josef Jungmann, Jan Kollár, Ravel Josef Šafařík and František Palacký.

iron continuity exists in European thought which is more powerful than every revolution and every idea, which has created its own vocabulary, its own terminology, its own myths and themes, without a knowledge of which European intellectuals cannot communicate. Recently I read a shattering document about the knowledge of world literature possessed by future teachers of Czech, and I wouldn't like to imagine what their knowledge of general world history is like. Provincialism doesn't only have its impact on the nation's literary achievements, but is a problem of the nation's whole existence, especially its schooling, its journalism and so on.

A little while ago, I saw a film called *Daisies*.[5] It concerned two splendidly repulsive girls, supremely satisfied with their own cute limitations, and merrily destroying everything which they didn't understand. It seemed to me then that I was watching a profound and very topical parable about vandalism. What is a vandal? He certainly isn't an illiterate peasant who burns a hated land-owner's castle in a fit of anger. A vandal, as I observe him around me, is socially secure, literate, self-satisfied and with no very good reason for trying to get his own back on somebody. A vandal is an arrogant, limited person, who feels good in himself, and is willing at any time to appeal to his democratic rights. This arrogant limitedness thinks that one of its basic rights is to change the world into its own image, and because the world is too big for it to understand, it chooses to change the world by destroying it. In exactly the same way, a youngster will knock the head off a sculpture in a park because it seems to insult him by being bigger than he is, and he'll do it with great satisfaction, because any act of self-assertion satisfies man.

People who live only in the immediate present, unaware of historical continuity and without culture, are capable of transforming their country into a desert without history, without memory, without echoes and without beauty. Vandalism today is not just something that is fought by the police. When representatives of the

5. *Daisies*, a film directed by Věra Chytilová, made in 1966, and one of the leading films of the Czech 'new wave'. In May 1967, a young communist deputy, Jaroslav Průžinec, attacked Chytilová by asking: 'How much longer will these artists go on poisoning the lives of honest working people, how much longer will they tread our socialist progress into the mud?' Kundera refers to him below.

people or the relevant officials decide that a statue or a castle, a church, an old lime-tree, is pointless and order it to be removed, that is just another form of vandalism. There's no substantial difference between legal and illegal destruction and there is not a great deal of difference between destruction and prohibition. In the Chamber a certain Czech deputy recently demanded, in the name of twenty-one deputies, a ban on two serious, 'difficult' films, one of them, by an irony of fate, *Daisies*, a parable about vandals. He uncompromisingly denounced both films and at the same time declared quite explicitly that he didn't understand them. There is no real contradiction in such an attitude as this. The biggest sin of these two works was that they were above the heads of those who did not like them, and thus insulted them.

In a letter to Helvetius, Voltaire wrote a wonderful sentence: 'I don't agree with what you say, but I will fight to the death to defend your right to say it.' This expresses the basic ethical principle of modern cultural life. If we return in history to a time when this principle did not apply, then we are taking a step from the modern age into the Middle Ages. Any suppression of views, especially any violent suppression of incorrect views, tends eventually to militate against truth, because truth can only be arrived at by a free and equal dialogue. Any infringement of freedom of thought and speech, however discreet the means and however subtle the name for such censorship, is a scandal in the twentieth century and inhibits and shackles the flourishing of our literature.

But one thing is beyond dispute: if a flowering of our art has occurred, it is due to the fact that intellectual freedom has been broadened. The fate of Czech literature is at this moment vitally dependent on the extent of our intellectual freedom. I know that when they hear the word 'freedom' some people immediately get their backs up and object that the freedom of socialist literature must surely have its limits. We know that every sort of freedom has its limits, limits which are determined for instance by the level of contemporary knowledge, education, prejudice and so on. Except that no new period has ever tried to define itself in terms of its own limitations! The Renaissance did not define itself by the limiting naïvety of its rationalism, for this was apparent only in historical perspective. Romanticism defined itself by saying that it went beyond and outside the limits set by classical canons and by making a new discovery which it was able to master outside those limits. And so also the words 'socialist literature' will have no real meaning until they mean a similar liberating act of transcendence.

The trouble is that in our country it is always considered to be a greater virtue to guard frontiers than to cross them. The most diverse, transient socio-political circumstances are supposed to justify the various limitations which are put on spiritual freedom. But the only great politics are those which place the interests of the age before transient interests. And the greatness of Czech culture is the vital interest of the age for the Czech nation.

This is even more true in that today the nation has quite exceptional opportunities open to it. In the nineteenth century, our nation was living on the periphery of world history. In this century, however, it is living right in the very centre. As we know quite well, the fact of being in the centre of the world's stage is not always a matter of milk and honey. But on the miraculous soil of art this hardship becomes a source of great wealth. Even the bitter experience of Stalinism can be turned paradoxically into something of unique value.

I don't like it when people equate 'fascism' with 'Stalinism'. Fascism, based on a quite open anti-humanism, created a situation which was fairly simple from the moral point of view: it left humanistic principles and virtues untouched because it appeared as their antithesis. Stalinism, however, was the heir of the great humanist movement, which even within the Stalinist disease preserved many of its original attitudes, ideas, slogans, expressions and dreams. To see such a humanistic movement turning into something exactly the opposite before one's own eyes, taking along with it the last traces of human virtue, replacing love for mankind with cruelty to people, love for truth with a renunciation of it, and so on, to watch this process going on, opens up incredible insights into the most fundamental aspects of human values and virtues. What is history, and what place has man in history, and anyway, what is man? None of these questions can be answered in the same way after that experience as before it. No one could emerge from this period of history the same as he was when it began. And of course, it isn't just a question of Stalinism. The whole story of this nation from democracy, fascist slavery, and Stalinism to socialism (coupled with its unique national problem), has something quintessential in it, something which makes the twentieth century what it is. This experience perhaps means that we are able to pose more meaningful questions, to create more meaningful myths, than people who have not gone through this anabasis. This nation has perhaps been through more than many other nations have during this century, and if its genius has been alert during that time, it may well know more than most others as well. This greater knowledge could change into a liberating crossing of previous boundaries, into the ability to surpass the limits of previous knowledge about man and his destiny, and thus give significance, maturity and greatness to Czech culture. For the time being these are just possibilities, just chances, but there have been many works appearing in the past few years which show that these chances are very real.

But again I have to put the question: is our nation aware of these possibilities? Does it know that these are *its* chances? Does it realize that historical opportunities don't occur twice? Does it realize that to lose these chances means to lose the twentieth century for the Czech nation?

'It is universally recognized', wrote Palacký,[6] 'that it was the Czech writers who would not allow the nation to perish, but resurrected it and gave a noble purpose to its endeavours.' Czech writers took on the responsibility for the very existence of their nation and they bear it still today, because the standard of Czech letters, their greatness or insignificance, courage or cowardice, provincialness or their wide humanistic outlook, determine to a considerable extent what is to be the answer to our most important national question. Is it worthwhile for the nation to exist at all? Is it worth having a language? And these terribly fundamental questions, which lie at the root of the existence of the contemporary nation, are still waiting for a conclusive answer. That is the reason why everyone who through his bigotry, his vandalism, his philistinism and his narrow-mindedness sabotages the cultural revolution which has largely already begun, is sabotaging the very existence of this nation.

6. Fantišek Palacký (1798–1876), Czech historian and politician, author of a famous history of the Czech nation, and the leading historian of the Revival. In April 1876, shortly before he died, he made a speech in which he said, 'Our nation is in great danger, surrounded, as it is, by enemies in every direction; but I do not despair; I hope it will be able to vanquish them, if it has the will to do so.'

Karel Kosík
Our present crisis (extracts)

Literární Listy, 11 April—16 May 1968

. . . Our present crisis is primarily a discussion about the *meaning* of national and human existence. Have we sunk to the level of anonymous masses for whom conscience, human dignity, a sense of truth and justice, honour, decency and courage are nothing but useless verbiage, which get in the way of the search for comfort, or are we able to solve all the economic, political and other problems in accordance with the needs of a human and national existence? . . .

Our present crisis represents not just the collapse of everything old, obsolete and inefficient, but at the same time an opportunity to create something new. Either it will become a transition point to a new indifference and routine, or it will be understood by revolutionary social and political forces as a rare moment of history when it was possible to create a new policy, new social relations, a new way of thinking and new forms of political alignment . . .

Every practical step which frees us from that remarkable conglomeration of bureaucracy and Byzantinism, from that monstrous symbiosis of the state with the pagan church, hypocrisy with fanaticism, ideology with faith, bureaucratic greyness with mass hysteria, has of course a much greater value than the most ostentatious proclamations about freedom. But those as yet small steps which we have taken to repudiate political crimes cannot conceal or postpone the urgency of providing answers to basic questions which so far we have not even touched upon, and without which socialism, as a revolutionary alternative for the people of the twentieth century, is unthinkable: we have to ask again who man is and what truth is; what is being and what is time; what is the essence of technology and science, and what is the significance of revolution.

Ivan Klíma
One project and one party

Literární Listy, 25 April 1968

It's amazing that everyone swears by the word socialism. If they are all in favour of the same social system, it's rather suspicious. Either they're really hiding something, or their ideas about what they say they are in favour of are so vague that they really can all be for it. No one, of course, takes any risks if he declares he is in favour of good and justice, of comfort and peace, in the same way as everyone can oppose fraud, corruption, violence and injustice.

The conditions we have lived in in this country up until now have been closer to what we oppose. After all, there can't be many people today who would disagree with the assertion that it had very little in common with socialism. But on the other hand, we have opening up before us the prospect of realizing what we are all in favour of, a truly humane socialism, the old goal of a scientific, rational model for a socialist system.

But what is it that we are actually in favour of? What kind of social system? What exactly is it that we are saying that we support from one day to the next?

We know that socialism socializes the means of production, that it is a system of directing society scientifically, that it promises to abolish man's alienation – from himself and from his work. It makes work creative again and gives dignity once again to a man who works conscientiously and willingly. It is supposed to reward every person according to his deserts. And then there are all those vague ideas: a genuinely humanistic society, freedom, culture for everyone, equality. But just have a look at our twenty years of socialism! If the ideal of socialism is the best that was ever suggested by man, how can we explain away the continual 'deformations' which have always been created by it – Stalinism, and the police bureaucracies it has bred in a number of countries; Maoism; the developments in Albania and Cuba and of course in Czechoslovakia as well? Can we so confidently and completely ignore such persistent warnings as these? Can we just keep on talking about 'deformations' caused by a few individuals, or by some disembodied force 'up there', or by imperialist plots? Isn't it possible that the root of the tragedy lies in the system itself?

The socialist scheme, which is always described as being 'scientific', bears all the marks of the times in which it originated, times which are becoming very dated at the same time as the ideals which they generated, and which are getting lost in the past. It was a period when homage was paid to reason. A time of faith in the saving rationalism of science. A time which destroyed God and the eschatological myth and longed to replace it with something . . . With what? With reason of course, and science. A time when people believed that man and his needs could be assessed in their entirety and that he can thus be manipulated for his own good. A time which did not have any ideas about psychology. And it believed therefore, naïvely and sincerely, that it was possible to construct, in the same way as religion did, an ideal which is equally attractive and applicable to everybody . . .

The moment power tries to realize the unrealizable it must inevitably come up against the resistance of the majority of the people. And then it can either back down or use violence. And what remains of the old dream then?

Ultimately, violence reigns.

We should ask the question again. Is it possible to build, and is there any point in building, a rationally directed social organization? Is it possible to do it today? Can one presume that man, whose psychology has been formed over thousands of years, is able to transform his basic attitudes in the space of one or two generations? Up until now, experience seems to have shown us that the answer is no. An absolutely rationally organized society deadens the movement of ideas and is as much the beginning of the end as complete chaos is. Experience shows that when millions of human beings are organized and urged towards one single vision of human perfection, towards a single aim, a single happiness, when a single God, a single Reason, a single Plan, contains them all, then catastrophe is approaching.

If society is to be rationally directed today, it can only be in the opposite direction, with a quite opposite aim from that towards which this rationality has been directed up to now. The problem will certainly not be how best to subordinate people to a single model and a single viewpoint, but how to relate them to each other and how to weld all the contradictory ideas, interests and aims which people from every part of society have into a workable whole, how to expand as much as possible people's scope for broadening their experience and ideas so that these projects don't clash with each other, but combine to help the whole of society to work better. People are talking about reviving private enterprise to a limited extent in certain areas of the economy, so as to allow society to develop more freely, and especially to give people initiative in the production process. But why only consider one way of breaking away from a single system? Aren't there groups of people whose convictions and ideals might lead them to want to do something in exactly the opposite direction: to set up communes, of course on the basis of voluntary membership, which might be able to abolish monetary relations and all their consequences in society; or to introduce direct democracy and lay the foundations of an attitude towards work on a purely moral basis? They would thus be able to offer a completely different kind of relationship between people, a scale of values different from those which apply in the society outside, to people who long for a way of life and self-realization based on them.

Everybody needs something extra, whether we mean by that his God or his culture, his reliance on himself or on others, his need to make sacrifices or to sacrifice himself – the thing that separates him from the crowd, that makes him unique. It is this which makes him a man. A society which takes over the direction of people's most basic human needs and tries to channel them in one direction has no future and can only end in catastrophe.

Action Programme of the Communist Party of Czechoslovakia (extracts)

Rudé Právo, 10 April 1968

We want quite frankly to disclose what the mistakes and deformations were and what caused them so that we can remedy them as soon as possible and concentrate on the fundamental changes in our lives that we are facing at the moment.

After the Twentieth Congress of the Communist Party of the Soviet Union, which inspired a revival in the development of socialist democracy, the Party adopted several measures intended to overcome bureaucratic and centralized methods of management and to prevent the class struggle from being turned against the working people. Many communists and whole working collectives tried to open up a way for the economy, the standard of living, science and culture to develop progressively. The more obvious it was that class antagonism had been overcome, and the foundations for socialism laid, the more urgent it became to stress that all social groups, classes and nationalities in Czechoslovakia should cooperate and that methods should be changed from those that were used during the early days of socialism . . . The survival of methods from the time of the class struggle provoked an artificial tension among the different social groups and nationalities, different generations, communists and non-Party members. Dogmatic attitudes prevented a much needed revaluation of what the character of socialist construction should be.

The measures that were taken did not therefore bring the right results. On the contrary, over the years difficulties accumulated until they formed a tight vicious circle. Subjective ideas to the effect that the construction of a socialist society depended only on an accelerated extensive development of production were not straightened out. This led to the over-hasty expansion of heavy industry, to an excessive drain on manpower and raw materials, and to costly investment. Such an economic policy, enforced through directive administrative methods, no longer corresponded to the economic needs of the country and resulted in its material and human resources being exhausted . . . Czechoslovak industry became technologically backward, the development of public services was slowed down, the market's equilibrium was upset, the international status of the Czechoslovak economy dropped, especially in foreign trade: in the end there was stagnation and a certain fall in the standard of living . . . Socialist enterprise did not expand. In economic life, hard work, independence, expertise and initiative were not appreciated, but subservience, obedience and kowtowing to authority were.

A deeper reason why out-of-date economic methods were maintained was that the political system itself was deformed. Socialist democracy did not expand, the revolutionary dictatorship deteriorated into bureaucracy and held up progress in every aspect of life in Czechoslovakia. Thus political mistakes were added to the economic difficulties . . . A great deal of the efforts, activity and energy of Party and state workers was wasted. And when we add to this the external political difficulties of the early sixties, then a serious economic crisis ensued. It is this that has caused the difficulties with which the workers are confronted day by day . . . the catastrophic state of housing, the precarious state of the transport system, poor quality goods and public services, the lack of a civilized environment to live in – all factors which tangibly affect the human being and are the vital concern of a socialist society. Bitterness grew among the people and a feeling that in spite of all the successes achieved and effort expended, socialism was making progress with great difficulty, with fatal delays and with many imperfections in the moral and political relationships between people . . .

Socialist democracy did not develop in the Party itself . . . criticism was silenced or even suppressed, and mistakes were not corrected. Party bodies took over the tasks of state and economic bodies and social organizations, and this resulted in an incorrect merging of the Party and state management, to the monopoly of power in some sectors, to unqualified interference, to the undermining of initiative, and to the growth of a cult of mediocrity and unhealthy anonymity. Irresponsibility and lack of discipline increased . . . And all of these questions became areas where those forces which were insisting on fundamental changes clashed with those which held reactionary and outdated opinions.

In the past decade the Party has frequently put forward the demand for the development of socialist democracy . . . It was stated quite clearly in the theses prepared by the Central Committee of the Communist Party for the Thirteenth Party Congress that 'the dictatorship of the proletariat has fulfilled its main historical mission in our country,' while the direction for the further development of our democracy was no less clearly outlined:

> the system of socialist democracy – with the state, social organizations, and the Party as the leading force – tries quite intentionally to emphasize the differing interests and attitudes of the working people, and to settle them, in a democratic way, inside the socialist organizations of society fairly, bearing in mind nationwide needs and goals. The development of democracy must go ahead hand in hand with the strengthening of a scientific and professional approach to social management.

Nevertheless, certain harmful characteristics of the centralized directive decision-making and management apparatus still survive. In relations between the Party, the state, and social organizations, in the internal relations and methods of these individual areas, in the relationships that exist between state and other institutions and individuals, and in the evaluation of the importance of public opinion and of people being informed, in the effects of cadre policies – in all these fields there are still too many things which are disturbing people's lives, while at the same time preventing really professionally competent and scientific decisions from being made and encouraging highhandedness. The reasons for all this lie above all in the fact that relations between different departments of our political system have been built up over the years as a means of carrying out the orders given from the centre, and decisions have hardly ever been the result of democratic procedure . . .

The real purpose of democracy must be to achieve better results in practical tasks . . . to satisfy the interests and needs of the people. Our democracy has to be a more profound democracy. It must give such a degree of civil liberty that the superiority of socialism over the limitations of bourgeois democracy will be proved, and socialism will become an attractive example for progressive movements even in industrially advanced countries with democratic traditions.

Three
The Past Re-examined

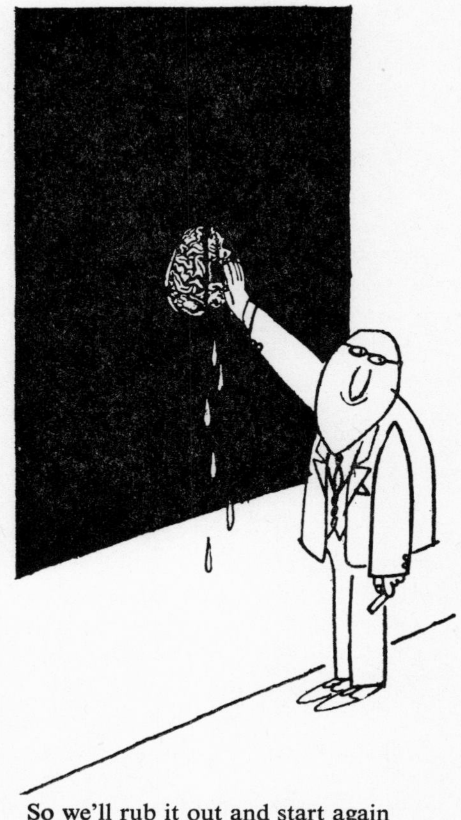

So we'll rub it out and start again

. . . the thing that had attracted, even infatuated me, about the Communist movement was the feeling, however illusory, of being close to the helm of history. In those days we really were making big decisions about the fate of men and things . . . The elation we experienced is commonly called the intoxication of power, but with a little good will, I could choose a rather less severe way of putting it: we were bewitched by history, intoxicated at having jumped on its back and being able to feel it beneath us. Admittedly, in most cases this did develop into an ugly lust for power, but all the same, just as all human dealings are ambivalent, there was at that time, and with us youngsters in particular, an altogether idealistic illusion that we were inaugurating a human era, an era when man – every man – would be neither outside history nor under the wheel of history, but would direct and create it himself.

Ludvík, the hero of Milan Kundera's novel *The Joke*

In the year 1948 we fell out of a train. Czechoslovakia at that time fell out of the train of progress.

Jan Procházka in an interview given to Agence France Presse, reprinted in *Literární Listy* 15 May 1968

The past dominated the whole of the revival process; the name itself implied retrospection. As the Party leadership saw it, the untainted ideals of before 1948 were to be reincarnated and used to expunge the all too vivid memory of the distortions and the deformations committed in the name of those ideals over the past twenty years. But before this could happen, the whole of the nation's past had to undergo a merciless examination; as Hamšík puts it: 'Rather late in the day we are in a situation in which we need to understand the past in order to be able to transcend it and really head in a different direction.' The 'tailoring' of the past for political and ideological needs had to be rejected in principle and remedied in practice.

The First Republic, its foundation and its course were 'rehabilitated'; T. G. Masaryk, the first president and father figure of what had before been disparaged as the bourgeois republic, was returned to his rightful place in the history of the nation.

But the truth frightened the conservatives because it undermined the power which they had, or rather had possessed, over the past and thereby over the minds of the people. What they had stopped had been the establishment of any real continuity, while in its place an official account of everything had been laid down in true Orwellian manner. Hamšík and others noted this practical importance of the past, and also stressed that without its restitution the moral character of the nation would continue to suffer, the Czech and Slovak would live on like 'a man torn out of history'. Revelations about more recent events, however, dominated 1968.

The events of 1948–68, and in particular what were known as the 'deformations',[1] had to be explained. Clearly a great deal had gone wrong since 1948, when young communists, such as Jiří Ruml (see 'My twenty years') had 'jumped head first into politics', and everybody now wanted to know why. Until the whole truth was revealed, and the factors which had made possible the transformation of the rule of the Party of the people into a totalitarian dictatorship analysed, there could be no real chance of preventing a repetition of the history of the fifties and sixties.

The political trials were seen as the embodiment of the chasm between ideals and practice; as a reality they had disillusioned many people as to the true value of any ideal. 'I gradually became

1. 'Deformations' was a term which embraced whatever 'mistakes', breaches of justice and crimes were considered safe to admit according to the Party policy of the day. In 1968, for the first time, all the injustices, politically motivated trials, and dismissals were included publicly in this category. Although arrests and dismissals began immediately after February 1948, and continued, in considerably mollified form, right up to 1967, the main part of the 'deformations' took place between 1949 and 1955. Estimates of the 'gross' figure of those who suffered varied from 100,000 to 130,000 for the whole period. The main trials took place between 1949 and 1955, the Centre trial of 1952 (Slánský and thirteen others, see note 9) being the largest. The report of the official Central Committee Commission appointed in April 1968 gives the figure of 178 executed for the 1948–52 years.

convinced that many sublime ideas lose their magic when it comes down to practical reality . . . It just depends on who is interpreting them and how' (Ruml). The Party and the Revolution in abstract were of little use, and it was the great advance of 1968 that it brought such 'untouchable' concepts within the sphere of practical judgement, criticism and even condemnation.

Facts about every aspect of the sad history of those twenty years, which Vaculík had utterly condemned, filled more pages of the press, and absorbed more time at meetings, than any other subject. Attention naturally centred on the most spectacular of the deformations, the arrests, torture, faked charges and 'theatrical' show trials from 1948 to 1956. At the beginning of this period the death of Jan Masaryk,[2] the son of the first president, was publicly questioned, and the Prosecutor General was asked to investigate it. At the time it had been surrounded by secrecy, in order to clear the Party and the communists in general (the Soviet Union was also suspected) of all suspicion. The vague admissions which had been made by Novotný that everything had not been in order with the notorious Centre trial expanded into nightmare accounts of how the Party had deliberately murdered its own best leaders by employing methods worthy of the Nazis (see 'Interview with Investigator XY'). An endless supply of former political prisoners fed the media with their own personal experiences in those years (see Jirásek for the non-communist view) which showed that the deformations had not been limited to a few large trials, but had permeated every sector of society.

Responsibility for these 'illegalities', for the entire range of crimes, from judicial murder to administrative malpractice, was discussed in the press. From the point of view of the new leadership the real culprits had to be unmasked and punished in some

2. The death of Jan Masaryk in March 1948 (he was Minister of Foreign Affairs) as a result of falling from a window, had been hushed up at the time and had remained a taboo subject for twenty years in Czechoslovakia. In 1968 the doubts that had stayed in many peoples' minds about the verdict of suicide given in 1948 were raised publicly, in particular by Sviták's call to the Prosecutor General to re-open his investigation of the entire matter. In the course of the period, the press, radio and television actively contributed to the 'search for the truth', and Soviet involvement was alleged (which provoked a flat denial from Tass). The whole case showed that, at least in the examination of the past, the new leadership were willing to fulfil the promises they had made.

way in order to prevent the entire burden of guilt from falling onto the Party as a whole, something which could not be tolerated (see Husák). Those of the new leadership who had themselves suffered in the fifties, such as Husák, Smrkovský and Pavel,[3] had a personal interest in seeing that those who had been responsible for the all-important decisions were made to answer for those crimes. This became the most powerful lever against Novotný himself,[4] and for his expulsion from the Party (he was actually only suspended, together with other prominent Party leaders of that period, at the May plenum).

The public showed a greater interest in finding the 'smaller' Urváleks and Bacíleks and Novotnýs, and some more conservative politicians thought that the naming of these judges, prosecutors, investigators and Party officials led to the 'maligning' of 'honest' people, and only helped those who wanted to undermine the Party's position (see Husák). Dishonest elements had begun to exploit the re-examination of the past which the Party itself had sanctioned so generously, Smrkovský told the public. Certain excesses could of course be seen. The revelations about the past activities of some of the workers in the prisons and courts drove them to commit suicide,[5] but there were no witchhunts. In view of the enormity of the crimes involved there was a surprisingly restrained tone in the mass media and amongst the people. Even the former political prisoners themselves, who made up K231,[6] in-

3. Smrkovský had been imprisoned from 1951–55. Husák was arrested in 1951, sentenced to life for Slovak 'bourgeois nationalism' in 1954, and released comparatively late in 1960. Josef Pavel, appointed Minister of the Interior in April 1968, had been imprisoned 1951–5.

4. The suspension of Novotný (with other former Party leaders) was obtained at the May plenum on the question of his responsibility for the deformations. His repeated denials were answered by a scathing speech from Husák, and by historians who pointed out in a calmer manner that he had been in the political secretariat since 1951, and had been first secretary since 1953, after which date several of the trials had taken place.

5. Dr Sommer, the former head doctor at the Ruzyň prison, where the Centre trial interrogations took place, committed suicide after several articles and testimonies had appeared about his past activities. The vice-chairman of the Supreme Court met a similar end, and rumours circulated that as many as twenty-six State Security members had committed suicide (*New York Times* 30 April 1968).

6. K231, which grouped former political prisoners together, was founded at

sisted on the careful gathering of evidence before any accusation was made.

The Party was not prepared, however, to allow any changes to be made in the statute of limitations,[7] which protected the overwhelming majority of criminals from prosecution, and where proceedings could still be started the authorities did their best to prevent any of the 'executors' from being sentenced. Political responsibility was to be defined in accordance with the position held; in Karel Kaplan's words: 'the degree of responsibility was directly related to the position in the power structure'. But although political responsibility was thus 'rehabilitated' in theory, the Party was not in the least willing to allow any political trials to be held; the convenient argument could be used here that this would only be a return to the same methods which had already been condemned. Party discipline alone was to be applied after long and deliberate Party investigations.

The official attitude to another practical aspect of this retrospection, the rehabilitation of victims who had received prison sentences, was less restrictive. Novotný had been forced to start this mammoth task, but had hardly scratched the surface when he declared, after the 1963 rehabilitations, that the injustices of the past had been remedied.[8] The policy after January was a thorough and complete rehabilitation of all who had suffered, including the non-communists who had been shamelessly neglected before 1968. The need to rehabilitate everybody became the lowest common denominator of the revival. Every politician declared his full support for this act of justice, and with the rehabilitation of a few local

---

the end of March, and grew rapidly to over 50,000 members. It was attacked as a platform for anti-communist and anti-socialist views, although its leaders categorically denied any political ambitions for the Club. It derived its name from law 231 of 1948, on the protection of the Republic, under which the majority of its members had been sentenced.

7. By virtue of the amnesties and the statute of limitations, all offences except murder which had been committed before 1958 were immune from prosecution. Seven ex-Security men were arrested for murder, but the charge was not proved.

8. As early as 1961 Novotný had declared that all the wrongs of the past had been remedied, but in 1963 over 400 more people were rehabilitated, a measure which was intended to silence all calls for further delving into the deformations.

survivors of the prisons or the forced labour camps, democratization was frequently considered to be in 'full flood'. A law was passed in late June which made provisions for the speeding up and simplification of the judicial process, and laid down how much compensation was to be given. But it still adhered to the priciple that 'the consequences of revolutionary measures' could not be altered.

More important in the long term than these practical expiations, unique though they were to the Soviet bloc in their thoroughness, were the theoretical deductions drawn from the past. First the terms themselves were rejected as 'alibistic' euphemisms:

> So-called deformations are no deformations, but normal, necessary and everyday manifestations of totalitarian dictatorship. They are not tumours on the peaceful body of socialism which can be cut out, but gangrene which permeates the whole method of rule. Totalitarian dictatorship is itself a deformation, and to remove this deformation means to remove totalitarian dictatorship.

Such was Ivan Sviták's view in 'With Your Head Against the Wall', *Student*, 17 April 1968. Dobrovský (see 'The personality cult as an excuse') attacked the over-used term 'personality cult' as one which was meant 'to conceal and not to reveal reality', which relieved the Party and the system of responsibility by placing it all onto one man. Old 'explanations', such as the international atmosphere, the class war, the evil influence of Stalin and Beria, were now declared to be wholly inadequate.

Kaplan, who made the most detailed and penetrating survey and analysis of 1968, came to the same conclusions as all those who allowed their reason to overcome any reluctance to admit the failures of Revolution and Party. 'The point about the fifties', wrote Kaplan (see 'Thoughts on the political trials') 'is not that they were a deformation of an essentially good system but that they were basically a bad system.' The question also inevitably arose whether the fact that all Marxist-Leninist-based systems had undergone a period of deformations meant that the fault lay 'deeper than political practice', and lay in the theory itself, in the preparation of the phase of the 'dictatorship of the proletariat' (see Dobrovský).

From the point of view of the reforms of 1968, however, the

most important conclusion made from the re-examination of the past was that it had all been the result not of any accidental conglomeration of circumstances, nor of the domination of events by any 'evil' personality, but of a bad system. The search for guarantees against a repetition of the past had therefore to be directed not towards any 'perfection' of the old but to the creation of the new (see Mlynář in 'On the Theme of Opposition'). As Karel Kaplan put it: 'To prevent the political trials from ever happening again, it is necessary not only to change our ideas about politics, but also to produce a new political system.'

Jiří Ruml
My twenty years

Reportér, 28 February 1968

... Twenty years ago, when we were twenty, we jumped head first into politics, as though we were jumping into uncharted waters. There was an element of bravery in this, but also of foolhardiness; there was a lot of enthusiasm and a lot of rash behaviour, a lot of spirit and less intelligence. You're like this when you're young, and we had an opportunity which had been long denied, to be there while something new was being created. And we were duly rude and inconsiderate about the hesitation and lack of understanding of older and perhaps more experienced people.

We won a great victory. Later many people joined us because they were sympathetic, others from inertia and still others from fear. We did not always recognize and distinguish these motives sensitively enough. We wrote proud proclamations, overworked our fellow men, and if the voluntary approach didn't always work, we gave orders. The revolution 'hasn't time' to try to persuade, it calls for decisive action. We shall govern the wind and the rain, so why not people, and he who's not with us is against us, he will be swept away by the storm. And so we kept our eyes wide open; the enemy might be anywhere, even inside the Party. It wasn't long before we 'found' him there.

The trials began. Today, it's easy to say 'Those were evil times,' but at the time we believed we were doing right. The accumulated 'proofs' seemed to us to be credible enough. The 'criminals' had posed a threat to what we had been building with such effort and enthusiasm, to what we had been living for.

A little later, the people who had led us into the struggle left the stage, those with whose names we had linked our successes. This was bad enough in itself, but the real shock came only when we found out that they had been very far from infallible.

We did not learn until later, and then only little by little, that people had been locked up and executed, first with the excuse that 'the condemned got caught up in a wheel which they themselves had started to turn,' and later with the excuse that 'false evidence had been used against them'.

We 'rehabilitated' people. According to its definition, this word means the restoration of a person's good reputation, dignity, rights, standing and innocence. But unfortunately not the restoration of life. This interpretation was not fully realized in many of the other cases of rehabilitation. We certainly pronounced the sentences with much greater ceremony than we quashed them with. In the process of rehabilitation, what we in fact obliterated were the traces of those who had originally pronounced them, either directly or indirectly. And this is where the conflict between our knowledge and our conscience deepened, leading to the paradoxical situation that the more someone knew about these things, the less his conscience seemed to bother him.

People's dissatisfaction grew, because the economic difficulties were multiplying as well. A person who won't recognize political mistakes is hardly going to acknowledge the causes of economic failures. And after all, these mistakes were rooted in wrong policies, in ill-considered long-term plans, in the very beginnings of our uneven development. People had tried again and again to reverse this undesirable development, but their strength gave out, disintegrated. Their voices fell on deaf ears, they weren't listened to. And so, slowly but surely, indifference spread among the nation. Indifference to what had to be done and to those who gave the orders, indifference to people and their fates. Everyone, or almost everyone, looked after his own patch of land, rather than the common fields. We became resigned . . .

Many times in my work as a journalist, I've met with the assertion that certain ideas are unassailable, that they are quite simply sacrosanct. Often in this connection I've heard those magic words, 'Trust the Party', quoted. 'The Party requires . . . You have disappointed the Party . . . The only time you err is when you err from the Party.'

And when afterwards I worked out, in peace and quiet, what it all meant, I found out that I was supposed to believe in something which one individual had said and which perhaps in six months' time would no longer apply: that it was not the Party, but Comrade So-and-So who required this and that, and that I had betrayed the trust of another Comrade So-and-So, who after a time had himself proved a 'disappointment' all along the line; that I shouldn't have listened to what an expert had to say on the subject of growing maize, but that I should have waited for the Party to give its judgement. And when I said anything against an individual, I was immediately accused of attacking the Party.

The truth is that a lot of people are looking for alibis. Why should someone have had someone else thrown out of his job? It was the Party that wanted it. Why should someone else have agreed to an unnecessary building project? But of course it was the Party's idea. But it must surely always be some actual person! Otherwise no one has really made a mess of anything, we are all responsible for everything. And doesn't it matter how high up the ladder you are? Surely the degree of responsibility changes according to one's position!

So I gradually became convinced that many sublime ideas lose their magic when it comes down to practical reality – ideas like humanity, honour, and truth. It just depends on who is interpreting them, and how. They can be abused. That is why for some time now I haven't liked to worship ideas, because anyone can use their dazzling brilliance to blind people. 'There are things we won't discuss with anybody,' said those who believed certain ideas to be unassailable, although at the same time they were talking non-stop about democracy. Think how debating circles were formed on the streets before February 1948, in which all that mattered was the strength of your argument. Then, no one could wag his finger and shout out: 'You mustn't say that, you're not allowed to say that!' One had to defeat one's opponent with a fact, one had to demonstrate where he was mistaken or where he was lying. But we are used to not being allowed to doubt the words and deeds of 'the leading force of society', even if those words and deeds are sometimes at variance. Consequently, there is not even any need to persuade, because it's all in the constitution, so what debating is there to do?

So slowly discussion stopped even at meetings called for that purpose, because no one was willing to bring thunder and lightning down on his own head unnecessarily. Consequently there grew up a 'unity', not as a result of the confrontation between views, but in their falling neatly into line. The other political parties became 'united' as well, and so did the mass organizations, because the more advanced a socialist society is, the more conscientious its members are. Conscientiousness is displayed by agreeing with basic directives. The person who has the rubber stamp also controls public opinion.

This system demanded obedience, which means reliable people who will respect the trust placed in them. Who values trust more, a talented person or one who would otherwise find it difficult to support himself? It turned out that there was more 'reliability' in those who didn't want to lose their positions. The professional revolutionary was born. People are not stupid; they will learn the ropes. But I can already hear someone saying: 'That's an insult to honest endeavour!'

I have never doubted our peoples abilities: in comparison with other, more developed people, they are above average, albeit untapped. If we had more of such capable people, and not those 'capable of anything' in decisive places, we should have had fewer decisions made which had to be put right later, and we would have definitely made more progress, with much less trouble. As for fidelity to ideas: why should a well-behaved and obedient person be preferable to and more faithful than the others? Perhaps only because he fears for his own private socialism. Except that he can't admit this in public.

As a result of all this, two levels of consciousness were produced in us. Among ourselves, in the circle of our acquaintances and close friends, we can tell the truth. But outside we mustn't say the whole truth, or even any of the truth at all, so as not to weaken the movement. A special code grew up; we say and write something different from what we think. And because we've been doing it for a long time, we even believe in both. Or at least we pretend to. Those who won't observe the code are trouble-makers, demagogues and adventurists, undisciplined and dangerous people. They outlaw themselves from our midst because they've broken the rules of the game. But who in fact is really sapping the movement's vitality?

I have never been satisfied with promises of bliss in an after-life. Perhaps it is because I am not a believer. But of course I'm not satisfied either with the promise that things will be better for future generations, that the happiness of which we're laying the foundations will only be enjoyed by future generations. So far no revolution has satisfied all man's aspirations and achieved the aims it set out for itself. I don't want to be thought of as a visionary. I think socialism was designed for man here and now, for him to enjoy in his own lifetime. The difficulty is that when it has strengthened its position, power always begins carefully to protect what it has achieved. It arms itself against attacks from left and right for so long that it becomes fossilized. It loses a capacity which is peculiar to every living organism, that of being able to renew or replace worn-out, damaged, lost or destroyed organs or cells with new parts.

If the organism that is our public life does not regain this capacity, we are looking forward to great changes quite fruitlessly because things have a habit of repeating themselves, although perhaps in a different way. Now there is a chance to change words into deeds, and such a big opportunity rarely occurs. But of course it has to be grasped.

Anna Tučková
Interview with Investigator XY

Slánský and Co.,[9] or it never rains but it pours

Reportér, 29 May 1968

It isn't my aim in this article to provoke someone to throw himself out of a window or hang himself. I'm attempting to use one person's story to cast some light on the smoothly running cogs of a monstrous machinery, to find out who it was who prepared the death sentences, for they involved not just those who were sentenced but also those who were responsible for the sentencing, and to discuss how they were prepared.

When XY was arrested in 1955,[10] a search of his flat revealed brochures with speeches of Slánský's and Šverma's, the protocol from the Rajk trial, one pair of old handcuffs, three pornographic playing cards, several anonymous threatening letters, and also the Order of February and the Order of the Republic. It seems from his personal papers that he had risen as far as Lieutenant-Colonel, that in 1953 he was awarded 30,000 crowns, and that when he started to get drunk regularly he was transferred from the Ministry

9. Slánský and Co. The Centre trial, as it was known, was held in November 1952. It was the largest political trial to have taken place in Czechoslovakia, or in post-war Central Europe. All the accused were former leading communists, headed by the alleged leader of the fabricated conspiracy, Rudolf Slánský, who until 1951 had been secretary general of the Party (second-in-command to Gottwald who was chairman of the Party (1945–53) and president of the Republic (1948–1953). Of the others in the Centre, Geminder, Frejka, Frank, Clementis, Reicin, Šváb, Margolius, Fischl, Šling and Simone were executed, and London, Löbl and Hajdů received life sentences, but were all released by 1960.

10. The 'XY' of this article is Lieutenant-Colonel Doubek, Chief of the Investigation Department of the State Security and head of the investigations for the Centre trial. He was arrested in 1955, and after two years custody was sentenced to nine years for using 'illegal methods', but was released in 1958 and provided with a good position in Čedok (the national travel agency) for which he worked as one of the Czechoslovak representatives at the World Fair in Brussels.

of the Interior into the leading ranks of the prison administration. He didn't even last there. He was released and in 1954 took up a position in the firm Motokov. In his cadre profile it was stated that 'for reasons of ill-health it is recommended that he should be given the opportunity to work outside the Ministry of the Interior'. This cadre report is dated 22.10.54, i.e. nearly a year after the revelations about Beria and almost a year after those on whom XY had worked had been executed.

How is it possible that none of those responsible and well-informed people thought of reasons other than health reasons? If XY had not become an alcoholic – and that in itself is nothing to be surprised at, for from what will be described later, it will be easily seen that he had good reason to want to drown his conscience – would he have stayed on at the Ministry? Obviously yes, like many others.

How did XY get into the Ministry? He was neither a pre-war policeman, nor a professional spy. Nor did he have a record of collaboration with the Gestapo, as in some cases. His life was quite ordinary, which doesn't say very much for a system which succeeded in turning a former medical student, a member of Mladá Kultura, into an inquisitor. During the occupation XY was placed in various factories to work, and after the liberation he worked in the Central Committee of the Communist Party of Czechoslovakia, at first in an economic department and later in the cadre department. It was there that Karel Šváb[11] selected him, supposedly for a three month work brigade, to strengthen the security of the Party.

When three months had elapsed, and XY expressed the desire to return to the Secretariat, he was not allowed to do so – Šváb told him to look on his work in the Security as a Party task. And so he stayed on, because one doesn't argue about Party jobs . . .

The machinery, driven along by the theory of the intensification of the class struggle and of the need to uncover enemies within the ranks of the Party itself, was already working. It could only have been stopped by such a fundamental step as the one Tito decided to take. Piecemeal resistance and piecemeal protests were not strong enough: they were swept aside or at any rate got round somehow. In 1949 XY started to investigate the traces of Rajkism

11. Karel Šváb, former head of State Security, arrested and executed in the Centre trials.

in Czechoslovakia. Gejza Panka, Alice Kohnová, Vlasta Veselá, Kurt Markus and others were interrogated.[12] Veselá rejected charges of collaboration with Field and started a hunger strike. When this didn't work, she poisoned herself with drugs, and the avalanche rushed on – Löbl, Šling,[13] more and more people were arrested . . .

The protocols[14] were intended to formulate quite clearly what those under investigation were guilty of, and to preclude their defence, since this was undertaken by the court. The investigating organs did not exist to interrogate a man about the good things he had done, but to prove that he was guilty on the evidence of the bad things. But how was it possible to prove him guilty? To help young investigators a manual was published, written by XY among others, on the basis of lectures given by Soviet advisers . . . XY says that the Soviet advisers taught us that our greatest asset is the person under investigation, and so it is even possible to bastardize that beautiful humanistic motto of Gorky's, that man is our most precious asset.

A cunning enemy does not leave compromising material behind him and it is therefore necessary to force him to confess. It is essential to exhaust the subjects under investigation both physically and mentally, and this is the reason for all the constant standing and walking and wakings in the night. They have to be convinced that the Party has thrown them overboard. The purpose was to bring about a 'break' in a person being investigated. When this was achieved, then they signed anything. With some, appeals were made to the person's Party loyalty: the person being investigated was persuaded that he could atone for his mistakes in the eyes of the Party by confessing. This method of investigation was used for instance on Clementis, who was constantly bombarded

12. Communists, some members of the International Brigades, who were arrested in connection with this record on various pretexts. Veselá committed suicide in prison.

13. Both among those sentenced with the Centre. Löbl, a deputy minister for Foreign Trade, was released in 1960, rehabilitated in 1963. He became director of the Bratislava State Bank, and published the first full account of the Centre trial in Czechoslovakia in 1968 (published in English by Elek, 1969). Šling was the leading secretary in Brno, and was executed in connection with the Centre.

14. The protocol in this context means the confessions of the accused which he had to recite in court.

with the accusation that once, at the time of the Soviet–German Pact, he had parted company with the Party and that he could only redress what he had done by confessing. XY quotes one of the chief investigators as saying, 'Don't be afraid, he'll confess to anything, because his attitude towards the Party is right.' If one adds to this the fact that many people, and Geminder is one example, apparently died with the cry 'Long live the Communist Party of Czechoslovakia!' on their lips, then suddenly one feels as though one is walking around inside Kafka's castle.

Slánský was at last 'the big case' which they had been waiting for. Nothing was left to chance; every confrontation was thoroughly planned. These preparations were analysed in detail at meetings of the investigators with the advisers and translators. The questions and answers were all decided beforehand. Not one line of the protocol was written while Slánský's resistance remained unbroken. Slánský persisted in rejecting the charges, and the investigators accused him of wanting intentionally to damage the Party, which had already publicly revealed all his activities. Up until his suicide attempt he was interrogated in an office, while later he was led to interrogations blindfold, with his hands tied, and then his feet attached to a ring in the wall. He stood up for himself and from time to time had fits when he shouted and banged his head against the wall . . .

When one of the investigators stayed alone with him in the room, Slánský asked him if he could go to the lavatory. The investigator went into the corridor and called the guard, and quick as a flash Slánský slammed the door shut and locked it, and when he didn't find the service revolver, hanged himself on the string of the alarm system from a window catch. They broke down the door and found him unconscious. The prison doctor revived him with injections and artificial respiration, and was later decorated for it . . .

The preparation of the trial was itself very thorough. Judges and prosecutors and defence council were chosen and for days on end they studied the protocols, the confessions of witnesses and the documentary material. They were told that they could ask only those questions which were mentioned in the protocols, and they did not have any contact with the accused. Bugging equipment was installed in their flats, so that a check could be kept on their reactions. Investigator XY worked out a draft indictment, which was submitted, but the advisers didn't like it. So they worked out another version, which was translated into Czech from the Russian and submitted to the Praesidium of the Party. The accused were selected in such a way as to take in every sphere of society, every sort of activity upon which the Centre could encroach. From this arose many illogicalities, and XY was himself surprised that Margolius also appeared in court as one of the accused. An adviser told him that Margolius's case involved huge sums of money and that this made a powerful impression on the public.[15] The production of the trial went off without a hitch, and those who took part in it were later decorated . . .

In this nation which gave birth to Švejk, not even Ruzyň[16] could avoid being involved in a case like the one which follows. Some investigators, mainly former factory workers, complained to the Minister, not, unfortunately, about the violations of the law, but that because of the uninterrupted interrogations the eight-hour working day was not being kept to. One of them was even found to have solved the problem of his Saturdays and Sundays by locking Comrade Smrkovský into solitary for those two days. XY, the chief investigator, wondered for a long time why Smrkovský always did something wrong on Fridays so that he had to be punished, until he discovered the real reason . . .

In this atmosphere of absurdity, the finale, after the trial, was utterly out of proportion to all that had gone before. When all the eleven condemned men had been executed, investigator XY happened to be with adviser Galinka. The driver and the investigators who had been charged with the disposal of the ashes reported back. They declared that they had put them into a sack, had driven with it into the country outside Prague, and had scattered them over a slippery road. The driver laughed as he had never before got fourteen people into the Tatraplan all at once, three of them alive and eleven in a sack . . .

Investigator XY, after his arrest, was sentenced for having exceeded his duties as a public functionary. His decorations were taken away from him. In 1958, far earlier than many of those

15. Rudolf Margolius was Deputy Minister of Foreign Trade.

16. A prison near the airport where the majority of the Centre interrogations took place, the most notorious of all the prisons.

whom he had investigated and who continued to sit in Mírov, Leopoldov and other prisons, he was released and employed in an enterprise which he represented at the Brussels World Fair. The highest State and Party authorities intervened on his behalf, and the whole history of his past was to be regarded as highly confidential.

In 1964 he went into retirement, and is said to have completely succumbed to alcoholism.

All these facts may well shock us. But far more shocking, and far more significant, is the fact that a detailed confession lay in the safe of the First Secretary of the Communist Party from 1955 on. Not just from this one, but from a number of other testimonies, the Party leadership at that time must have known for certain what had gone on during the trials, and what happened to the others who had been unjustly and illegally imprisoned. As early as 1955 the Party leadership could, without any hesitation, have condemned these methods and put them right. It would have saved a lot of people years of suffering and saved the Party and socialism a loss of prestige. And the fact that no open admission was made even in 1956 after the Twentieth Congress of the Communist Party of the Soviet Union, when a number of organizations and also the non-Party public were demanding an explanation, is a crime. Because even if some Party leaders did not necessarily know what was going on at the actual time of the trials, they must have known by then. And it was their Communist and human duty to speak out, to inform the Party and the public, to take steps to see that the law was restored. And today it is much more difficult to do this because of all the lost years.

If we are going to believe once more that the teachings of Communism offer possibilities for the future, and that we have to commit ourselves to this better tomorrow, then the whole truth must be told.

Miroslav Jirásek
Another viewpoint

Práce: 28 April 1968

I am one of the people who was sentenced to a long term for treason and espionage by the State Court. The Prosecutor Munk did actually propose the death penalty for me at Pankrác,[17] but I regarded that – as I did the whole trial – more as a farce than as a serious threat. Why should I deny it? When all is said and done we have nothing to be ashamed of, and I'll say straight away that even though as a former member of the Chancellery of the President of the Republic, Dr E. Beneš, I have not yet been rehabilitated, the hundreds of thousands of bags that I have sewn up in Leopoldov have been far more useful to the country than all the work which has led up to the chaos which Professor Ota Šik talked about at the meeting of Prague youth in the Congress Palace on 20 March 1968. And I'm not taking into account the shifts I worked in the Jachymov Mines[18] before the bags and feathers of Leopoldov. Even at that time it seemed to me that the shifts I was working would do no good at all for our country.

People used to say in those days that there were two kinds of people in Czechoslovakia: those who were already locked up and those who would be. Of course, it wasn't true. We who were behind bars consoled ourselves with the thought, and it's just as well that it was just a consolation and not a fact . . .

I was arrested as I came home with my little daughter from the doctor's. The men who were waiting in my flat said that they had only come to ask me about something, and that there would be no arrest. But as soon as we got outside the house, they handcuffed me and we went to Ruzyň, where I spent a whole year without even five minutes in the open air. I have here in my hand a statement from the Supreme Court in which it states that as far as my allega-

17. A prison in Prague.

18. In the Jachymov Mines uranium was mined largely by political prisoners. All the produce was sent to the Soviet Union.

tion of illegal investigatory methods being used against me is concerned, this allegation has been found to be justified . . .

And then there was the trial, a trial without any witnesses, without evidence, a trial in which Prosecutor Munk and the judges with their fat and pompous Chairman of the Senate were the masters. That was no court, and I had the impression that it wasn't really anything to do with me but with someone else, it was all untrue, completely unreal. Dr Aron, who as Defence Council defended me, came to see me shortly before the trial and told me through the bars that he hadn't seen any briefs at all, they hadn't even been offered to him, and that he didn't know how he was supposed to defend me.

I was arrested in March, and was allowed to write my first letter to my family in December. I wrote home that I was thinking about Dante's trilogy and in particular about the last section. Because nobody knew anything about Dante's work at the prison, the letter was released from the custody of the investigators and my family got to know what inquiries pending investigation were all about. My stay in Pankrác, before the trial and after it, was an absolute rest cure for me compared to Ruzyň, even if there was still no lack of bastards there. After more than a year in solitary in Pankrác, I was put into the Jachymov command. They took me away in handcuffs to an assembly point, and from there to camp 'Fraternity', which was a ridiculous name. The commander was the well-known sadist Pták, who welcomed us with the words: 'Now you'll work, work, and work again, and we'll make tarts out of your wives and sisters.' This man is even today – as far as I know – still commander at Pankrác, and has been promoted. During his time as commander, an underground bunker was built at the camp, which was a cell for solitary confinement, six foot by six, and about four foot high, in to which I went and out of which after a prolonged stay I was dragged unconscious.

Another camp, also crawling with bugs, was camp 'Equality', whose legendary and feared commander was the worthy Dvořák, once a dentist, also known as Paleček. Even this man still walks around Prague as if nothing had ever happened. He beat up prisoners and has crimes on his conscience. He was an intelligent man and thus all the more insidious and dangerous. He liked to talk and in a note I sent home, I took down his conversation word for word. A little bit of it follows:

PALEČEK: You are a dangerous man, a follower of Masaryk, dangerous to the régime. Your way of thinking is hostile to us, and now you ask us for certain privileges, like staying on the surface instead of going down the mine . . . You told us once that you wanted no favours from us. And what we know about you and the information we have on you doesn't put you in a favourable light. You are an out and out reactionary.

JIRÁSEK: That's your own tragic misunderstanding. When someone isn't 100 per cent with you, you think he's 100 per cent against you. But if you want to talk, then please let's talk as equals and don't use punishment as your argument.

PALEČEK: Go ahead, say what's on your mind. Are you for the régime?

JIRÁSEK: I have my reservations. I agree with some things, I disagree with others.

PALEČEK: What do you disagree with?

JIRÁSEK: I agree with the nationalization of large private fortunes, but not with concentration camps. I am against such a lack of freedom for people that when someone rings the door bell in the morning they are afraid that the secret police are standing there waiting.

PALEČEK: Of course mistakes are made. But they are made by people, and it's vital to make a distinction between the Party and people. Individuals can be treacherous, but the Party never can.

JIRÁSEK: I'd like you to explain that to me. The Party is a fiction to me because it cannot exist without the individuals who make it up. Where is the distinction between the Party and the people who form it? How do you yourself tell them from each other? Apparently, therefore, people who opposed Slánský were against the Party, and those who were for him were in favour of it.

Gustav Husák
Speech to the West Slovak Regional Party Conference, 21 April 1968

Reprinted by permission from the
BBC Monitoring Service's Summary of World Broadcasts
EE/2751/C1/10–13.

. . . The question of the redress of the wrongs which have happened here during the past twenty years is being felt very acutely by the general public. It is not just the trials which are involved. Whereever we turn we come across a sea of demands and complaints, many grievances which have built up through the years . . . We cannot bypass these things. The Party is coming forward with the initiative for redressing all of the wrongs, the grievances, and sufferings which have been inflicted through the application of incorrect methods and incorrect principles.

The rehabilitations are given so much significance today in the eyes of the general public that some people think that we can abolish February 1948, or that we can go back to 1945, or even that that we might rehabilitate the old Slovak state . . . We are not out to dismantle socialism: what we do want to do is to dismantle the incorrect methods and the wrongs which were committed . . . and these are two different things. Now, when the rehabilitation law is being formulated, this point causes a lot of problems; how to formulate the law to draw a subtle line between redressing the wrongs and violating the principles of socialism. For example, do we think that it was right in principle to turn the farms into collective farms? I do think that it was right. Do we think that the methods which were used in many cases, and by which peasants were sometimes unjustly victimized, were incorrect? I do. Thus, when redressing the wrongs, we have to keep the result, i.e., that cooperative farming is the progressive basis for farming in the future . . .

Often Comrades and even non-Party people come up with actual cases, but these people are reasoning backwards. They are not looking for the authors – the people who were politically, or in some other way, responsible for the arrest, investigation and condemnation of an innocent person. Instead they pick on the people who made themselves conspicuous during the procedure, the prosecutor or the judge, anyone who can be seen . . .

Clementis, Novomeský and I held high Party and state functions in 1949, and with the consent of certain highly-placed people and the Security organs a secret investigation was initiated against us . . . Comrade Löbl is here. He had been in jail since 1949; he knows all about the whole affair. I repeat, this was an agreement between leading Comrades in the Party and the Security organs. Then, about six months later, as a result of these secret investigations, it was decided to recall us from our functions and to criticize us politically. A secret investigation continued meanwhile, run by the same people, a group of politicians and a group of leading workers in the Security service. Six or seven months after we had been criticized and recalled from our functions we were arrested, and after another thirty nine months of investigation we had a trial in which the prosecutor and the judge figured prominently. I have been asked at a number of political meetings about who it was who sentenced me and who the prosecutor was.

If I have chosen not to mention these names, it is not because I want to protect these people, because, after all, they had consciously violated the law in my case, as they knew what was going on . . . But the prosecutor and judge were actually insignificant, minor figures when compared with the directors who made all the top-level decisions and had even determined the sentences and punishments in advance.

Why then should I malign these small insignificant people, even if they did violate the law and behaved spinelessly? After all, those who directed them have sat and some still sit on the Central Committee of the Party.

I am bringing up this subject, comrades, so that in our search we will look for the real culprits and not just for the people who happen to be the most accessible. I think that in this respect the Central Committee should speed up its review of the political and possibly also the legal responsibility for the trials which took place in those years. A political commission exists and it should speed up its work. I am glad that the Central Committee has also adopted a resolution to investigate the case of Comrade Novotný. These problems have to be investigated and the public informed about which functionaries and which people were actually responsible for the deformations. This is necessary to put the people's sense of justice at ease, and also, comrades, for another reason: to cleanse the whole Party.

There is another curious aspect to this issue. Today everybody is talking about our difficult political and economic situation, and the problems we have to solve in the coming years, but nobody wants to take on the reponsibility for the past and for the political and economic mistakes that have been made in this country. I'm thinking especially of Comrade Novotný's speech to the Central Committee plenum. His assertion that he acted essentially correctly during all those years must be refuted as impudent demagogy. Yesterday, Comrade Ervín Polák was telling us here about Novotný's share as far as the problem of the trials is concerned, and this could be added to endlessly on the basis of concrete facts . . .

We don't want to prevent anybody from expressing his opinions freely. However, presenting an opinion at a meeting where one speaks for oneself and presenting an opinion on the radio or on the television, where one addresses millions of people, are two entirely different things. I believe that all of us here, and all the millions of people besides us, not just the person who at one particular moment has access to the microphone or stands by it, should have the chance to speak on the radio or in the press. It is a problem of public control and responsibility. But in this connection, as I have said, we should remember that there does exist today a trend to malign certain honest people and to outlaw them from public life . . .

I want to reject quite firmly the tendency towards holding our whole Party responsible for the deformations, even though I see that this is happening in the villages and the districts where minor functionaries are being attacked . . . We must not humiliate people unnecessarily or allow them to be humiliated. On the one hand, we have to rid ourselves of people who have been clearly compromised. But on the other we should intercede for people who are personally honest and worked bravely in the past . . . We are adopting democratic methods, and we must learn to carry out these transfers with moderation, to make an art out of doing it. Particularly at this time we must be able to carry out these measures in the interests of the Party . . .

Dušan Hamšík
The trials

Literární Listy, 28 March 1968

Although these questions have been preoccupying me now for a number of years, I have got no further in my exploration of them than the Censor's Archives, the forbidding bundles of private correspondence in the anterooms of power, and the tortured private lives of those destined to fall from public life. These people were removed from the limelight of fame into prison cells, and ultimately, after coming to death's door, lived among us for many years in a kind of ghetto, in disgrace, like forgotten outcasts. There are even some dead people among them: Slánský, Geminder, Frejka, Frank, Clementis, Reicin, Šváb, Margolius, Fischl, Šling, Simone, and others . . . In actual fact, what we are concerned with here is a series of scandalous judicial murders . . .

By why dig all this up again? That's what a lot of people would say, and they are not just people whose consciences are troubled in one way or another, people who perhaps actually played only a minor part. *It's almost twenty years ago now, things have changed and time has healed the wounds*, and the people who think like this are not just those who took part in one way or another, but also those who were the victims and lived through it all. There is obviously a lot to be said for this compassionate attitude. To prove the point we need go no further than a summer resort near Prague, where a former interrogator and his victim live not very far from each other: both are now pensioners, both are physically and mentally broken, both of them are victims in their own way and both have had a bad time of it since. The once tortured man and his torturer now meet for lunch in a holiday restaurant and neither of them blames the other for anything.

Of course there's no point in random recriminations: dead people can't have their lives given back to them, and you can't give history back to a person and let him have his life over again, which would be the only genuine rehabilitation. And there isn't any point either in looking for the people who are really guilty and punishing them, because the instinct for revenge which might be produced as a result in the popular awareness is a debasing thing, very far removed from the noble suffering of those who have looked right into the face of the mystery of life and death. It would serve no purpose to allow some loud-mouthed radicals to turn the demand for justice into the demand for revenge, in the name of those wronged, in their brief attacks on one thing today and something else tomorrow . . .

Of course the extent of the guilt of the actual perpetrators, the interrogators, the prosecutors, the judges and others, should once more be examined and evaluated. But this will only provide answers to a few of the questions which have to be asked and explored. To punish these people – even if the punishment is a very severe one – might merely lull us into a false sense of security, which would satisfy our consciences and create a false impression that everything has been nicely taken care of: after *crime* comes *punishment*, even if it is a bit late, justice has been done, our slate is clean again and we can carry on afresh. The trouble is that this neat criminal formula, which incidentally is very dubious from the criminological point of view, collapses completely when the *criminal* appearance and dénouement of events is really only a mask which conceals their real *political* and *moral* nature. This apparently radical demand for the punishment of the culprits, therefore, however justified it may seem to be, is similar in its extremism to a merciful attitude at the other extreme. Moreover, it really isn't at all radical, because it leaves the whole vast area between these two extremes untouched, an area which is full of problems which involve us deeply and which are fundamental for an understanding of the whole matter. We won't rid ourselves of the urgent need to solve these problems by punishing the actual culprits as severely as possible. These problems will still remain if we allow ourselves to give in to the traditional urge to take an eye for an eye and a tooth for a tooth.

Why do the trials of the fifties and the problems connected with them disturb us so much? Why can't we agree, for instance, with the well-meaning attitude of those who say that we shouldn't go back twenty years into the past when today we are different people, in different situations, going in a completely different direction?

The Past Re-examined

The past is a peculiar thing. It's rather pathetic to notice how politicians again and again make the same mistake of tending to treat the past as their servant. They tailor it to their own particular needs, they leave bits out here and add others there, under the completely false impression that they and only they are the logical culmination and the highest point of recent history. They can often succeed, if they are skilful and have shrewd apologists to help them to fill their own actions with mystique, and legends and myths which may last for many years and be influential long after the people who originated them are dead.

Obviously we are influenced much more than we realize by the past; it remains in us, in our unconscious, even sometimes against our will. At the same time there are a great many historical facts, trends and details which we can't see. They make up a kind of continuous strip of unofficial history, without which so-called 'official' history seems to be incomplete, fragmentary, neither accurate nor comprehensible. A social consciousness which has not had the chance to learn about, absorb and come to terms with the facts that have a life of their own in archives, libraries and the memories of the people who actually participated in creating them is rather like someone who is ill but unable to undergo a more exacting course of treatment until he recovers from a cold. Unrevealed, unacknowledged, unsolved and unresolved problems are not just adding up but positively piling up, and they have become mystified, so hard to see, that they have taken on an irrationality which they never should have had. As a result, because the past has been moulded and manipulated to suit a particular narrow purpose, the present is also deformed. The artificial and illusory continuity fabricated for us produces in reality a burdensome sense of discontinuity – the mark of a national crisis . . .

Once again, an old question crops up. Who is it who does his country a good turn? The person who conceals its mistakes from it, or the person who points them out critically and helps to rectify them? No one generation, no political party, no class or movement, however young, idealistic and revolutionary in its outlook, is insured in advance against the old self-deception of patriotism. The distinguished German sociologist and publicist Harry Pross writes that nationalists act as if by overlooking the unpleasant facts they are strengthening the national character. Of course, he is referring to the Germans, and he adds, 'That character then proceeded to develop accordingly.'

The consequences of such an uncritical attitude as this for the character of individual Czechoslovaks . . . are more apparent now and better recognized than they once were. It produces a common social type: a man torn out of history who feels links neither with his past nor with his future, a man who recognizes only himself and the present moment, vulgar and proud, without any scruples about banning, suppressing or stamping out everything which does not resemble himself and his self-confident ideas. A society in which this kind of person predominates or simply dominates, a type which has strutted self-importantly through history from its very beginning, must always fundamentally rethink the meaning of its existence as soon as it rids itself of domination by this type. We are living now at such a moment: a time to take stock and consider the future, a time of revaluation and of searching for new programmes . . .

And so once more, and in a broader context, we are back again with the political trials of the fifties. We are turning back to them not in spite of the fact that we have changed, are in different situations and heading in a different direction, but precisely because of these facts. Obviously we feel that we don't need to hush everything up, or to go on mouthing clichés about time erasing everything. The very opposite is true: we need to see things in a very clear, calm way, and to have them unevasively and unhesitatingly explained to us, though perhaps we can allow ourselves to get excited occasionally at the extraordinary nature of the facts that are being divulged. But their drama is unnaturally exaggerated by their having been for so long concealed and forbidden. Rather late in the day we are in a situation in which we need to understand the past in order to be able to transcend it and really head in a different direction. Socialism is still young in this country, but not so young as not to have already created a certain epoch of history, still unfinished. After all, it has now lasted for the same length of time as did the First Republic from beginning to end. If we try to prevent society from knowing about itself and reflecting about its own nature, thinking that this prevention is in its interest, we really are working against its interests, preventing it from developing.

For many people, analysing, defining and illustrating a problem means starting from everyday occurrences, from things that happen the most frequently, from things that are obvious, close at hand and easily accessible, and therefore most typical. This approach should not be denied someone who believes that it's useful. But surely the truth can be seen much better in prominent and abnormal events and actions, those in which conflicts are intensified to their extremes and in which bloodshed may even occur. It seems to me that by looking at what is conspicuous and exceptional we get a much clearer idea about things that are ordinary and typical than we do if we just look at dull, mediocre things.

What we hear, after all, is that the political trials were a sudden, accidental frenzy, something which blazed up for a short time and died away again. It is now recognized that they were a case of criminal overindulgence, pure and simple, and that things are no more complicated than that; the whole affair is therefore closed and dismissed and people say there's no point in returning to it, that it's only scandalmongers looking for cheap sensation who keep on harping on it and keeping it artificially alive. This interpretation apparently gains strength because it is not denied that in these catastrophic rigged trials people who were absolutely innocent were condemned and executed, a fact which has no parallel in Czechoslovak history either before or since. The astonishing fact of these unprecedented judicial murders rivets people's attention and pushes the political and historical atmosphere and the conditions in which they could have been perpetrated into the background. What's more, the most extreme of these trials were concentrated in the space of just a few years – they were never repeated in their original form – which once again seems to support the view that they were exceptional and fortuitous. And so, as with similar trials in most of the other socialist countries, the Beria–Stalin conspiracy is blamed, its criminal hands reaching out and bringing into our country something which had no roots there, something which was absolutely foreign to us.

There is of course some truth in all this. The part played by Beria's representatives, or 'teachers' as our assistants called them,[19] in fabricating the accusations, searching for the 'guilty',

19. Beria, Stalin's Security Chief, sent 'adviscrs' to Czechoslovakia in 1949 to help the Czech security forces in their work. Some 26 'advisers' virtually

interrogating them and then judging them, is nowadays an open secret, confirmed among other things by the fact that after Beria had been discredited these representatives were executed in the Soviet Union. The actual conditions and circumstances surrounding our trials will have to be fully investigated and elucidated when the time is ripe and the spirit willing, and we should not just confine ourselves to our country alone.

And yet facts do not make up the whole truth. After all, to refer only to the Beria–Stalin circle seems to be rather unpleasantly reminiscent of the evasiveness of which we are so quick to accuse other people. If the Germans say that only an imperialist élite, the extremely closely-knit financial oligarchy, was responsible for the rise of Nazism, having misled and misused the nation, we are inclined to feel that this is the nation's attempt to absolve itself. We consider that it is lying to itself in order to rid itself of any responsibility for its deceit and its own crimes, a responsibility which varies according to the degree of individual participation from the lowest to the highest rank, but which in some way includes everybody – the nation as a whole, the nation as a continuum, and therefore of course, people born after the Nazi period.

We are all aware that not even the most savage dictatorship, not even the most powerful reign of individual terror can rely for long just on terror as a weapon, that to a certain extent it has to depend on the people's consent, that to assert itself it needs the active participation or passive non-cooperation of certain groups of the nation. The responsibility of the actual rulers, which of course hardly needs emphasizing, is not so relevant if we begin to approach the problem in this much broader way.

What does remain a painful and glaring problem, indicative of the kind of human situations created by such a system, is the position and attitudes of those people who disagreed right from the beginning and yet did not have the opportunity to voice their dissent properly. And in this respect, although it wasn't according to some of our wishes and we strongly condemned it at the time, and

---

ran the entire process of arrests, interrogations, charges and trials. Most of them left after Beria's own fall and death in 1953, but some of them were still to be found at the Ministry of the Interior even in 1968. Denunciations during 1968 of their vital role in the 1950s brought sharp denials from Tass.

even though some of us weren't alive then, we are all collectively responsible for the political trials – the nation as a whole, as a continuum. They are a blot on our past, a burden on our history, by which our standards of good and evil are determined. We can't just throw the whole affair to one side: we can only come to terms with it by understanding and transcending it.

We should beware of those campaigns of hatred which appeal to what is debased and primitive in people's hearts, and arouse hard feelings and a bitter desire for vengeance. In the sort of atmosphere which they create, the prosecutor is able to make impressive speeches, the judge can pronounce sentences and the hangman put on his gloves not only without having any cause to be afraid, but even to the applause of the masses. It would be embarrassing to quote here some of the pliant, acquiescent speeches from the past, the resolutions demanding the severest punishments and the poetic adulation of cruelty. For me this atmosphere is typified in the picture of the little flaxen-haired girl, who stands up excitedly from her school bench, blue eyes full of yearning for justice, saying 'Hang them all!'

When we refer to the Beria–Stalin conspiracy we are only hinting in an oversimplified way at the more general, broader background to our political trials. At that time the wartime coalition against Hitler was collapsing, the United States was not concealing the usefulness of its monopoly of the atom bomb, Stalin was reacting to this in his own way, and the Cold War was suddenly in the air. In the European countries, the period of searching for individual models of socialism which would correspond with national traditions, psychology and the wishes of the politicians, and more or less with the people's wishes, too, was over. Rapidly and compulsively, the Stalinist model was everywhere introduced. The political trials were undoubtedly an instrument of this policy.

But it would mean putting far too much emphasis on the magical, demonic power of Stalin's personality, against logic and known facts, if we were to try to deny that the soil was ready in our own political and social climate for the acceptance and introduction of the Stalinist model. Munich, the loss of independence and lastly wartime developments, brought about such metamorphoses in the thought of the nation that the majority saw in socialism the best hope for the future. Also the dependence of Czechoslovakia's foreign policy on the powerful Soviet Union in order that our national independence should be guaranteed, was really the only solution which was favoured by all realists. In spite of the fact that they represented different class interests, this foreign policy was the creation of Beneš just as much as of Gottwald. It was a national solution which no one in the past or the present wants to change because it expressed what was demanded by reality both in a broader European context, and also in our own national interest. It is based on our friendship and alliance with the Soviet Union.

During the years 1945–50, in communist and non-communist circles, some very interesting ideas about the *Czechoslovak road to socialism* could be seen to materialize. Expressed politically in the National Front, a body not merely formal but dynamic, they consisted of the desire to establish a democratic socialism corresponding to Czechoslovakia's very advanced economy and cultural and political life. In these different aspects of our life, ideas were being elaborated and partially put into practice which naturally bore traces of our national weaknesses but whose practicability and popularity had still to be proved.

Perhaps it would be true to say, in a metaphorical sense, that Rudolf Slánský and others were tried *as representatives of this specific Czechoslovak road to socialism*, while its non-communist representatives had left the country or otherwise disappeared. In contrast to his actual conduct and his role at the time of the trials, Klement Gottwald[20] was also one of the accused, as he was one of the authors and originators of this road to socialism. When we think that Gottwald in actual fact identified himself with and played a part in denying, destroying and condemning his life-long work, to which he had devoted all of his talents and his intelligence, and for which he had made considerable personal sacrifices, we are appalled at the profundity of the tragedy which at the end of his life not only overwhelmed him and his personal relationships with friends and comrades of many years standing, but also the whole movement which he represented.

20. Klement Gottwald, head of the Communist Party leadership in Moscow during the war. Chairman of the Party 1945–53, president of the Republic from June 1948 to 1953 when he died, shortly after returning from Stalin's funeral.

But it wasn't just that Gottwald and other politicians had gradually to change in order to be capable of following another line. It is characteristic of the sombre logic of the whole affair that they were gradually replaced by a different set of leaders who were essentially more suited to the new system, who moulded it and were moulded by it, from those at the top to those at the bottom. And so we find that the political trials of the fifties, however isolated from each other they may have been, stand at the beginning of a far-reaching and lengthy *social process* which has up until now been neither explained nor concluded. As late as 1954, i.e., after Stalin and Gottwald had died, Osvald Závodský was executed.[21] And not just Communists were sentenced – the Milada Horáková trial is typical of many others.[22] The most active people, people who had really taken part in the building of history, foreign soldiers from the West and the East and resistance fighters in general, were systematically and brutally excluded from influential positions in public affairs: it's difficult to find words to express the tragedy of their fates. Everything that was vigorous, original, that was different or offended against conventional standards was suppressed. In 1961 a group of Communists was imprisoned and persecuted because they did not share the view of the Party leadership on Yugoslavia's version of socialism. Although the methods of repression used never again went as far as the death penalty, nevertheless they were all the more ingenious, more diverse, they penetrated all the more effectively into the fundamental structure of our lives. All of us have become different people.

Can we be satisfied with this interpretation which holds that the trials were a kind of accidental frenzy? Errors can be relatively easily corrected. Although the trials took place in the space of just a few years, nevertheless the process of exonerating ourselves from them – and this doesn't just mean carrying out the actual rehabilitations – has made a number of very strange detours up

21. Osvald Závodský, former head of State Security, arrested 1951 and executed in 1954.

22. Milada Horáková, a National Socialist deputy, who was tried in 1950 as a leader of a conspiracy against the republic, a non-communist Centre trial, after which she and three others were executed. Czechoslovakia thus won the primacy of having executed a woman on political charges. She was rehabilitated in 1968.

until the present moment, and now we feel ourselves to be still just at the beginning of the process. The political trials were admittedly something eccentric, but all the same it is significant that at the moment we should concern ourselves with them. They represent a raw nerve, one of the foundation stones of the age, and their very uniqueness impinges on many other different factors.

It only remains for us to admit that they were indeed a manifestation of some system which has so far not been named. That expression 'the cult of the personality' cannot possibly be used to describe a problem so wide-ranging and profound, and it is hardly satisfactory from a Marxist point of view, even if it is used to refer to a personality as outstanding, forceful and versatile as Stalin's. Can one personality, however strong it may be, determine the appearance and nature of politics, economics, culture, state administration, military matters, and the psychology and all the other aspects of day to day life? In what circumstances can the soil of socialism become a fertile soil for a concentration of power such that it cannot but invite comparison with non-socialist and anti-socialist systems? How far does a régime based on personal power have an influence on economic theories and how do they then influence the power structure? Which has the strongest influence, and how do they interrelate? What is the effect of historical factors and traditions, with which every movement, whether it likes it or not, is burdened? And how does this movement react to the contemporary distribution of power in the world outside? How does it respond to its opponents, and its opponents to it? What are its inner limitations and weaknesses, where do they come from, under what circumstances are they playing a significant part and when don't they matter very much? What role do the leading personalities play, what influence do they have, what is their psychological make-up, and what are their personal standards?

One could go on asking many more such questions without finding the answers to them. We cannot look for them in individual figures, because for the most part it is the whole of the working-class movement which is concerned, its various phases of development and its situation at the present. Our own communist movement has been a part of it, our politicians have shared its attitudes, they have been formed under its influence, and at an early date it was already a mass movement.

But we should be asking many questions about ourselves too. In what conditions did we ourselves show our willingness to adopt this system? What social forces, which sections of the population, pushed it forward? And what needs did they have, what illusions and what intentions? Which of our leading politicians became its mouthpieces and representatives? And to what extent was it really an expression of the wishes of the people? What is it in our national consciousness, in our historical self-awareness, in our feelings, our characters and our morals, which is not able to resist lies and degeneration? And how was our national character influenced by the occupation, during which acquiescence and compromise, the will to survive, to wait and see, to hibernate, became common qualities among us?

It isn't a question of conducting some kind of exhibitionist self-searching or of encouraging what would be an embarrassing moral vehemence, which would both be deceitful, artificial and repugnant. For the course of events, the completely understandable and human need to live meaningfully under any circumstances, reveals certain moral attitudes which from force of habit become stereotyped and appear to be normal and natural. They are close to us, intelligible; we recognize them and perhaps even respect them, but it needs an objective view, somebody outside us, to show us how wrong or unreliable and supposititious they are.

A little while ago I was telling a friend of mine off for having taken part in some rather shady business, and I pointed out to him the fact that his freedom was not so limited that he couldn't at least refuse to participate. He replied by sending me a long letter of explanation, which contained among other things the following sad sentences:

> I have never formed any personal theories for myself. For more than half my life I have been a communist. I helped the Party, just as most of its members did incidentally, to its successes and its failures. I always defended it, believed in it and I never once abandoned it. And I shall carry on doing so. Retire into private life? I'd have to be as good and strong as the man I used to be. And I am no longer that person. Youth is finished and it's a long time before I get my pension.

This letter reminded me of a discussion I once had for a whole day with an old respected communist, by then retired, who in his day had played an important part in the preparations for the political trials of the fifties. I went along to see him some years ago with a group of historians, who had studied all the available sources, and really knew all about the most intricate details of the trials and just needed to check a few points with him, points concerning his own share and responsibilities. A fierce argument began, during which he defended himself like a lion, with all the vigour and volatility of an old hunter. But the well-prepared arguments of the historians were unanswerable. And in the end, finally worn down by their insistence, he said, 'I firmly believed that it was in the sacred interest of the Party. They entrusted the jobs to me because they knew that I would always and in every way obey the Party. And even if they had told me: "Put your head in the gas oven, we're going to gas you. It's in the interest of the Party," I would have obeyed, I would have put my head in the gas oven.'

Shortly after this incident he died. His death seems to me to have been more psychological than physical. He could not come to terms with the fact that what he had done out of sincere conviction and good-will could possibly have been evil and criminal as well.

The moral judgement, 'But he meant well', is neither an excuse nor a mitigating circumstance. To mean well, to be reliable and obedient, are not criteria of eligibility to hold office. What is more important is the ability to make personal decisions and to take personal responsibility, and not just to follow the orders of some high-up, anonymous person. When an individual acts on instructions from above, it is he himself who becomes vitally important, and not just the person who gave the instructions.

Perhaps by looking at things in this way we can catch a glimpse of hope, of hope that the as yet all too brief history of democratic socialism, which was interrupted by the political trials, has not come to an end. Perhaps, indeed, it is only just beginning.

Karel Kaplan
Thoughts on the political trials

Nová Mysl, No. 8, August 1968

The political trials must be seen as a very significant episode in the history of post-war Czechoslovakia. They grew out of an international and a domestic climate. They are one of its most tragic products. They made a very deep impression on society, because they were conspicuous for their negation of the ideals and aims which society had set for itself in the name of socialism . . . They were a classic example of the population of a country being manipulated. It wasn't just the accused who were manipulated, but also those who did the interrogation, who sat in judgement, and those who were witnesses or gave expert advice. Tens of thousands of citizens, communists and non-communists, who were invited to believe in the trials, and who were influenced from all sides, by the press and radio and other means of propaganda, were the victims of manipulation on a mass scale.

I think the political trials helped in the consolidation of the political system in the sense that the system developed as the result of a political and social tension, in the world and the state, and the system was at the same time the product of this tension and served to relieve it. It was distinguished by one quality in particular – its ability to renew the impulses which had brought it into existence. It created tension and nervousness by itself, and thus perpetuated its original *raison d'être*. This explanation takes account of the fact that the period of tension had such a long life-span even after its disadvantages had become obviously apparent. And it was especially the trials which provided the system with one of the reasons for its existence.

The gravest social result of the trials was the atmosphere of fear, mistrust and suspicion which bored its way more and more deeply into human relations. It reached not only into the highest circles of functionaries, but also increasingly into the provincial districts and into the factories. Barriers were erected between non-communists and communists as well as between communists themselves. The enemy's hand was seen behind every economic failure, behind everyone who expressed disagreement with decisions that had been made by an organization . . .

The tension in society grew to unbearable proportions. The natural rhythm of political life, of economic activity and cultural work, was paralysed. But society could not live for ever in a state of such tension, particularly when the pressure of unfavourable international influences began to diminish . . . I don't subscribe to the thesis that the present finds in history an answer to its own problems. But in spite of this, I should make the suggestion that by looking at the black pages of post-war Czechoslovak history, we may be able to make a contribution to ideas on how our socialist society should now develop. We will all be able to agree that the bitter experiences of the fifties must not recur . . .

To prevent the political trials from ever happening again, it is necessary not only to change our ideas about politics, but also to produce a new political system . . .

The point about the fifties is not that they were a deformation of an essentially good system, but that they were basically a bad system . . . If we want to prevent all the negative features of the past from being repeated, there is no other choice but to 'rehabilitate' political responsibility, or to put it more precisely, the responsibility of politicians for the decisions made by the organizations in which they work, for things they themselves do, and for the policies they advocate . . . Today, we often come across people who must take responsibility without a shadow of doubt and who try to shirk this responsibility, to squirm out of it, to blame somebody else. They can often be heard to say: 'But we didn't know anything about it', 'I myself can't be blamed, for even though I was in an important position, it wasn't me who made the decisions, it wasn't up to me, other people made them for me,' etc. . . .

However, a politician must accept responsibility for giving his approval to something he didn't understand, for the fact that he wasn't really up to carrying out his function and yet went on in the same position. Once he has entered politics, once he takes office, then he must be answerable for anything which is connected with his job. It's unthinkable that somebody should admit responsibility only for the good actions and blame others for the bad. And it's equally unthinkable that someone should occupy a place among the country's highest authorities at a time when thousands of people were suffering unjustly, and should declare that he wasn't aware of this fact. How is it possible that he did not see, know about or sense such massive breaches of legality, how could he have been a politician? . . .

The direct or indirect responsibility of the Communist Party as a political body has to be related to its position in society at that time, to its broad political conceptions. It was the force behind the creation of the power mechanism, and it occupied a monopoly position in that mechanism, which itself created the illegalities. It determined the political policies of the state, and defined how socialism would be put into effect. In 1948, Gottwald had already drawn attention to the fact that in taking over power in the state, the Communist Party was at the same time assuming complete responsibility for what happened in the state . . .

Certain groups of people, Party functionaries and state functionaries, people in Security and judicial departments, Party organs and institutions, bear direct responsibility. But the actual amount of responsibility, the degree and share of individuals and organs, is completely different. But one thing can be said as a general principle: the degree of responsibility was directly related to the position in the power structure, in the power mechanism . . .

Finally, I should mention another of the characteristics of the period: indifference. The indifference of functionaries and rulers to their fellow citizens, colleagues and comrades, some of whom they had known for a long time, was a notable feature of the period of the trials. Human relationships changed, were disrupted, cooled. People who were accused and arrested remained isolated. No one had the courage to speak out on their behalf: injustice and wrongdoing did not seem to stir anybody. The fact that the people were manipulated to such an extent at that time undoubtedly had some influence on this . . . The Communist Party had its general secretary arrested and executed; the Party remained silent. It was the same with the ministers and deputies, people called for the highest punishments and did not defend them. Indifference reinforced by the influence of propaganda gained the upper hand, and in some cases people were so transformed that they were actually capable of being aggressive against those who had been wrongly accused. The atmosphere of the time was evil, and it strengthened the feeling of resignation . . . Society and its indifference helped to create this atmosphere. And this indifference is everybody's responsibility, our entire society is scarred by it. We are scarred by the past which we carry with us into the future, and we have no alternative but to overcome this indifference.

Luboš Dobrovský
The personality cult as an excuse

Reportér, 22 May 1968

The expression 'the cult of the personality' has been interpreted in various ways, but usually in some limited context. Referring to certain aspects of socialism, it came into our vocabulary after Khrushchev's speech to the Twentieth Congress of the Communist Party of the Soviet Union, which also laid down which period of time and which particular personality the expression could be used to refer to . . .

The reaction to Khrushchev's speech, the embarrassment and confusion in people's minds, both in the Soviet Union and abroad, the moral problems of communists both as individuals and as members of Parties, the question of Budapest, and before that Poznan – all this apparently served to justify the original limitation which was put on the use of the expression, and even gave rise to critical questions as to whether the term 'cult' had not been given too broad a definition. The very manner and timing of Khrushchev's speech about the personality cult is typical of the situation in which it originated: it is an artificial term which is not the result of a profound analysis of the past period, or of a review of the system of organizing society. Its purpose is to conceal and not to reveal reality: it is an attempt to relieve the Party of responsibility for the negative features of that stage of development of society which is associated with the 'cult' . . . Khrushchev and the Central Committee, relying on public opinion that had not been officially informed and could only base itself on imperfect sources of information and rumours, were able to clear the names of some people who had been unjustly sentenced, but at the same time to leave out other names with impunity, and without any danger of unpleasant questions being asked . . . The amount of information given to the public was relatively small, even though the facts were quite shattering, and it was this which meant that the subjects for rehabilitation could be chosen with the future developments of home and foreign policy in mind, and that the social system could be retained in the same form as it had been during the personality cult. The only difference was to be that instead of mass repressions there would be just the suppression of individuals, who could be accused in a legally justifiable fashion . . .

Up until now, all the social systems which have based themselves on Marxism–Leninism, and all the different kinds of state in which the Communist Party has assumed power, have gone through or are going through a period characterized by rigged trials, by a violation not only of state legality, but of laws, which, thanks to civilization, have become a natural, normal part of every moral individual. There must be somewhere a fault other than just that the wrong people were chosen. The fault must even go deeper than political practice, and lie in the theory itself. It can be found in the inadequate preparation of the legal, or rather the constitutional, phase of socialism, that initial phase which we call the dictatorship of the proletariat. The revolution itself, its first steps in the military and social spheres, may have been carefully prepared, but the society which was formed soon after these first steps were taken became unscientific and coarse, lacking respect – in the case of the Soviet Union for the wealth of thought in Russia's past, and in Czechoslovakia's case for the traditions of a reasonably well-functioning system of democracy.

Four
On the Theme of Opposition

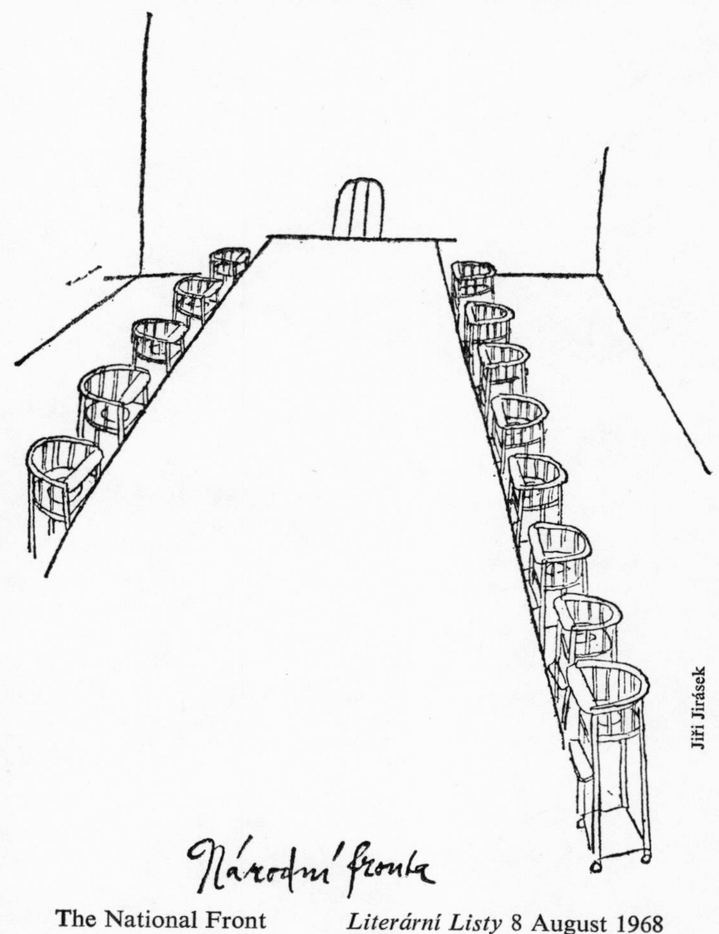

The National Front *Literární Listy* 8 August 1968

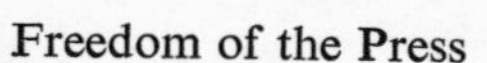
Freedom of the Press Democracy Opposition party

The revival process, which turned its attention to the history of the past, and expressed people's sense of crisis and dissatisfaction, was essentially a political reform movement. It was in concrete political reform, and not just talk of 'liberalization' or 'democratization', that guarantees could be given that there would be no repetition of the 'deformations' of the past.

The new decentralizing ideas which had been pioneered in the economic field in Czechoslovakia had to be applied in the political sphere. Practical conclusions had to be drawn from the theoretically established thesis that the era of the class struggle and class antagonisms had given way to that of socialism, in which there were only differentiated group interests.

Novotný had tried to isolate the implications of this transition to a socialist republic by restricting the changes to the New Economic System, but with the victory of the progressive faction in January the ideas about a new, pluralist political system which had been worked out by the team headed by Mlynář were gradually adopted officially. The main aim was to rule out any possibility of a repetition of the over-concentration of power which had characterized the old régime, with its domination of the Party over the people and of a small group or an individual within the Party.

On the more theoretical level, the citizen had to be made to feel not the object but the subject of political decisions. This was the essence of democracy, that he should participate in the decision-making in a society where the means of production were already communally owned. For this, a new political system had to be created: 'It is, therefore, not a matter of "perfecting" the system which was worked out in the fifties,' says Mlynář. 'One is therefore fully justified in talking about the abolition of the existing system . . . None of the characteristics described can be "perfected"; every one of them must be eliminated' ('Towards a democratic political organization of society'). The explanation that the system had been 'deformed' was thoroughly rejected: perhaps the system had been wrong altogether, some people suggested.

The separation of the offices of first secretary of the Communist Party and president, which had been the issue which had ousted Novotný from the first secretaryship, was to be an example to be followed throughout the structure of society. Control was to be placed in more people's hands. The 'universal caretaker' concept of the leading role of the Party was to be abandoned and to be replaced by influence through members of central government or 'interest organizations' with seats in the National Front, who also happened to be members of the Communist Party. This was a very serious threat to the dominance of the Party. The exact size and range of the Party's influence in this new sort of role was intentionally ambiguously defined in the Action Programme, which seemed to resign power in one sentence only to take it up again in the next, an obvious source of confusion:

> The Party's aim is not to become a universal caretaker of our society, to bind every organization and to regulate every step taken in everyday life with its directives. Its mission lies primarily in arousing socialist initiative . . . and in winning over all the workers . . . At the same time, the Party cannot turn into an organization which would only influence society through its ideas and its programmes . . . Communists must over and over again struggle to engage the voluntary support of the majority of the people for the Party line.

But it did not explain on what basis the Party should take the initiative to engage the support of the non-Party members.

Independent organizations, such as the trade unions, the Union of Youth, etc., were to provide one of the new checks against over-concentration of power in the Party. Perhaps more significant was the statement in the Action Programme that the leading role of the Party was not granted to it once and for all, but that it had to be earned by the Party. 'The Party cannot impose its authority: this has to be won again and again by Party activity. It cannot enforce its line by means of directives but . . . by the truthfulness of its ideals.' It would not employ any power means to maintain itself in the leading position but had to persuade all those who opposed it by the strength of its arguments. This statement put the Party in a dilemma, since its logical consequence was that the Communist Party might have to give way to another party. As Pithart points out in 'National Front or Parliament?':

> Unfortunately it seems that reading between the lines of the political section of the Action Programme, the only assurance one can get is that the only universal and at the same time autonomous political body remains the Communist Party . . . The impression is given that the Party will have to fight to maintain its leading position . . .

But the man in the street should not be taken in unless these promises are supported by guarantees. This is exactly the distinction that was always being made during 1968 between 'democratization' and democracy.

One of the main safeguards laid down was the principle of democracy within the Party, under which, according to the draft Party Statutes, the minority had the right to go on advocating its views even after they had been rejected by a majority vote, as long as the minority did not refuse to carry out resolutions once they had been taken. In this way, *democratic* centralism was, in theory, to be restored among the Party members and the people – a development which displeased observers in Moscow.

A further safeguard offered by the new leadership in the Action Programme was the rejuvenation of the National Front. This institution, which had existed until 1968 in the same form since the communist takeover in 1948, provided an ineffective front organization for the monopoly of power by the Communist Party. Within it were grouped the other political parties – the People's Party (Christian-based) and the Socialist Party, the successor of Beneš's National Socialist Party, and in the Slovak National Front the Freedom Party and the Slovak Revival Party – as well as social organizations ranging from the Czechoslovak–Soviet Friendship Society to the Beekeepers Union. All these members accepted the basic programme of socialist construction, which included, among other things, alliance with the Soviet Union together with the acceptance of a constitution which legally perpetuated the leading role of the Communist Party. Everybody admitted that the National Front had no effect on the making of policies, but it was now seized on by the reformers as the best channel through which to remould the political system. All the existing institutions were to be used in Mlynář's and the Action Programme's scheme of transition to the pluralist system. This was made more easy by the fact that these institutional appendices of the defunct democracy had been preserved through the twenty years of dictatorship, and it also made it far more easy for the reformers to forestall more radical criticism of the inadequate scope and speed of their approach.

Criticism did come on the crucial issue of opposition. Few people criticized the other proposals, as there was nothing to fault in the idea that the Party would leave the rest of society to make its own decisions, that it would not install its own men in all the leading positions. This only had to be administratively guaranteed. But the logical consequences of the drastic changes in the concept of the Party's leading role were not admitted.

The remnants of dogmatic ideas, and the fear of Moscow, the fear of charges of revisionism that were ultimately made by the Soviet Union against such a comparative hard-liner as Císař, prevented progressive reformers like Mlynář, and also of course Dubček himself, from extending the concessions they had made to ending the class struggle.

Mlynář did at least show signs that he acknowledged the theory of the two-Party system as not being completely out of the question and as possessing its own virtues ('Towards a democratic political organization of society'). In practice, however, any political party outside the National Front, and thus any Party which had not already accepted that the Communist Party had the best qualifications to lead society, was unacceptable and out of the question in 1968. This official prohibition did not express the opinion of many of the Party members, since in a survey carried out by *Rudé Právo*, not a paper with an unduly 'progressive' readership, 57 per cent of the more highly educated communists and 54 per cent of the less educated communists considered that an election between two parties was one of the essential safeguards of socialist democracy. And more noteworthy still was the fact that 38 per cent of the more highly educated communists did not think that the leading role of the Party was essential to a *socialist* democracy (*Rudé Právo*, 27 June 1968).

In the free-for-all criticism which went on in the revival process, this issue of the leading role of the Party and the question of opposition were widely discussed. Václav Havel, the poet and playwright, did not think that any of the guarantees offered by the official proposals was good enough: 'Power in the end respects only power, and a government can be made to improve itself only when its existence, and not just its good reputation, is at stake.' Only free elections between real alternatives, and not just between candidates on the National Front, could ensure a permanent democracy. Havel thought it completely illogical for people to exclude this possibility by arguing that everybody in Czechoslovakia was agreed about the fundamentals of the socialist system, and that any non-National Front platform would mean a return to the pre-1948 struggle for power, with the political anarchy and confusion of pre-war Czechoslovakia. But in a speech given on 29 May, Dubček explicitly rebuffed ideas such as Havel's: 'We must discount the possibility that the development of socialist democracy in Czechoslovakia could at present include the formation of an opposition party outside the National Front.'

A contest for political power as such was nothing anti-socialist in itself; even Mlynář recognized that, and Havel, Sviták and Pithart all underlined this point. To take the criticism this far was relatively easy; even if it did not have any results. What proved to be far more difficult was to find a real basis for an alternative party which would not be just another debating club or interest organization not primarily concerned with gaining political power. Some put forward the old non-communist parties as potential political opponents, although their revival in the pre-invasion period left a great deal to be desired in terms of strength and activity.

The People's Party, even though it did take some time to change its leadership and activate its extremely rusty organization, recorded substantial gains in membership during 1968. At the beginning of the year it had 21,362 members (*Student*, 3 April) and by about August, 65,000 (*Lidová Demokracie*, 20 August). The Socialist Party showed far more initiative in starting out on the road towards an independent policy, although nothing official of any note came from either of these parties, and it managed to grow from 10,705 (*Student*, 10 April) to over 20,000 by late June (*Smena*, 27 June), a fairly large increase. The increases were due more than anything to the old members wanting to join again. The large religious sector accounts for the gains of the People's Party, rather than any energetic recruiting by the party itself, although both parties became more active in the summer.

KAN, the club which included Sviták and Havel, although still only a debating club in August, was nevertheless primarily concerned with politics and, according to *Reportér*, 3 July, grouped about 15,000 non-Party people together. KAN existed specifically for the four fifths of non-Party citizens who had been until 1968 non-people as far as any authority or real participation was concerned.[1] They had been a suppressed majority, according to Alexander Kliment in *Literární Listy* (14 March):

> For twenty years ... non-communists were deliberately and consciously atomized; they could not associate together, they did not have and still do not have their own public forum, most of them could not fill important social functions, and they could not unite, nor, as a result, could they distinguish between themselves. Non-communists in fact just do not know each other; they are an anonymous, passive, mysterious quantity to themselves and also to the communists.

The new policy declared equality for these people, the 'cadre ceiling'[2] was to be abolished. But this equality was taken further in the creation of KAN than the Communist Party leadership had intended.

KAN frightened the Party, and a campaign was launched which directed itself primarily at KAN and the other potential political opposition group, K 231, whose existence was seen by the more conservative members of the Party as an institutionalization of anti-communist grievances.

The third, and potentially most dangerous, prospect was the attempt to renew the Social Democratic Party which had existed in Czechoslovakia as the first workers' party long before the Communist Party, and which had been forcibly fused with the Party in 1948. Because of its old traditions of being a workers' party and because of the consequent difficulty of calling what had once been a part of the Communist Party anti-socialist, a great deal of pressure was exerted against its efforts to revive. The press was asked not to write anything about the attempt, and even such a progressive paper as *Práce* did not publish a single one of the hundreds of letters which were sent in by workers in support of the renewal of the Social Democrats (see *Svědectví*, No. 38, 1970).

With these signs that the promises about a truly democratic

1. The Club of Committed Non-Party people was formed in April 1968 on the basis of a discussion club dealing with political questions. Like K 231, branches of the Club spread rapidly, and it was accused of trying to turn itself into a political party as it declared its intention to put up candidates in forthcoming elections.

2. This was the name given to the practice of reserving any important, and especially any politically significant jobs, for members of the Party.

system, which would challenge the control of the Communist Party, were being taken at their face value, the attacks upon the idea of the formation of any political party outside the National Front increased, and the word opposition was used more and more in the old loose sense which made it easy to condemn. The Social Democrats, KAN and all the others were literally outlawed by the Ministry of the Interior, which declared that no new political organizations had any hope of their applications being accepted (*Rudé Právo*, 25 May). Naturally, Soviet pressure accounted for much of this tough attitude on the question of opposition. Nevertheless, all the signs – as shown by the report for the Fourteenth Congress – were that the Dubček leadership was not even in theory, let alone in practice, prepared to test, at least for the next five years, whether the country thought that they deserved their power or not. A really free choice between the Party and any other political force was not on the cards.

And so, at the end of the period, Havel's analysis of the rift between the Party and the people still remained acceptable:

> I'm afraid that a wider and more active political force will never manage to form itself in the non-communist majority of the nation as long as the non-communist point of view does not succeed in winning for itself basic *moral and political recognition* . . . It is really very difficult to commit oneself earnestly and on one's own to something, without a basic guarantee that a communist error is once and for all not worth more than a non-communist truth. And if many a non-communist recognized a communist error even at a time when the communist did not have an inkling of his mistake, then the non-communist must be given credit for this . . . If this is not possible, it means that communists are a special type of supermen . . . and that non-communists, in principle, are always wrong even when they are right . . . If communists have the occasional right to be wrong, then the non-communists must have the right to be right sometimes. Otherwise the whole thing is nonsense.

Karel Kosík
Our present crisis (extracts)

The crisis of a political system:
Party and non-Party members.

Literární Listy, 11 April 1968

. . . Our present crisis is not just a political crisis, but also a crisis of politics. It asks questions not only about a particular political system, but also, and above all, about the meaning of politics. Our political system up until now mystified everything and obscured not only its own nature, but also the nature of politics in general. In order to surmount the crisis, this mystification has first of all to be removed . . .

The root of our political crisis lies in the fact that the citizens of this country no longer want to live as Party or non-Party masses, without full rights or without any rights at all, while those who are in power can no longer carry out their leading role by means of a police–bureaucratic dictatorship, that is, through an unlimited monopoly of ruling and decision-making, a monopoly which is based on arbitrariness and the use of force. A radical solution of this crisis is possible only if the system of police–bureaucratic or bureaucratic dictatorship is replaced by a system of socialist democracy. The difference between the two systems is a fundamental one. One is based on the partial or total lack of rights of the Party and non-Party masses, the other on the equality and full rights of all socialist citizens.

The masses and political manipulation complement each other. When someone talks about the masses – whether he is thinking of Party or non-Party masses – he is presupposing a certain political system in which a large number of people ('the masses') are denied their own political will, thereby enabling an alien will to impose itself from outside. In this system man does not exist as the subject of political life, of political thinking and decision-making, or of civil rights and obligations, but only as the object of political manipulation. People are not born as 'the masses', they only become the masses. They become 'the masses' in a system which in practice divides society into two groups, into the anonymous majority and into the manipulators. Anonymous masses are people without their own identities and responsibilities. In a system in which there are masses, anonymity and irresponsibility reign not only on one side, but on both sides. The anonymity of the masses is matched by the irresponsibility of the manipulators. A system of masses and manipulators is a system of universal irresponsibility. And at the same time, the system is one of complete mystification because political thinking is replaced by political clichés, and the system functions only by creating a mass false consciousness as a precondition for its existence, and rejects as heresy or sacrilege any attempt at political deliberation. The dialectical method, as well as common sense, is excluded from the process of decision-making.

This system works without really knowing its own nature, and its various component parts exist in a state of confusion about themselves and each other. The non-Party masses believe that the Party masses are a homogeneous collective, which knows about everything and decides about everything. The Party masses believe the political leadership to be omniscient and omnipotent rulers who make decisions on the basis of exact and comprehensive information. The political leadership looks down on the Party masses as perpetual minors without minds of their own, and who are therefore incapable of deciding for themselves what they can and should know, what they can and should do. They believe that the non-Party masses are supremely satisfied with their right not to know anything and not to decide about anything, and with their duty of just making observations now and again – in general 'toeing the line'.

A system of conveyer belts, of cog-wheels and nuts and bolts, of human souls being engineered, of iron discipline and of a rigid historical theory, can and does function only because, and for as long as, it reduces everything to a common denominator of political technique and technicality. In a system of transmission belts and levers, everything has to be a transmission belt or a lever. The 'Party masses' are the transmission belt by means of which a second belt called 'the non-Party masses' is set in motion. The transmission belt system is a system of complete political deformation which turns communists into 'Party masses' and non-communists into 'non-Party masses'. The system is one of masses and anonymity.

The system does not form people, or their qualities and abilities. It just makes use of those abilities, interests and passions which are necessary to keep it going. The fact that in a particular political system 'natural selection' operates in such a way that people of average intellect, people with bent backbones, pliable characters, obedient and trusting people, people burdened with prejudice and governed by jealousy, reach the top, does not imply that these are man's natural qualities; the problem is that it is these qualities and these abilities that such a system requires in order to carry on functioning. Any other quality and ability is, from the point of view of what the system needs, superfluous or harmful.

A system based on such a relationship between Party and non-Party members both forms and on the contrary deforms the content and meaning of political leadership. Since Party and non-Party members are nothing but a manipulable mass with no, or only partial, rights, deprived of political subjectivity and thus of freedom and responsibility, the political leadership becomes identified with the monopoly of power. To be the leading force in such a system implies having a monopoly of power and he who has a monopoly of power therefore plays the leading role. This reality has its own logic, the implications of which those who hold power are not ready to accept: the person who has absolute power must also accept full responsibility; the person who can make decisions about everything and everyone, must accept responsibility for everything and everyone.

In a system of transmission belts, the leading role is identical with the ruling position and cannot be asserted except by means of orders, supervision and restrictions, and by using pressure and political monologue. The identification of the leading role with the ruling position gives birth to one of the gloomiest mystifications in the history of socialism. Politicians talk of the 'leading role of the Party', by which they mean, however, the ruling position of a power group. This confirms the fact that in a system of transmission belts the Party splits into a ruling minority which claims the exclusive right to speak on behalf of the Party and the working people, and a Party mass which just fulfils the function of another transmission belt.

In the mystifying identification of the ruling position with the leading role, disturbing questions about the nature of leadership and the administration of government are quite simply never asked. Are progressive political thinking, the ability to formulate plausible theories, maturity and courage, good taste and refinement essential to the leadership? Should the leaders stand out as people whose thinking, behaviour and moral code might be an example to society and every responsible individual? Or is a very negative social example set, so that society is faced with the question of what it can possibly learn from a privileged group which settles its internal political quarrels by murder and intrigue, whose leading representatives often suffer from loss of memory and bad behaviour, and who excel in mediocrity rather than in intelligence or distinction?

Zdeněk Mlynář
Towards a democratic political organization of society

Nová Mysl, No. 5, May 1968

Political problems have rarely been so much at the centre of attention as in recent months. In the past, politics were often very confused, there were many things that made people bitter, but now people expect this to come to an end. They expect a new policy to be put into effect which will not repeat the same old mistakes.

It seems as though people are very generally agreed about this. But the situation is not so rosy when it comes to the question of deciding what the new policy should look like, what the nature of the best possible future political system should be, so that we can make sure of the best possible guarantees against the mistakes of the past, and satisfy people's needs. We are promised that it will be a socialist system and at the same time a deeply democratic one, and that it will guard us all from being misused by power and be based on a legal system and laws; such general statements are all very well meant, and they are good within their limitations. But they hardly give us a clear enough picture of the ways in which such a goal can be realized . . .

A political system is primarily a system of relations which are created in social life by the shaping and implementation of specific policy decisions, by specific policy line and in the execution of policy. It is primarily a system of relations between society (which extends from the individual to the people in general) and political institutions (the state and its organs, political parties, political organizations of the interest group type such as the Trade Unions, youth organizations, agricultural organs, etc.). Furthermore, it includes the relations which exist between all these various institutions . . .

To a certain extent a political system has its own ideology, which consists of a set of opinions and ideas about the aims of the given system, about the values which this system supports and promotes or, on the contrary, limits or directly suppresses, a set of views and ideas about the means by which these defined ends should be attained. Every political system has such an ideology, and it is a serious mistake to imagine that perhaps only socialist systems are 'ideological' in this sense, and that other systems are not. But the truth is, however, that the socialist systems are more obviously and more frequently directly and heavily influenced by an ideology, that – especially in the case of a dogmatic socialist ideology – ideological assumptions have sometimes played a very decisive role, and political decisions have sometimes been directed by ideological dogmas even when 'life itself' . . . was speaking strongly against such decisions. It is for this reason that, in our history, there have been so many similarities, even very painful ones, between our political system and those political systems which were governed or are still governed by religions, even to the extent that 'heretics' have been politically persecuted and inquisitorial methods used.

Political systems, in this general meaning of the term, never come into existence purely as a result of ideas alone. They are always the product of practical reality, of a project for a system, *plus* the specific historical situation of the country as a whole, its economic and political reality, its traditions and national character, its cultural personality, etc. That is why it is ridiculous to identify a political system only according to the class structure of a certain country; and it is also ridiculous to imagine that if we can find out what the specific 'faults' of a certain political system are and we admit that we know this, then we can create the right 'project' of development for the future, that all these different influences will stop having an effect on our course of action, because in fact they will go on having an impact . . .

I'm discussing these things right at the beginning because now especially it seems as if we can become the victims of an illusion similar to the one I mentioned above, at a time when it may seem as though it is only a matter of our finding a sensible 'project' for the future. But on the contrary, the economic and political realities which exist – both the good and the bad – will contribute to the creation of our new political system, as of course will our traditions . . .

On the Theme of Opposition

The measures proposed by the Action Programme of the Communist Party in the political sphere started the reform of the Czechoslovak political system: we want, in other words, gradually to give a new quality to all of the ties and relationships which are part of the political system. It is therefore not a matter of 'perfecting' the system which was worked out in the fifties. What is involved is the attempt to create a new system.

One is therefore fully justified in talking about the abolition of the existing system. Some people are perhaps frightened by the use of such a word because they can only envisage 'abolition' as the overnight destruction of everything and a period of social upheaval ... What is it that has to be removed, and replaced by something new?

The political system which was established in Czechoslovakia between the years 1949 and 1952, and then developed until 1956, and which in the last twelve years tried to reform itself in a number of ways (which, it is true, eliminated some of its particularly dangerous and anti-democratic features), can be characterized as a system fully adapted to the dictatorial enforcement of one sole interest, an interest embodied in the decision-making processes at the centre of political power.

Historically, this political system grew up during the years of the final stage of the struggle for power between the bourgeoisie and the working class. It emerged during the period of international tension known as the Cold War, and at a time when the system which had been created in the Soviet Union in the thirties was increasingly being made out to be a generally binding model for all political systems of the socialist type. The Soviet system was fully justified by the conditions which gave rise to it, but it had at the same time grave deformations because it had already suppressed many of the fundamental relations of the democratic systems.

In general, for a short time after a revolutionary upheaval, a system of revolutionary dictatorship always works in favour of the victorious forces of the revolution. The basic links between the political institutions are so designed that orders from above can be very quickly executed ... As long as such a system must solve the specific short-term tasks of the revolution, such as the suppression of the class overthrown in the revolutionary struggle, the liquidation of its economic, proprietorial and social supports ... and as long as it must solve the problem of the replacement of the whole power élite . . . then it is almost inevitable that a dictatorial system of this sort will be established.

During this short period, the dictatorship usually gains the support of the majority of the population. In whatever way it is actually in conflict with a number of important aspects of the fundamental bases of democracy, such a revolutionary dictatorship may nevertheless be democratic in the sense that it is one form of the rule of the people, in the sense that the will of the majority is being enforced, and in the sense that there is voluntary (often fanatical) support for the revolution.

The problems begin, however, when the revolutionary encroachments into social structures (of property and class relations for instance) are successfully completed, and the political system which was created to achieve them persists in society, and goes on enforcing a single interest. The guarantee that this power will act in the objective interests of the revolutionary class, and that the possibility does not exist for arbitrary government, can no longer be given. This is exactly what happened in Czechoslovakia in the fifties . . .

The basic features of this system could be characterized in a rather oversimplified way as follows:

(1) A monopoly power centre was created in the political system, which was in the end separated into a number of supreme Party, state and certain social interest organizations. In fact, political decisions . . . were made in one centre, by a small group of people, and in many cases even by just one person.

(2) The whole political system had in the end a variety of different organs, Party, state social administration and also the political parties in the National Front, the economic bodies, etc., but in fact there was a monopoly of all these political organs; an internally fused Party-state system of mainly central organs was in operation.

(3) In the process of decision-making, the variety of the interests, needs and viewpoints of different groups of people in the socialist society, and of different individuals, was only allowed very inadequate expression . . . The system allowed this partial freedom, and often even organized it in the form of various campaigns of discussions and 'suggestions', but the actual implemen-

tation of these suggestions or of the interests of the people was in the end wholly dependent on the power centre . . .

(4) The different interests, needs and standpoints did not have the *independent platforms* which they needed to express themselves . . . to make any impact on politics.

(5) A fundamental feature of the . . . old political system was direct restriction of the influence of public opinion . . . Censorship and the power to curtail the people's right to assembly played an increasingly large part as one of the pillars of the whole system . . . the political atmosphere was hostile to political democracy.

(6) All the institutions and component parts of the system at a lower level than the centre of political power were turned more or less into instruments for the *execution of central directives* . . . The directive-centralist system thus placed tens of thousands of functionaries 'down below' in a position where it often seemed to them that they were the creators of socialist policy, and in which they served in an honest and self-sacrificing way, whereas in fact they were above all fulfilling the function of supports of the redundant system. This is now the source of one of the most crucial moral-political problems of the present time. Criticism and anger are directed at these *misused* people, criticism which should really be directed at the *consequences of the system as a whole*. The fact that thousands of these lower functionaries resent the injustice of the way they have been treated could threaten to reinforce the apathy felt by many people on the subject of reform, and is certain to increase the dangerous likelihood of conflict. Alternatively, there is the equal threat that they could be misused yet again by the supporters of the old political system who could try to set these thousands of sincere people against the programme of reform, and against a movement which they claim is 'against the interests of the people' and is leading to the 'bullying of honest communists and functionaries'.

The whole of the existing political system, which has been described quite shortly and simply in the six points above, must be changed, removed and reformed. *None of the characteristics described can be 'perfected'; every one of them must be eliminated . . .*

There is a fundamental and direct connection between the new economic system and the need to create a new political system. For the *social reasons* which made necessary the destruction of the old centralist and bureaucratic system of the directive management of the economy are in general the same reasons which make it necessary for the existing political system to be superseded. Political management by a system of decision-making from a single centre threatens to lead to the stagnation of social development, threatens to create a situation in which the internal dynamic of socialism will not work . . .

The basic problem is the position of man in socialism. This may sound like a very abstract idea to some people, but what I mean is a very concrete thing which is felt in everyday life. Socialist man is not a private owner and therefore the stimuli which are created by private property relations have disappeared. If in these conditions we try to keep people, either as individuals or as members of a certain group, in the position of *objects overwhelmingly directed from above*, one tendency will be more and more in evidence: people will begin to separate the pursuit of their own private interests and needs from the pursuit of the collective, group and social interests.

They understand anyway that they have no influence over the collective interest, and will therefore leave this to other anonymous creatures (we know the expression, 'Let them decide and solve the problem'). But people do realize that they can have a direct influence on their own private circumstances and therefore use their initiative to find ways and means of ensuring the best standard of living *for themselves*, from their material conditions to the amount of free time they have.

The traditional Utopian ideal of collectivism as the basis for a new social order was turned under the old political system into a situation where *official collectivism* has become just a hollow-sounding phrase. It is now a cloak under which a person can build his atomized private life, or produce the most favourable conditions for his own individual 'survival'. And thus, one of the most characteristic features of the breakdown of the official ideology of the old political system is the huge disparity between the formal political activity of nearly every 'upright citizen' and the *completely different values* for which this same citizen increasingly shows a preference in his private life. It was mere 'window dressing' for a citizen who was part of some organization to go to the right meetings and take part in various activities, to present himself at elections and vote without being forced to do so for the prescribed candidate, when in reality he increasingly expended his most important activity and talent on his private interests, regardless of whether this activity was connected with the formally professed fetish of 'the social good' or not. And so we were led to the phenomenon which we can see today, that the people who are really the most 'honest', those who are devoted to the ideas of collectivist communism, etc., *objectively* perform in some situations the socially negative role of sectarians. And incidentally it is these facts which will be among the strongest barriers the democratization process will come up against . . .

Unless there is a change in the position of people in the political system, this state of affairs will not change; without an alteration in people's economic relationships (which the new system should be trying to create), an efficient and dynamic socialist economy cannot be created . . . And only in this way will people begin to turn their initiative, activity and talent away from advancing their own private affairs, towards the goal of the social whole, to the search for ways to satisfy their own needs and interests *in harmony with* the whole development of society . . .

Of course, this is a thesis, a premise. But it is one which does hold some water. It is based on a concept of socialism as a social order which will preserve the *active forces in European capitalist development* . . . the necessary independence and subjectivity of the human individual. It is in conflict with other conceptions of socialism which do not have this end in view, and which are based on the historical conditions of the development of other civilizations, for instance of the East, as we can clearly see in the Chinese conception of socialism.

The main features of the new political system in Czechoslovakia

In general, it has been suggested here that *more than one* kind of political organ must be created. The political system which is based on this principle is called a *pluralist system*, and it would therefore be true to say that an experiment is going on in Czechoslovakia to create a pluralist society for which there is at present no real analogy among the socialist states.

Towards a democratic political organization of society

A pluralist political system is quite often identified just with the existence of a large number of political parties. But I do not think this is really right, and all the less so for a socialist society. It is very easy to understand why this question is so much discussed at the moment in Czechoslovakia . . .

What is clear above all is that the direct fusion of the Communist Party with the state, and the idea of the leading role of the Communist Party . . . is one of the critical points of the old system. So a guarantee is needed to make it impossible for this to happen again. Therefore, the fundamental problem of the development of socialism is thought to be the formation of an opposition. Some people think that it is even necessary for an opposition party to be *outside the National Front* and to be created immediately, because even the whole idea of the National Front as a platform for dispute between the different political interests seems to some people a kind of fraud, when they take into account what the National Front has stood for in the last twenty years.

I am not one of those people who think that the idea of the development of the National Front as outlined in the Action Programme . . . is the last word on the theory and practice of Marxism or of socialism. But I do think that the idea of a model of for instance two political parties, which would operate on something like the principle of the well known system of opposition in Great Britain, is not only not out of the question, but, on the contrary, has its own logic and virtues. There is nothing anti-socialist in principle in this idea as a *mechanism* of governing, just as there is nothing anti-socialist in the mechanism of the so-called division of power . . .

When I look at our current social situation, the present state of the political system and the practical possibilities for it to be transformed, it does not seem to me that the attempt to create political parties outside the National Front, parties which would put forward programmes and a platform of opposition and attempt to win state power at elections . . . would be a guarantee of our democratic development.

I don't want to frighten anyone by saying this, but I should like to state the fact that there is enough scope in the situation as it is at the moment for all the other forces in this society, given maintenance of the principle of the National Front, to oppose the tendency to a monopoly. And I say, 'the principle of the National Front' on purpose, not wanting it to continue on its present basis. The possibility of the independent development of political parties themselves cannot be ruled out. It could take place by their being reconstructed, integrated with other groups, or by the constitution of a new party, *but this should be on the basis of the existence of a National Front*.

Action Programme of the Communist Party of Czechoslovakia (extracts)

The leading role of the Party – a guarantee of socialist progress

At present it is most important that the Party practices such a policy that it fully merits its leading role in society. We believe that at present this is a condition for the socialist development of the country.

The Communist Party enjoys the voluntary support of the people; it does not realize its leading role by ruling over society but by serving its free, progressive socialist development in a devoted way. The Party cannot impose its authority: this has to be won again and again by Party activity. It cannot enforce its line by means of directives but by the work of its members, by the truthfulness of its ideals.

In the past, the leading role of the Party was often conceived as a monopolistic concentration of power in the hands of Party bodies. This corresponded to the false thesis that the Party is the instrument of the dictatorship of the proletariat. This harmful conception weakened the initiative and responsibility of the state, economic and social institutions, damaged the Party's authority, and impeded it in carrying out its real functions. The Party's aim is not to become a universal caretaker of our society, to bind every organization and to regulate every step taken in everyday life with its directives. Its mission lies primarily in arousing socialis tinitiative, in showing the ways to and actual possibilities of communist perspectives, and in winning over all the workers to them using systematic persuasion, as well as through the personal examples of communists. At the same time, the Party cannot turn into an organization which would only influence society through its ideas and its programmes. With its membership and its bodies, it has to develop the functions of a practical organization and a political force in society . . .

On the Theme of Opposition

As a representative of the interests of the most progressive part of all the state – thus also a representative of the aims and perspectives of that society – the Party cannot represent the whole gamut of social interests. The political expression of the many-sided interests of society is the National Front. Its nature expresses the unity of the social classes, interest groups and the different nationalities in this society. The policy of the Communist Party must not lead to non-communists getting the impression that their rights and freedom are limited by the role of the Party. Far from it: they must see in the Party's activity a guarantee of their rights, freedom and interests. We want to achieve, and we shall achieve, a state of affairs in which the Party, at its basic organizational level, will have informal, natural authority, based on its ability to work and manage society and on the moral qualities of its functionaries.

Within the framework of the democratic rules of a socialist state, communists must over and over again struggle to engage the voluntary support of the majority of the people for the Party line. If Party resolutions and directives fail to express correctly the needs and potentialities of the whole of society, they must be altered. The Party must try to make sure that its members – as the most active workers in their particular sphere – have a corresponding weight and influence in society, and hold functions in state, economic and social bodies. But this, however, must not lead to the practice of appointing Party members to functions without regard to the principle that the leading representatives of institutions of the whole of society are chosen by society itself and by its various components, and that the functionaries of these components are responsible to every citizen and to every member of social organizations. It is necessary to abolish the discriminating practice and creation of a 'cadre ceiling' for people who are not members of the Party.

The most important thing is to reform the whole political system so that it will permit the dynamic development of socialist social relations, combine a broad democracy with scientific, highly qualified management, strengthen the social order, stabilize social relations and maintain social discipline. The basic structure of the political system must, at the same time, provide firm guarantees against a return to the old methods of subjectivism and highhandedness from a position of power. Party activity has, so far, not been turned systematically to that end; in fact, obstacles have often been put in the way of such efforts. All these changes necessarily call for work to start on a new Czechoslovak constitution . . .

It must be perfectly clear throughout our system of management in the future who, which body and which official is responsible for what, and what are their rights and duties. To this end each component part should have its own independent position. The substitution and interchanging of state bodies and economic and social organizations with Party bodies must be stopped completely. Party resolutions are binding for communists working in these bodies, but the policy, the right to direct activities and the responsibility of state, economic and social organizations are independent entities. The communists who work in these bodies and organizations must take the initiative to see that state and economic bodies and the social organizations such as the trades unions, the Union of Youth, etc., take the problem of their activities and responsibilities into their own hands.

The whole National Front, the political parties which form it, and the social organizations, will take part in the creation of state policy. The political parties of the National Front are partners whose political work is based on their joint political programme. Their partnership is naturally bound by the constitution of the Czechoslovak Socialist Republic and is based entirely on the socialist character of social relations in our country.

The Communist Party of Czechoslovakia considers that the National Front is a political platform which does not separate the political parties into government and opposition in the sense that opposition to the state policy – and that of the whole of the National Front – would be created and a political struggle for power in the state waged. Possible differences in the points of view of the individual component parts of the National Front, or a difference in matters of state policy, should all be settled on the basis of the common socialist conception of the National Front policy by way of political agreement, and the unification of all the separate parts. The formation of political forces striving to contradict this conception of the National Front, to remove the National Front completely from its power position, was ruled out as long ago as 1945 following the tragic experience of both our nations in the pre-war development of the then Czechoslovak Republic. This is obviously unacceptable to our present republic.

The Communist Party of Czechoslovakia considers the political application of the Marxist–Leninist conception of the development of socialism to be a precondition for the correct development of our socialist society. It affirms the Marxist–Leninist ideal as the leading political principle in the National Front and throughout our political system. It will assert this ideal by seeking, through its political work, the support of all the different parts of the system and especially the support of the workers and all the working people, so as to ensure that its leading role is held democratically . . .

Voluntary social organizations must be based on truly voluntary membership and activity. People will join these organizations because they are expressing their interests, and therefore they have the right to choose their own officials and representatives who cannot be appointed from outside.

Petr Pithart
National Front or Parliament?

Literární Listy, 18 April 1968

The Action Programme of the Communist Party is a compromise. It is a surprisingly successful one in the context of the voices and the reproachful silence which reach us from the neighbouring friendly countries. And it is obviously adequate for our domestic conditions, especially for what the present Central Committee of the Communist Party could achieve. On the other hand, what is startling is the defeat it has suffered at the hands of the apparatchiks, with their elusive vocabulary and their skill . . . Perhaps it is not a defeat it has suffered, perhaps it surrendered voluntarily . . .

In the part of the Action Programme which deals with the development of the political system, the public has been struck most of all by several apparently puzzling paragraphs dealing with the political parties and their role . . .

Suddenly, like a *deus ex machina*, we come across the words – National Front. In its time this internally divided body played a by no means unambiguous role. But today it just exists, that is to say it has not been formally disbanded. Recently, it has been the organization which puts on state celebrations, nominates election candidates and 'regulates' the influx of new members into the other political parties, and yet suddenly, out of the blue, we find that it is revived in the Action Programme as the 'expression of the alliance between different classes and interest groups and the nations and nationalities of our society'. The lack of arguments to support this statement is so conspicuous in contrast to the Programme's general verbosity that you get the impression that the long since dismissed National Front is just being used as a way of avoiding replying to one of the most crucial questions – that concerning the position of non-communist parties and therefore the pluralist or monist character of our future democracy.

National Fronts and other alliances like them usually indicate a certain agreement on the values which will not be disputed politically, at least for the time being; they represent a certain agreement about what is in the common good. A National Front is the parenthesis within which the political haggling, the struggle, is confined.

But does the Action Programme make out a case for the existence of the National Front as an absolute necessity? Would it be true to say that the more there is going on outside this parenthesis containing the National Front, the poorer is democracy? Who is it who has decided to make the National Front the be all and end all, and who was responsible for its second regeneration now? There seems to be no point in the National Front unless it comes into being as a result of the natural need of independent political parties; it certainly cannot be instituted or imposed from above. And how else is it possible to interpret the fact that it has been suddenly roused from twenty years of slumber (though at times perhaps it reacted like a sleepwalker) if it is not being imposed from above? . . .

The Programme rules out the possibility of dividing parties 'into government and opposition in the sense that opposition to the state policy – and that of the whole of the National Front – would be created and a political struggle for power in the state waged'. And yet politics is among other things a struggle for power; to exclude this from politics is to exclude politics from the life of society (and only politics can be democratic) and to replace it with manipulation, or, to use the more traditional expression, management. It seems that the long-term monopoly of power gives those who wield it the impression that a struggle for power can only take place on the streets . . . and that its only result is the end of the idea of socialism, the end of the state, the end of everything, though this 'everything' really refers only to the loss of its own power positions . . .

Unfortunately it seems that reading between the lines of the political section of the Action Programme, the only assurance one can get is that the only universal and at the same time autonomous political body remains the Communist Party. Although in some of the ways that the thoughts are expressed the impression is given that the Party will have to fight to maintain its leading position, that in the future it will have to show itself to be worthy of it, and that it will have to win its authority 'by the most devoted service to the free development of society . . .', nevertheless, even the man in the street who is not very well versed in politics could not be taken in unless these promises are supported by mechanisms which guarantee that there will be no civil war, nor a return to Stalinism, if the Party has to defend its position in a democratic fight.

Obviously no politician or political party would want this to happen, but the possibility of such an eventuality has to be reckoned with unless provision is made in the mechanism of power for as peaceful and civilized a change throughout the ruling set as possible. It is characteristic of political bias that a collective and organized effort is made to achieve power for a certain social group . . . But it is the mark of the democratic process that it takes into account the possibility of losing power once gained and that the bridges for the old holders of power to retreat across are kept in repair.

Apparently it cannot be too strongly emphasized to impatient, expectant non-Party members that it wasn't possible to expect from the Action Programme that the Communist Party would perhaps 'allow opposition', call for the formation of other political parties, or voluntarily retreat to the same place from which the People's Party and the Socialist Party are starting today . . . On the other hand, it was justifiable to expect from the Programme's conception of the position and function of Parliament that the lawful or constitutional foundation and independent existence of political parties would be allowed. But the National Assembly, as the creator of state policy, is evidently to be dependent not only on the constitution, but also on the line established by that convenient connecting link which neutralizes political parties, the National Front . . .

That same National Front would come forward with a single candidate for the elections to Parliament and the National Committees. It appears to be a vicious circle. A binding policy simply cannot be laid down from two centres: the idea of a political system including a National Front must tacitly assume that either the National Front or the Parliament and government are not functioning. If both centres are functioning, then it is either a false impression or a political crisis is just around the corner and the old pre-January times are back . . .

A political party is a political party only when it enters elections with its own programme and its own candidates: otherwise it has in fact only the same effect as any interest organization relying on the strength of its membership. To enter elections, however, means talking to every citizen as a potential voter, and putting forward alternative programmes which are generally intelligible and capable of appealing to the whole of the population if possible. The possibility of choosing independently between these alternatives is the essential basis of pluralist democracy: political parties then act as controls on power.

Thus it becomes all the more urgent for the interplay of political forces to be provided with some rules that will give them at last all the same chances, and that will ensure that any group which 'confesses' that it has political ambitions . . . will not generate embarrassment, fear or even terror among the people looking on.

Václav Havel
On the theme of opposition

Literární Listy, 4 April 1968

If some of the ideas which have so far appeared in various official speeches about the possible form of a political opposition in present day Czechoslovakia sometimes give the impression that their propagators want to have their cake and eat it too, then we shouldn't be too surprised. If in the Communist Party, in the course of a few weeks, the more progressive and democratically minded people can win over the conservatives, this doesn't by any means show that in just as short a space of time the members of a movement which, throughout its history since its victory, has not made a single attempt to change the principle of one-party rule are capable of seriously facing up to the idea of an opposition, which until recently was so shocking to them. If, nevertheless, they are going so far as to allow a public discussion about a formerly taboo subject, then this is probably a good opportunity for everybody who has something to say on the subject to take up the challenge and to say it.

To begin with, why is it that the ideas put forward so far seem to sound so half-hearted?

We hear quite often that as a result of our present and future freedom of speech, which is said to be the essence of democracy, the natural controlling function of an opposition will be carried out quite simply by public opinion, kept well informed by the mass media. Such an idea assumes that one can trust the government to be guided to all the necessary conclusions by the force of public opinion. The trouble is that democracy is not a matter of faith, but of guarantees. Even if we admit that the public 'competition of views' is the first condition, the most important way of achieving and the most natural result of democracy, its essence, i.e., the real source of our guarantees, is something else: the public and legal '*competition for power*'. At the same time public opinion, for example the press, can effectively control and thus improve the quality of the ruling power only when it too has access to an effective means of control, that is, when it can influence public decision-making, as through elections. Power, in the end, respects only power, and a government can be made to improve itself only when its existence, and not just its good reputation, is at stake. In so far as public opinion loses the possibility of influencing the government, so the possibility will increase of the government manipulating public opinion through a limitation of its freedom, either by changing the law or illegally. Not only that: if the 'competition of views' is substituted for 'competition for power', then the doors would be opened to undemocratic processes. If for instance television or public meetings, rather than Parliament, had the right to dismiss ministers, then the citizen would have no legal control over the power mechanism, and would not be protected against its misuse.

I also think it an illusion that the internal democratization of the Party, willing to tolerate something in the nature of an internal Party opposition, would provide a sufficient guarantee of democracy. I hold this view not only because, in principle, the only true democracy is one which is valid to the same extent for everybody, but also because it has been the bitter experience of every revolution that if the political group which assumes power does not renew its control from outside in time, it must sooner or later lose its internal self-control, and begin slowly but surely to degenerate. For if the group in power is not sustained by controlling pressures from outside, to improve its quality as a whole, then all the internal controlling pressures in the group, improving the quality of the leadership, also inevitably weaken and die out. The group fossilizes instead of regenerating itself all the time spontaneously, and becomes more and more profoundly alienated from reality. The results of this process are well known. When the situation becomes uncontrollable, the first unexpected disturbance causes an explosion, and a period of bloody palace revolutions, coups, lobby conspiracies, nonsensical trials, counter-revolutions and suicides follows. The 'competition for power', which had at one time disappeared from view, suddenly reappears, and begins to effect everything in a much more insidious way because it is not happening out in the open. The lack of legal guarantees, which the group was not able to renew in time, now rebounds on it like a boomerang. The group liquidates itself. In other words, if the Communist Party does not allow the quickest development of strong controls on it from outside, it will have no guarantees that it will not again slowly degenerate in the future. It is obvious that internal Party democracy cannot last for very long unless the whole of society is democratic. It is not internal Party democracy which guarantees the democracy of the whole society, but vice versa.

Another idea which has appeared – that independent individuals might be able to function as an opposition in elections and various public bodies – is to my mind a classic example of an attempt to cut the ground from under the opposition's feet before it has even come into being. A handful of private people, with no political background, without any possibility of coming to a collective agreement about procedures, candidates, coordination, and a broad concept of the nature of political activity, and with only a few local communal rights and duties, would have to stand against a perfectly organized and disciplined political party, with an ideology, an apparatus, press and propaganda organs, and a programme for the whole of society. In elections, these independent candidates would not be able to base their activity on a good general knowledge about what was happening in society; they would not have a programme, nor the advantage of belonging to a particular section of society which would propose them. And thus, unlike the candidates from the leading party, they would be deprived of the classical, time-tested means of guiding the electorate, the overwhelming majority of whom cannot and do not make distinctions between candidates as individuals, but can always be relied on to distinguish between more general familiar political concepts. Also, this 'opposition' would have no chance to develop any effective and coordinated political activity that would compete with the communists. To put it simply, without an organized political force, possessing by virtue of the very fact of its being organized certain specific powers, the leading Party cannot seriously talk about a 'competition for power' and imagine that it is exposing its monopoly position to any serious test of its quality.

Another type of eventual control or actual opposition that is sometimes suggested is in social and social interest organizations. But not even these – in spite of the fact that some of them might in time gain a certain amount of political influence – are a fundamental solution. Based on principles other than those of political conviction, and designed for a purpose other than that of sharing the political power of the state, these organizations can never satisfactorily act as a check on excess power, simply because they do not satisfy the basic condition of independence from what they are supposed to act as a check on. Membership of these organizations not only does not exclude membership of a leading or other party, but the highest officials of these organizations are almost exclusively members of the Communist Party, subordinate to higher Party bodies and responsible to them for their activities in the interest organization. And if we add to this fact the well known system of Party groups, Party lists of candidates and the disciplined system of Party voting (plus the election rules which make it practically impossible for even a majority of non-communist voters to elect an opposition candidate), then we can understand that, in spite of all the changes in the practice of manipulation which we shall surely see soon, it is still difficult to talk about control from outside the Party.

The most logical and acceptable solution would be the constitution of an opposition in the way which is most often suggested in official circles, by the revival of the existing non-communist parties in the National Front. Of course, we cannot exclude the possibility that forces capable of becoming an opposition might be able to assert themselves in these parties, but I myself do not have much faith in this solution. Over the past twenty years, these parties and their representatives were allowed only to agree in a slavish way with everything that the Party said. I am afraid that during this time they have compromised themselves to such an extent that their advantages, such as their existing organizations, their press, etc., cannot outweigh their main disadvantage, which is the difficulty they would have of regaining lost confidence. Further to this, it would be quite easy, and not unjustified, to criticize this as 'a return to outmoded and obsolete forms of bourgeois democracy', as is often heard in official circles when the idea of opposition is broached. Above all, it would be little more than an attempt to try to drag back into the light of day the remains of the pre-February political forces, which even at that time were very questionable.

The half-heartedness of all these ideas, then, seems to be due to one fact: none of them makes it possible to have a real election.

Indeed, and let's be honest about this, you can only talk about democracy seriously when the people occasionally have the opportunity of freely electing who is to govern them. This assumes that two comparable alternatives exist, two equal and mutually independent political forces, each of which has an equal chance of becoming the leading force in society if the people so choose.

In other words, as long as our society needs the Communist Party to exist as a party, the demand for a second political party as its fully fledged and sovereign partner in the 'competition for power', as a permanent guarantee of its control from without, will also exist. So I see the only logical way, and, in our conditions, the only effective way of reaching the ideal of democratic socialism to be a revived *model of two parties* based on a socialist social organization. And as these would not be parties based on class interest any longer, and which would therefore not put forward various ideas about the country's economic and social organization dictated by class, they would be able to relate to each other in a historically quite new kind of coalition. While they preserved full political independence in enforcing mutual control, these parties could at the same time also be linked by an agreement about their fundamental common aim, that of the humane, socially just and civilized self-realization of the nation through democratic socialism. This principle could be anchored and expounded in some kind of fundamental 'national programme', which would formulate, for example, the basis of foreign policy and so on, and would be accepted and adopted by both parties, and eventually by other social organizations. The manner and extent to which this programme is or is not fulfilled, as well as possible future modifications, would be assessed by the people at general elections, which would reflect their confidence in both parties in the coalition, as well as each of them separately.

Although it would quite amuse me as a writer, that is as a man working in the sphere of fiction and fantasy, I am tactful enough not to think up some would-be positive programme for some so far non-existent party and to project it into various areas of our social life. One cannot plan strategy without an army. Political programmes are not born of writers' typewriters, but of the day-to-day political activity of those who implement them, of their continuous reflections about the interests to which the movement is dedicated and of their continuous contact with social reality, with public opinion, expert analyses and so on. Therefore I will confine myself to some general remarks.

Today the strong and specifically democratic and humanistic nature of the Czechoslovak tradition is often stressed. At the same time, we tend to forget what this means in concrete terms; that there are in Czechoslovakia many truly democratically and humanistically disposed people who have not engaged in any political activity within the framework of the Communist Party because of their beliefs, or simply because they did not think that the practices of the Communist Party were sufficiently democratic and humanistic. These potential grass roots of a new party also suggest its possible intellectual framework, which could be based on the democratic and humanistic tradition and therefore form a kind of Democratic Party. Naturally this does not mean that this party would claim the right to be the only legitimate advocate of democracy, just as the Communist Party cannot claim to be the only true socialist force: democracy and socialism can only be categories in the entirety of a society whose development is in everyone's interest. And if the two main partners were to be the Communist Party and the Democratic Party, this would mean that their names would symbolically guarantee the two poles of a common coalition task – democratic socialism.

At the same time I would see in such a Democratic Party a kind of – and I hope this doesn't sound too pompous – moral revival, a moral regeneration of the nation. As is often pointed out now, the emphasis on things bigger than human beings, on general social ideals, in whose name the right of a man to his individual fate was suppressed in the years of dictatorship, has led this nation to the brink of a moral crisis. This was especially true when the system was progressively degenerating, a time typified by the system of directive government by a dehumanized Party bureaucracy, with its all-embracing phraseological ritual completely divorced from reality. And the present decline in working morale is nothing more than the natural result of this demoralizing system in the economic sphere.

Unburdened by the premises and consequences of this process, with which the Communist Party will have to grapple within itself for a long complicated time to come, this new Party could restore fundamental human individuality to its place in the centre of the stage, and re-establish the individual as the yardstick for society and for the system. Not that it would adopt the rather abstract term 'the individual' as a basis for a new phraseological ritual. It would, rather, have a simple and practical attitude, expressed in its interest in specific human beings, an interest which would not be filtered through various *a priori* ideological barriers separating it from the individual's immediate and exclusive concerns. The new party would speak out in several ways in the fight for specific human rights, demands and interests: by rehabilitating concretely, actively and unconditionally those values which were until recently regarded as 'metaphysical', such as conscience, love of one's neighbour, sincerity, compassion, confidence, understanding, etc.; by adopting a new attitude towards human dignity and a respect for the individual; by giving consideration to the moral calibre of its leaders. It seems to me that as a result opportunities would be available to people of various ages, groups, social positions, faiths and viewpoints, who, because of their concrete and radical humanism, were wrongly cast out onto the periphery of society and denied the opportunity to fulfil themselves socially. And the same possibilities would be open to the younger generation. From what I have learned about the efforts of this generation to fulfil itself, for instance from the various ideas of the student movement (which, by the way, I see as one of the few forces really working towards a real political independence), I should think that for various reasons such a spiritual climate might be quite suitable to it. I don't however mean to suggest that the young should be 'recruited' (the Communist Party failed to recruit them precisely because it did nothing else but try to recruit them all the time). Instead, they should be enabled to become the subjects of political activity, not its objects.

So much for the theme of the 'second party'. In conclusion I would like to mention something which I think is very important. I'm afraid that a wider and more active political force will never manage to form itself in the non-communist majority of the nation as long as the non-communist point of view does not succeed in winning for itself a basic *moral and political recognition*. This must spring from the acceptance of certain self-evident truths, and must show itself in certain unequivocal political actions aimed at the righting of wrongs which no one so far has attempted to put right.

It seems to me that without this recognition, as an explicit moral basis for any further activity, the non-communists can never be really confident of the possibility of any of their plans succeeding. This is not a surprising demand. It is really very difficult to commit oneself earnestly and on one's own to something, without a basic guarantee that a communist error is once and for all not worth more than a non-communist truth. And if many a non-communist recognized a communist error even at a time when the communist did not have an inkling of his mistake, then the non-communist must be given credit for this, however unpleasant it may be to do so. If this is not possible, it means that communists are a special type of supermen, who are right in principle even when they have made a mistake, and that non-communists, in principle, are always wrong even when they are right. In such a situation, non-communists would be really foolish to commit themselves to anything. If communists have the occasional right to be wrong, then the non-communists must have the right to be right sometimes. Otherwise the whole thing is nonsense.

Just what am I asking for? Nothing other than the demand for the complete rehabilitation of all non-communists, who have had to suffer for many years for the fact that they recognized certain truths before the communists themselves arrived at the same conclusions. This is a highly important point today, when people who were punished in the past for their conviction that a socialism which was prepared to sacrifice democracy and liberty supposedly to help its own development could not be a good thing – when such people are quite justifiably bitter because after all these years our establishment arrives at the same conclusion. That means that they were right, but at the same time the government does not show that it is prepared to admit this and to draw the necessary conclusions from it.

To give one small example: in 1949 and 1950, as a result of the purges, tens of thousands of talented students were forced to give up their university studies. Their only offence was to have disagreed, or to have been liable to disagree, according to their fanatical colleagues on the interviewing committees, with the political practice of the Communist Party; or simply they were not communists. It is hardly necessary to point out how much this and other actions like it have damaged the nation. Most of those who stayed here and were dispersed in various jobs could not go back to the profession of their choosing, and almost until today have had to fight their dubious personal records. The ones who emigrated are likewise lost to us, although by now many of them are professors at various American and West European universities. What I am concerned with here is nothing more than the conviction that it would be appropriate if those who once conducted these purges, and who today, full of newly resuscitated Young Communist euphoria, scream at conferences and students' meetings about the times of darkness, about freedom, democracy and justice, would make a gesture to support the rights of their one-time 'ideological opponents', who thanks to the irony of history are today still paying for the fact that they believed in these values twenty years ago. This might not be appealing to them, but would strongly confirm their progressiveness. There are things which can never be put right. But there are many things which could be remedied. One could give examples of more drastic wrongs, which affected many different classes of people, from farmers to small tradesmen, from university professors and writers to village priests. And a particularly important, and politically so far almost untapped force, can be found in the perhaps eighty thousand political prisoners from the fifties. People from many different walks of life, they have so obviously been through a hard test of their moral strength and character that it would be an unpardonable sin if this force was not actively integrated into the nation's political life.

There is something else, which is not as irrelevant here as it looks – the problem of the post-February 1948 political and non-political exiles. All of these people are still, in most cases, regarded as enemies of the people and of the country, in spite of the fact that most of them have committed no greater offence than to have been convinced twenty years ago that democracy ought not to be sacrificed to the socialist system. At the same time many of them emigrated because here they were threatened with imprisonment and persecution, or simply because they did not have the opportunity to work in their professions. Though they left illegally, it is doubtful whether from the point of view of the Declaration of Human Rights it can be seen as a crime when they did not have the possibility of emigrating legally, and when such an opportunity did not exist. Unless the state's attitude to these exiles is revised, then the situation here, among ourselves, cannot be fully normalized; after all, every democratic state takes pride in keeping its international reputation free from the stigma of having forced people into exile.

I don't think there is any longer a need to see this nation exclusively from the point of view of the February conflict . . . I am not saying this because I want to fight for the restoration of the pre-February 1948 situation – although at the moment we are laboriously trying to achieve a number of things which then were taken as a matter of course – because that is simply no longer possible.

Full political and moral recognition of the non-communist position will not be a simple matter by any means, and people's rights accruing from such a recognition will not just drop from the sky. It is up to the non-communist above all to take the initiative and to win these rights gradually. It is also possible that various non-communist forces may form without this recognition. But it seems to me that without it the activity which follows will always be half-hearted, hedged around with reservations and barriers, not entirely authentic, and therefore not very forceful. After twenty years of being made to feel an outsider, and of not enjoying full rights, it's difficult to enter the political arena.

Petr Pithart
Political parties and freedom of speech

Literární Listy, 20 June 1968

Today we are continually hearing that Czechoslovakia has a unique chance to establish and bring about a political system such as has never been seen before: that we have been called upon, even selected, that everybody in the progressive world is looking in our direction hopefully, and that it's up to us now, or perhaps nobody will ever have this chance again.

But we shouldn't have any illusions about one thing, which is that we are tragically isolated in our revolution, as one of our journalists in France was quite rightly told by one French communist.

Most of our allies do not understand us, or more precisely, do not even want to understand us. To large numbers of the radical Left in the West we are traitors to the ideas of socialism (by which they mean Maoism), 'revisionists', or at the very best madmen who intend to install the very system that they themselves are erecting barricades against. The Western establishments on the other hand are making speculations about the developments in Czechoslovakia, looking first and foremost after their own interests. The communist parties in the West certainly wish us well, but they also are forced to interpret the developments in Czechoslovakia from the point of view of their own interests, always thinking about elections. The state and the Party are growing together in Rumania, and in Jugoslavia real discussions about the setting up of another political Party are apparently still taboo. Many different people seem to be projecting their own frustrated hopes into our experiments, and these hopes differ as widely as the disappointments from which they spring. After all, not even we ourselves know exactly enough just what is going on here, because up until now we have not even proved that we are capable of analysing the system which we have been abandoning during the last few months.

These are some of the reasons why I treat these exaggerated visions of our epoch-making chances of installing some kind of quite new political system with great reservation. At the moment, it seems to me, we should analyse the situation as it exists, as well as the history of the past twenty-three years, rather than listen, for example, to the advice of such an otherwise sympathetic person as Rudi Dutschke, of whom more later. Paradoxically, this advice supports the hand of the conservatives or the forces of the 'centre', whose programme is a compromise.

Our real hopes lie in the wisdom with which we combine the most enlightened political structures which have worked or are at present working in various places in the world with our own democratic traditions, at the same time bearing in mind the specific needs of both our nations. This is not a recommendation that we should copy in a passive way. We shall want to look for untested models, and in the future we shall most likely be obliged to do so. But as far as the immediate task of installing a new political system is concerned, then to call for an improvement here can only be meaningful today if it means to want something extra: the autonomy of political parties, which would put up their own candidates in elections, and real freedom of speech. These are the so far unfulfilled minimum requirements for Czechoslovak democracy to exist.

To call, at this early stage, for improvements or reforms, to suggest, for instance, that instead of being channelled through autonomous political parties the people's will can be expressed in some direct way or that it can be expressed in a socialist syndicalism or corporateness which has so far not been outlined (apparently this would be a case of workers' autonomy, or of other common interest organizations legally expanded into a parliament with several chambers), and so on – all these suggestions are symptoms of an already incurable incapacity to learn from the tragic history of socialist ideas in practice up until now. To postulate these theories is possibly a gamble taken by impatient politicians and a few philosophers. On the other hand, they may just show how widespread and how understandable in its way is the unwillingness to break finally with the old monolithic system, an unwillingness masked because some progressive forces are merely pretending to be radical.

Naturally, a system with several political parties leads to a power struggle, or a struggle for a share in power. And the struggle for power, even if it takes place within an institutionalized framework, for example, in accordance with the election regulations and therefore peacefully, or shall we say in a civilized way, as a rule also creates a whole series of what are really undemocratic phenomena. In the end it can also create the rather sad, distasteful spectacle of politics going on behind closed doors, partisanship, government by professional party apparatchicks, favouritism, corruption, the continual vetoing of opposition proposals and a readiness to forgive each other's mistakes behind the scenes . . .

People who create irresponsible Utopian fantasies, who apparently no longer accept that power exists, or the possibility that it might be misused in the future, and demagogues who associate the free play of political parties directly with Preiss, the Živnobanka and the shooting of children at Radotín,[3] and also aesthetes who think that politics is above all a dirty and swinish game – all these people should be very firmly reminded today of the fact that the First Czechoslovak Republic, which no one wants to return to today because of all its other faults, sentenced, as far as I know, only eight people to death. The struggle of political parties for power, therefore, still remains the most reliable way of controlling power, however imperfect it may be – unfortunately. But even legally perfected control and 'brake' mechanisms, such as when power in the state is divided into three – legislative, executive and judicial – easily break down where a single political party has an actual monopoly of power . . .

In the heat of this sincere searching for the best possible political system for this country and also of the experimental efforts to preserve the old monolithic system in a more acceptable garb in the future, a very relevant and important question is raised: is not political pluralism today, even in the West, already really a thing of the past? . . .

It does appear that the two-party system in particular breaks

3. Preiss, pre-war Czech banker; Živnobanka, one of the leading banks of the First Republic; the shooting of children at Radotín, a reference to an incident in the First Republic when some children of strikers were accidentally shot during a confrontation with police.

down, although at first sight this should be the very system which . . . reflects the basic contraditions in society and hence facilitates their solution. But evidently it is exactly its straightforwardness which is its fundamental weakness. The possibility of being essentially in favour of the status quo or basically against it, these are the oversimplified alternatives which exist to make the decision-making processes of the people meaningful in the last third of the twentieth century. Paradoxically it turns out . . . that in the consumer societies a political system based on the existence of only one opposition party . . . can in the end mean that this party risks losing its ability, and above all its will, to think and act in opposition . . . Society then loses its capacity to criticize itself radically . . . The only other alternative then – however understandable it may be – is the vandalism of the American Negroes, or, in recent weeks, in somewhat different conditions, of the students of Paris; or else assassinations.

However little hope there may now be for the future of political pluralism in the advanced capitalist societies, we have to bear in mind that the West is after all the West . . . So I'll come back to the inadequate description of socialism as a social order whose political and economic system is based on the social ownership of the means of production, in an attempt to show that political pluralism can be a meaningful mechanism in socialist conditions. Provided of course that the socialization of the means of production is not considered to be synonomous with their acquisition by the state, for in a country where everybody is really a state employee no democracy has a chance, let alone a pluralist democracy.

Rudi Dutschke, among other members of the West European New Left, has spoken to us about our democratization process. During the visit he made to Prague, he summed up very succinctly the attitudes of those who feel themselves to be oversaturated and disappointed by liberal democracy, above all by the parliamentary systems in their countries. The New Left welcomes sympathetically all the latest happenings in Czechoslovakia, but is very much afraid that by installing a multi-party system we shall be following the capitalist countries up a blind alley, at the end of which the New Left thinks it is standing today, facing rank upon rank of police.

Political parties and freedom of speech

I should think that nowhere in the world is there so much confidence – often ill-considered and in many respects naïve – in the parliamentary system, in the free play of political forces, at least among the politically committed intelligentsia, as in Czechoslovakia today . . .

Alexander Dubček
Speech to the Central Committee of the Communist Party, 29 May

Rudé Právo, 4 June 1968

The Communist Party of Czechoslovakia is today the only political force in this country which has a scientific socialist programme. It is the principal guarantee of the good relations between the Czechoslovak Socialist Republic and the other socialist states and as a result ensures our stable international position. It is the unifying force of both our nations, Czechs and Slovaks, it amasses hundreds of thousands of workers, farmers, and the non-manual workers who enjoy respect and authority among their fellow workers. In its ranks are concentrated the overwhelming majority of the most creative forces in our society, scientists, technicians and artists. Party members are people who have won their positions of authority by their struggle against capitalism and against the Nazi occupation, people who were the initiators and organizers of the present revival process of socialism and of the development of socialist democracy. Its cadres form the predominant part of the administrative and managerial structure of our society.

All of this creates a *historical reality*, a situation in which there is no way ahead for a really democratic socialist development, without unleashing a struggle for power, other than the road along which the Communist Party of Czechoslovakia, as the strongest organized political force in this country, will lead the future process of development . . .

We want to create a system of political relations in our society, such a political system in which our Party will share decision-making and power with non-Communist parties, in which the Party will not be fused directly with the monopoly of the centre of state power.

At the same time, it would be distorting facts to maintain that the Party does not express the interests of society. We have to be sure that its leading position in society is above all based on the representation of the most progressive and far-ranging social interests. The problem is that the range of interests expressed by the political direction of our state and society should be as broad and concrete as possible. That is the real significance of our present efforts to develop the policy of the National Front, the basis of which is and should be a policy aimed at the intensification of socialist democracy, a democracy which should open up broad scope for everybody's active participation in socialist construction. It would however be a mistake to assume that the essence of democratization is a mechanical transfer of the formal democracy of the bourgeois parliamentary system into socialist society . . .

The National Front will certainly in the very near future clearly define the programme of its socialist basis. Violation or rejection of this will be incompatible with membership of the National Front.

The Communist Party of Czechoslovakia will submit its proposals, according to which such a programme would consist in agreeing with a socialist class and ownership arrangement of social relations and activity which would support their development. Further conditions are that activity should comply with the constitution of Czechoslovakia; that activity against the people's interests would be inadmissible, such as anti-communism, fascism and other activity which might incite nationalist or racialist conflict, or any kind of political activity aimed at the foundations of state and national independence as expressed by the alliance with the Soviet Union and the socialist countries. Furthermore, that the principle that the Marxist conception of the construction of socialism forms the basis of the development of our society should be observed, and that the leading political position of the Communist Party of Czechoslovakia is today a historical fact . . .

The fundamental difference between the bourgeois parliamentary system and socialist democracy is that the relationship between the political parties in the National Front must be a relationship of partnership and cooperation and not one of the struggle for the division of power in the state, as in the bourgeois political system. This does not mean that political autonomy, controversy and mutual dispute are excluded. Conflicts of opinion must be based on a common socialist programme. The guarantee of this programme is the leading role of the Communist Party of Czechoslovakia. For there is no other real programme for the construction of socialism other than the Marxist programme, based on scientific knowledge and the most progressive social interests.

We must discount the possibility that the development of socialist democracy in Czechoslovakia could at present include the formation of an opposition party outside the National Front, as this would be the road to a renewal of a struggle for power. Our Party will oppose such tendencies by all possible means, because in the present conditions . . . this would lead to an attempt to undermine first the position of the Communist Party of Czechoslovakia in our society and ultimately even socialist development. We therefore resolutely reject the establishment of any opposition party which would stand outside the policy of the National Front. And this is the principle that we adopted as early as 1945.

Five
What About the Workers?

Literární Listy, 4 April 1968

Bohumil Štěpán What about some advice as well

The representatives of the apparat are extraordinarily frightened of one force only, and that is the people. They are afraid of the people; they're not afraid of the intellectuals, who can be intimidated, some of them corrupted, divided or tamed a little, and suppressed using administrative methods.

But the workers, the people, that is just where the apparat feels the great danger to itself. Every democratic procedure, any real stand made by the people, is a threat to them.

Ivan Sviták, from a speech to the Central Committee of the Union of Film and Television Artists
Filmové a Televizní Noviny, 29 May 1968

The workers in Czechoslovakia occupied a strange position in the ideological thinking of communists before 1968. The class struggle was officially declared in the constitution of 1960 to have been superseded. The period of the dictatorship of the proletariat was over. Yet the working class, as distinct from the intelligentsia, the technocratic workers and the farmers and peasantry, continued to be talked about as a group whose interests most of all had to be protected. In fact, the defence of the interests of the workers was used as a pretext for repelling any threat to the dominance of the Novotnýite line.

Jiří Hendrych, Novotný's ideologist, in a speech given at the beginning of 1967, outlined the official attitude of the conservatives to the problem of the changing nature of the class struggle. What will happen to society now that the revolution has accomplished the classless society? What will our new definition of the working class now be? he asked:

We consider the basis of the progressive core of the working class (in which a new type of worker is already being formed, a worker for whom physical work is becoming increasingly linked with mental work) to be the group of highly qualified workers, whose number will go on increasing. A rapprochement of great strength is taking place between these workers and the technical intelligentsia. They will gradually become a part of 'the complete worker', as Marx called the product of the integration of the working class and the technical intelligentsia. This process is continuing to such a degree, with the advance of the scientific and technological revolution, that it is possible to consider entire groups of technical workers part of the working class, since they are acquiring its socially progressive characteristics.

The logic of the argument was that any development or change in social stratification can be labelled as 'working class' as long as it is 'socially progressive'. Hendrych saw new social groupings only in terms of the revolutionary class struggle, perpetuating an obsolete form of social conflict. New definitions could not be allowed to emerge. The tone of the argument came perilously close to some of the arguments used in the early days of socialism, when 'progressiveness' could be worn in the form of a cloth cap or working class clothes, and the bourgeoisie had to be subjected to the same torments that had always afflicted the proletariat:

> Children of bourgeois origin must choose manual labour so that they may at last do the work that their class always gladly left to the proletariat. They must become miners and foundry workers. There, underground, let them dig coal. There, in the glowing light of the furnaces and the red-hot iron, a brand new world will open for them, a world of active work. There will be their new high schools and universities. There we will hammer and educate them into builders of socialism.[1]

One of the aims of the 1968 revival was to nullify the impact of this kind of artificial stratification of social groups, and to come to terms with changing economic and social roles. While many people were aware of the dangers that might result from, for instance, a de-levelling of wages to reward the more able and hard-working, some form of initiative such as this was seen as one of the only ways of stimulating both the people and the economy. 'In tackling the exciting tasks of today,' said Dubček in a speech at the Allied Steel Works at Kladno, the industrial area near Prague, 'we must not see skilled and unskilled work, the work of manual workers and technicians, the interests of the working class and the interests of the intelligentsia, as being opposed to each other . . .'

1. A. Jungwirthová, a woman communist legislator. First published in *Lidové Noviny*, 27 April 1951, quoted in Táborský, *Communism in Czechoslovakia*, Princeton, 1961, p. 532.

'Our present crisis is one which involves every social group and every class,' says Kosík in his long important analysis of the Czechoslovak situation in *Literární Listy*. 'The so frequently reiterated slogan about "the united alliance of workers, peasants and the intelligentsia" has become a meaningless statement not because it is a cliché; it has turned into a cliché because the actual nature of this alliance has changed.' The ruling bureaucracy, he says, played a deforming role in society. It tried to 'confine workers to their factories, peasants to their villages and the intelligentsia to their libraries, reducing their *political* cooperation to a minimum'. The bureaucracy had a very serious effect on the workers, who, 'as a class, ceased to play a political role and became isolated from their most natural ally, the intelligentsia . . . While the ideology of the leading role of a class was promoted to the level of a state religion, any *genuine* public activity of the workers was reduced to a minimum . . .' The working class, he says, must once again become a real political force, for which it needs freedom of speech and of the press.

The workers were the *eminence grise* of the revival process. They were important more for their general inactivity than for the fact that they adopted positive and purposefully directed attitudes. They were courted by all the different interest groups, from the ultra hard-liners to the ultra progressives. The criticism levelled at Dubček by the old régime was that he was betraying the interests of the workers for the sake of new ideas and so-called 'democracy', while most of the reformers shared Kosík's view that Novotný had used the workers at the same time as he had protected his own position.

Novotný himself had always taken great pains to remind everybody of his own working-class origins – son of a bricklayer and a mechanic until the age of twenty-five, since when he had been a full-time Party functionary – and like so many of the workers' representatives, the 'professional revolutionaries', had not worked in a factory for decades. He based his campaign against the Dubček leadership after January on his appeal to the working class. In mid February, he spoke at several of the largest Prague factories, declaring that the January plenum and the change of first secretary had been a coup against the interests of the workers and in favour of the intellectuals and the economists, who only wanted to lower the standard of living and to take away from the workers all the power that they had won in 1948 and after.

Novotný tried to link the idea of the conservative politician with the workers' interests: 'If to be a conservative means to oppose the lowering of the standard of living of the working class . . . then I am proud to be a conservative' (*Le Monde*, 24 February 1968). The conservative defence against the reformers was thus directed in support of the supposed economic, social and class interests of the working class.

Reformist criticism of the policies of the past was almost unanimous. 'The police–bureaucratic régime above all depoliticized the workers. They stopped playing a political role as a class, and this function was taken over by the bureaucracy which identified itself ideologically with the whole of society, and represented *its own* monopoly ruling position as the leading role of a *class*' (Karel Kosík). 'What is certain is that in the arguments and debates which went on among the intelligentsia and between other groups, the word "workers" was used as a kind of armed veto' (Ludvík Vaculík). 'If the authors of the resolution characterize the past twenty years as a *proletarian dictatorship*, they are at odds with the facts, because what is happening at the moment bears witness to the fact that the workers, the intelligentsia and the people were ruled by the apparat' (Ivan Sviták). 'The system of bureaucratic despotism liquidated the rights of the working class, just as it did the rights of every citizen in the country' (Ivan Sviták). 'We have to ask whether that policy of ours was in the past really in harmony with the interests of the working class' (Josef Smrkovský).

Šik, Smrkovský and many writers and journalists tried to talk to the workers, but progress was slow. The inbuilt prejudices of the workers, conditioned by twenty years of broken promises and communist verbiage, made them regard the new leadership as just another re-shuffle, and, indeed, up until the end of March, they were quite justified in doing so. Although it was difficult to speak in simple terms about the interests of a working class, because of the growing inner differentiations of and difficulty of defining this class ('For a long time now I haven't really been aware of all the things that the word "worker" means in Czechoslovakia today' – Vaculík), it is possible to say that they had been neglected politically and now felt uneasy about their own identity and the emphasis put on the role of the intellectuals and the students in the revival process. One worker said at the end of May:

> When we don't see for ourselves that our work is better organized, that things are really getting better, it's obvious the people in general will say to themselves, 'We know all about this, we've seen it all before.' We know all about different kinds of revival processes, there have been enough reforms during all the years. We can remember at least five of them . . .

And another, at the beginning of April, 'Why don't people speak for us too, and why did Šik just talk to a closed group of functionaries, and as usual leave us in ignorance?'

General assurances about the need for unity of all classes for the democratization process were not enough to offset these doubts and fears. A positive effort was made to present the opinions of the workers in the press, partly as a counter to the conservative-dominated workers' conferences. In the exchange of letters between the technicians of the Doubrava Mine and Ivan Sviták, the whole issue of who is in fact speaking for whom is brought to a high-pitched head. Sviták accuses the technicians of the mine of protecting their own interests and jobs, and kowtowing to the apparatchiks. 'The Party is you, the actual people,' he says to the workers, 'and not the apparat.'

The task in hand was an enormously difficult one: to make the workers think independently, to undo twenty years of depoliticization created by the old régime. The tendency towards passivity was very strong. 'If only the people up there would shut themselves up somewhere, come to an agreement, and tell us in a straightforward way what will be happening from tomorrow onwards,' says one worker to Vaculík. Sviták's own campaign against Kolder, a conservative member of the leadership who remained in the Praesidium, and whose stronghold was in the North Moravian mining area, was successful, but the terms on which many of the appeals to the workers to support the revival were based proved too vague. The workers at least partially got over the myth of the ogre-like intelligentsia.

> I'm a worker and a member of the Works' Committee [says Ladislav Anděl] . . . I've been systematically following all the most important things in . . . the press . . . Nowhere . . . have I so far found so much as a

line . . . about writers and intellectuals attacking the working class. I'd like to know when and where it was. On the other hand, I've heard many brave things which openly defended the rights and interests of the working class.

They did not, however, understand the need to link the demand for rights for the workers to the demands of the journalists and intellectuals for freedom of speech, something that Sviták managed to express in 'The meaning of the revival'.

> The intellectual must quite openly tell the worker today, 'If anyone interferes with your right to strike I shall defend it as resolutely as I am defending freedom of speech for myself.' Similarly, the worker should openly tell the intellectual, 'If anyone interferes with your freedom of speech, I shall strike.'

Economic rights, the right to strike, to make wage demands and to press for better working conditions interested the average worker in 1968 far more than the democratization of the political structure of society. In 'The search for a common language', Vörös says: 'I don't care whether I work for Bat'a or for a state enterprise; the decisive factor for me is which place I'm better off in, and where it's better to work . . .'

Many of the workers thought they would be much worse off under the efficiency and the work differentiation of the New Economic System – or rather its theoretical efficiency, since it had not produced many results by 1968. Miroslav Jodl wrote at the end of May:

> Certainly, without a visible improvement in the economic situation, the 'men of January' will not succeed in winning the *active* support of the majority of the people. And until now, there has not been even the first sign of such an improvement.

All the protectionism of the old market would have to be discarded, all inefficient enterprises closed, and the rest left at the mercy of the market.

Šik and Smrkovský could tell the workers that they had been badly off in comparison with workers in the capitalist countries; but the old system had at least not demanded a great deal of hard work and they had never gone short of food. Unskilled workers had been especially well off under the levelling of wages of the old system, another 'advantage' that was being destroyed by the New Economic System. Even though Šik took great pains to point out that the economic difficulties which had been inherited from the Novotný regime could not be solved except by the tough application of the new principles, the appeals in 1968 from the new leadership to be patient and reasonable with wage demands, and to sacrifice short-term interests for long-term ones, carried about as much conviction with the Czechoslovak workers as they do in a capitalist country.

Švestka (see below) did, in fact, express the feelings of many workers when he wrote of the continued mistrust of the new policies on the rather mundane but nevertheless vital issue – where the workers were concerned – of social security. Despite the obvious political motives behind his views (Švestka was one of the more conservative members of the Praesidium), his critics (see Pavel Machonín) could only point to an embryonic workers' movement, and repeat the rather vague and, for many workers, largely irrelevant promises of democracy and the formation of Workers' Councils.

The solution to this problem of the passivity and suspicion of the workers was seen by many intellectuals and progressive politicians to lie in these Works or Workers' Councils. Theoretically they were a perfect answer. By means of their representatives, the workers would have a direct say in the running of their enterprises, they would become an integral part of the self-management principle of independent units throughout the country, and would thus be linked to the revival. Economically, the Councils would make them see the real difficulties to be faced, and they would behave reasonably since it would be in their own interests to do so. 'Activity which would really do something to change your position is the election and the activity of workers' self-management bodies, which would be both *with you and for you*, and would administer what is primarily yours' (Bartošek). The idealistic notion of these councils was challenged by Petr Pithart in an article in which he expressed his fear that even here the workers may be pushed too fast – 'The worst thing of all would be for the state to legislate about self-management, to make it compulsory. One cannot force anybody to be free . . .'

Despite theoretical differences about the exact form the Czechoslovak version of these Councils would take, an official concept was outlined by Šik. The only trouble was that what should have been the saving grace of the relationship between the workers and the democratization process was not received by the workers themselves with any enthusiasm. Many of them knew nothing about the whole scheme; in a survey published late in the period, almost half of the unskilled workers questioned professed complete ignorance (*Práce*, 13 August), and many of those who did know about it expressed doubts as to whether it was not another ruse by which to make the workers responsible for the production side and thus make it impossible for them to press their own wage demands. Others pointed out that it was putting the cart before the horse, as the enterprises had still to achieve real independence.

Švestka's remarks that at least the workers had had their social security under the old régime could only be countered by the plea that the workers had accepted change soberly and that they knew what was in their interests in the long run. There was a lot of evidence to support the claim that their basic political passivity and lack of experience had still not been overcome. 'People talk about Workers' Councils,' said one worker in July. 'Give us some advice on how to begin, what actually to do. We haven't got any experience of such things. We can't just call a meeting. We've got no right to do that. We haven't even got a hall which belongs to us' (see 'Groping in the wind').

The one encouraging sign for the progressives' efforts was the workers' committees for the defence of the freedom of the press (see Kubíček – 'An initiative from below'). Unlike the officially imposed Workers' Councils, these committees were spontaneously formed in the real tradition of socialist and Communist agitation. They provided the only concrete evidence of a genuine alliance between the workers and the intelligentsia, of the workers concern not only with higher wages and better conditions, but with democratic rights and liberties.

In the train of the invasion came patriotism. Patriotism accomplished what democracy and socialism had failed to do – convert the generally passive support among the workers for the revival into active support. The agonizingly slow process of change within the working class and its organizations caught up in speed and intensity with the rest of society. The months which followed

August saw the factories and the unions develop into a politically progressive force; the goal of the intellectuals' 'campaign' was achieved, but it had been overtaken by events. The Czechoslovak general strike on 23 August characteristically lasted only one hour, and in subsequent action or contemplated action, preoccupation with the well-being of the economy, and with prudence and wisdom prevailed. Not even the combination of national democratic socialism could make the Czech and Slovak 'revolutionary vanguard' lead from anywhere but the rear.

Karel Kosík
Our present crisis (extracts)

The crisis of classes and society

Literární Listy, 25 April 1968

Our present crisis is one which involves every social group and every class, and of course at the same time, the interrelationship between them. The so frequently reiterated slogan about 'the united alliance of workers, peasants and the intelligentsia' has become a meaningless statement not because it is a cliché; it has turned into a cliché because the actual nature of this alliance has changed. In its relations with the separate classes, the ruling bureaucracy played a deforming role in two ways: firstly, it tried to identify a modern society with a medieval guild, and to confine workers to their factories, peasants to their villages and the intelligentsia to their libraries, reducing their *political* cooperation to a minimum. And secondly, it deprived each of these classes of its individuality and transformed them into a politically uniform and expressionless mass. The ideal of the bureaucracy is a *closed* society, based on the sectarian limitations of the various classes, and on the rationing of information. The ground plan of society was supposed to be formed by corporateness, which would isolate the different classes as pursuers of their own particular interests, and make the bureaucracy not only the only representative of the general interest but also the exclusive mediator in the mutual exchange of information.

This bureaucratic practice had a very serious effect on the workers, who, as a class, ceased to play a political role and became isolated from their most natural ally, the intelligentsia. The intelligentsia, too, was artificially cut off from the working class. The police-bureaucratic régime above all depoliticized the workers. They stopped playing a political role as a class, and this function was taken over by the bureaucracy which identified itself ideologically with the whole of society, and presented *its own* monopoly ruling position as the leading role of a *class*. While the ideology of the leading role of a class was promoted to the level of a state religion, any genuine public activity of the workers was reduced to a minimum. They were given certain unalienable rights: they were allowed to repeat *ad infinitum* their criticisms of the shortcomings at their places of work, although the causes of course lie in society as a whole and therefore cannot be removed within the framework of a single factory; and they could solemnly express their opinion about information presented by the ruling bureaucracy and show their agreement or annoyance in plebiscites.

The fate of our present crisis depends on whether the working class will understand the discrepancy that exists between ideology and illusions on the one hand, and their real *political* situation on the other. Only if they then draw the necessary conclusions will they become once again a *political* force and again lead a social alliance with the peasantry, intelligentsia and white-collar workers.

However, the working class cannot play a political role in a socialist system without freedom of the press, freedom of expression and information. Without democratic rights it is both locked within the horizon of one factory or one workshop, and doomed to corporateness – it will always be exposed to the danger of the political bureaucracy ruling on its behalf. Their self-appointed 'friends' have always tried to make the workers believe that freedom of expression and of the press only concerns one group of people, the intelligentsia. But it is of vital importance for the workers to have democratic freedoms, because without them, they cannot carry out their historical emancipating role. How can they play a political role when they have no access to information, and can thus never know exactly and at the right times what is happening in the country? How can the working class play a political role when it is deprived of the chance to *interpret* information independently, when this rightful activity is done by someone else on their behalf and in their name?...

The conflict between the workers and the intelligentsia, which the ruling bureaucracy has been provoking constantly since 1956, was not only artificially created, but was also an artificial conflict. The real meaning of the conflict was that it incited one group, the workers, against another, the intelligentsia. It was also an attack on the wisdom, the critical thinking, the judgement, in short on the intelligence of one class of society, the workers. It was aimed chiefly at them. The meaning of the conflict will become quite clear when we understand that together with this campaign against the intelligentsia, against reason and judgement, there was a revival of primitive instincts: anti-semitism, mass psychosis and so on. As a result a dark alliance of superstition, prejudice and resentment was being secretly and sometimes even publicly organized against the possible alliance between reason and intelligence.

If this alliance of the three classes ideologically obscured the political role of the workers and the intelligentsia, even this mystification paled in comparison to the problems of the third partner, the peasantry, since the farmers played an insignificant political and social role. As a political and social problem, the countryside disappeared from sight, and with it vanished any consideration of the relationship between the state and the peasantry and the place of farming in a modern society...

Instead of the old obsolete alliance of Party and non-Party members, a new political alliance of communists, socialists, democrats and other citizens, based on political equality and full rights and basing itself on the principles of socialism and humanity might be created. Socialist democracy is either an all-inclusive democracy, or it is not democracy at all. Among its fundamentals are the autonomy of socialist producers, and the political democracy of socialist citizens: one degenerates without the other.

As soon as the working class reconstitutes itself as a political force (and this is impossible without a consistent democratization of the trade unions and the Communist Party, and without the formation of Workers' Councils), the conditions will be created for a new class alliance of workers, peasants and the intelligentsia. Each group would make its own characteristic and specific contribution to this alliance, and the whole would succeed in influencing, correcting and modifying the interests of each group, producing a useful tension and a fruitful political dialogue. This alliance would become the basis for an open socialist society, because the dialogue, conflict, tension and harmony of the various classes is a stimulant and a source of initiative and political drive. Such energies encourage the development of every aspect of society.

Alexander Dubček
Speech at the Allied Steel Works in Kladno, 2 March

Rudé Právo, 5 March 1968

The working class now faces the task of carrying out the most fundamental purpose of our revolution, to bring about the collaboration of the whole of an already non-antagonistic society . . . It's necessary for every communist, workers' official and for every worker himself to understand how the role of the working class is changing at the moment. Today the workers have to play an important part in the process of economic development, the democratization of society, and the development of their freedom, together with the freedom of the whole of society.

In tackling the exciting tasks of today, we must not see skilled and unskilled work, the work of manual workers and technicians, the interests of the working class and the interests of the intelligentsia, as being opposed to each other . . . Nothing could be more detrimental to the healthy development of Czechoslovak society than to set the interests of one class against those of another. The interests of the working class today can only be defended in the development of the whole of society, in the integration of all the classes and interests into society . . .

We are determined to give scope to all the creative and as yet untapped resources of the working class. To underestimate our workers and to believe that they are not able to undertake the very exacting transformation of their working conditions would not be a working class policy. The working class cannot free itself without liberating the other sections of society . . . The leading role of the working class consists in continuing the socialist revolution, in implementing and applying the revolutionary changes which have so far taken place. The working class must unite and stand at the head of a process of social integration and the democratization connected with it.

Action Programme of the Communist Party of Czechoslovakia (extracts)

All the social classes, divisions and groups, both the states and all the nationalities in our society are in agreement with the fundamental interests and aims of socialism. One of the big advantages of socialist development to date is that a decisive factor in assessing the standing and activity of the people of this society is their working merit and their social activity, and not their membership of this or that class or social division. The Party heartily condemns all attempts to set the various classes, divisions and groups in the country in opposition to each other and will try to remove anything which creates tension among them . . .

The Party depends, and will continue to depend, on the working class, as it has shown that it is able to carry the main weight of socialist endeavour. At the present time, we are relying especially on those who are aware of the real interests and tasks of the working class in the revolutionary construction of the whole society, and profoundly understand them, who are qualified in and devoted to modern technology, and who are efficient at work and socially active. For these are the people who contribute significantly to the development of Czechoslovak industry and to the whole society.

The working class began its revolutionary struggle in order to abolish every kind of exploitation, to break down all the class barriers, to make it easier for people to be free and to change the conditions of human life, to make way for man to really fulfil himself, and through all this of course to change itself. These long-term working-class interests have not yet been fully asserted. The workers, however, now have in their hands new technical, social and cultural means which allow them to go on changing their working and living conditions, to expand the elements of purposeful creative endeavour in their activity. We are determined to open up wide the road for the assertion of all the creative energies which the working class has but which still remain considerably untapped.

In the past, the workers did not always have the opportunity to express their immediate interests. The Party therefore will do its utmost to activate the social life of the working class, to give them scope to use all of their political and social rights through political organizations and trade unions, and to strengthen the democratic influence of collective teams of workers in the management of production . . .

Likewise it is necessary to understand that the character of our intelligentsia has gradually changed, it has become an intelligentsia of the people, a socialist intelligentsia . . . Today the workers will find in the intelligentsia a component part of themselves and part of their own inner strength. The constantly closer collaboration of the technical intelligentsia and the workers in production collectives is a way of proving that former class barriers are being surmounted. The Party will support the growing unity between the intelligentsia and the other working people, will fight against the recent tendency to underestimate the role of the intelligentsia, and will set itself against everything that upsets relations between the intelligentsia and the workers.

Ludvík Vaculík
What about the workers?

Literární Listy, 4 April 1968

For a long time now I haven't really been aware of all the things that the word 'worker' means in Czechoslovakia today. The definition of a worker according to the manual nature of his work just won't do. There is a very great difference between the machinist bent over her machinery in a shoe factory and the man who gives directions for moving around huge pieces of iron. Their pay, what they do with their free time when they finish work, their job-security, all these are very different. They do not have an equal status. The metal-roller is a kind of 'super' worker. We should see that very easily if at the same moment a strike broke out in the shoe factory and in the steel works. Where would Dubček go first?

Another point: workers by birth and by class origin coexist with those who have been forced to become workers; a part of the working class has, as is well-known, a bad class origin. And as well as that, in every factory, there are better-paid jobs, with better pension schemes, with healthier conditions, with better prospects for promotion or travel, in short, jobs just made for committee members of long-standing and for various brands of cooperative advisers. What are the characteristics of 'workers' like this?

And yet again, people who a long time ago began working in a place which has now completely changed in character go on counting themselves as workers. Such a long time ago, indeed, that certain among their number confuse 'secretariat' with 'proletariat'. I prefer to call them all professional revolutionaries, an expression which I have borrowed from Lenin.

For a long time now, I've been thinking of writing a piece on the theme of 'Who this state really belongs to'. In it I would discuss the odd fact that the average, uninformed worker sees the bad state of affairs in this country as the fault of the intellectual, whereas the intellectual knows that this bad state of affairs was in fact organized by professional revolutionaries in the name of the workers. To what extent with their knowledge, their willingness or unwillingness, their indifference or agreement, I don't know. What is certain is that in the arguments and debates which went on among the intelligentsia and between other groups, the word 'workers' was used as a kind of armed veto. So that's what I'd like to write an article about. But what's the use of an article? Someone should organize a large meeting at the Škoda Works to debate this subject, though we should be very careful who . . .

Of all the bad ways to choose in order to get an opportunity to talk with workers I didn't know, I picked a sad, notorious one. I asked the chairman of a local trade union committee in a locomotive works to arrange a meeting for me with people of his own choice. About twenty turned up, including six who were members of the Communist Party of Czechoslovakia, one who had left the Party because of the high subscriptions, one an old Social Democrat, one an ex-worker of some organization or other, one a young bloke with a moustache and one woman. I think they spoke frankly enough, but I doubt whether frankness is a very important quality in front of a journalist. People who aren't afraid have a tendency to show off just how much they're not afraid. I don't think that what they said was a particularly good sample of workers' thinking as such. It was a picture of what a certain group of workers, in March of this year, could say and were willing to say in front of a reporter from *Literární Listy* and in the presence of a functionary, whom I wasn't acquainted with and who probably came from the trade union, and who sat on one side and didn't say a word.

It was the day after a big meeting in the Prague Congress Palace. This event had had a disagreeable effect on most of us. An older worker said, 'It all seems to me like a plot against the working class. Who did Smrkovský refer to when he was talking about provocateurs?'

A non-Party worker said, 'Goldstücker is, well . . . let's say, a wise man, and he was, let's at least give him this much, wronged.[2] Kohout and Procházka I respected, but some of the answers were just given for the effect.[3] And at times it seemed as though they

2. Eduard Goldstücker, chairman of the Writers' Union in 1968. (see Notes on authors).

3. Pavel Kohout, a dramatist, who was very active politically from the beginning of the period; lighthearted in his style of expressing the issues, parti-

were like cheap-jacks who would be quite willing to sell rotten apples to you. You lot should be more patient with us; you may be able to understand this democracy quickly enough, but it'll take us longer. Whenever there is a worker joining a discussion on the radio, there are immediately six others trying to get on top of him. That creates a very bad impression. And these Reichstags, like yesterday in Prague, are a bad joke.'

Another voice: 'They want to give us democracy using undemocratic methods. They forced Lenárt to speak even when he was ill, and they almost interrogated Mestek with a lie-detector.'[4]

The young worker, who was otherwise in favour of the progressive course, said, 'What I see as a problem today is that the conservatives should get the full right to speak.'

There was general agreement that everything was happening only in Prague, and that all the democrats were going round trying to persuade the students and no one was talking to the workers, for instance, those at the Škoda Works. 'We can also have a demonstration,' said the woman.

'We can have a general strike,' called out the old man.

But for what and against what? As the woman, a Party functionary for some years, said, 'Today it seems as if everything we have done has been of no use! As if I ought to be ashamed in front of my own children of what I have brought them up into. We have worked our guts out here for twenty years; why didn't the people at the top do the same?' She asked me, 'Was the censorship

---

cularly at the March mass meetings. Jan Procházka, novelist and a vice-chairman of the Writers' Union. Was at one time considered to be on good terms with Novotný; lost his candidature to the Central Committee after his part in the Fourth Congress, and in the 1968 period was very outspoken, particularly concerning the Soviet Union relationship. Died in February 1971.

4. Jozef Lenárt, a Slovak who replaced Široký as Prime Minister in 1963, and was to begin with considered as one of the more hopeful new young Party leaders. He hotly defended Novotný at the December–January plenum, and was replaced as prime minister by Černík in April 1968. The instance referred to here is his speech defending his own record, which he made on television on 18 March 1968. Karel Mestek, minister of agriculture under Novotný, a committed conservative, who made some extreme and unsubstantiated allegations both about developments in the countryside and about the press, and was 'grilled' in an effort to elicit concrete charges on these issues.

really so bad that it's only now that we're getting to know about the sort of fascist methods that were being used?'

'The greatest censorship was under the First Republic. This reporter here was only a tiny boy at the time, and he probably doesn't know about the blank spaces that used to appear in the papers,' called out another worker. He doesn't know that the present censorship confiscated even those blank spaces so that he could not see what had been going on at all.

The non-Party worker: 'I was expecting this to come. And we should be thankful that it's come in the form it has. The communists introduced the system without consulting anybody else. If we had functionaries like Zápotocký,[5] there would already have been a strike! The students talk because they're organized. We aren't organized, because the trade union, well, that's just a cover-up for the Communist Party!'

And just as violently as he had rejected the 'leading role of the intellectuals' in our present democratization, he criticized the example of disorder and corruption which had been set; how silver medals had been distributed during the enterprise's anniversary celebrations; how more money was given to people who occupied a function than to those who worked. By simplifying matters, the main part of the blame was palmed off onto the economic management: 'All those people who came and went and talked to us now have positions in the departmental management and in the ministry, and we have had to stay here and clear up the mess after them!'

The former Managing Director had told them they would produce 400 locomotives a year, and at present they are making seventy. Wasted investments. Who among the general public knows that all the women workers get a month's unpaid holiday? And go take a look at the scrapyard, at all the work that's been thrown out there! They built a railway system for the cranes, and then they took it down again. Who's responsible for all this?

'The Communist Party set up the system,' points out one

5. Antonín Zápotocký, a leading pre-war communist, who was prime minister in the Gottwald government (1948–53) and became President after Gottwald's death (1953–57). He was a great trade union leader, was chairman of the Revolutionary Trade Union Movement 1945–50, and is referred to above in this capacity.

worker, but another rejects this: 'How can you blame Lenárt and Novotný for this?'

'Don't give me that: from the moment Novotný got into power, we've just been robbed!' said a former apparatchik. 'We were robbed of our output, our wages, but we put up with it, because socialism should have made up for it. And today? The intellectuals are swines because it was they who contributed towards the losses. The so-called "new economic system" is a swindle, which is based on the assumption that the same people will stay on at the top, because after all, dogs don't eat dogs. When a worker messes something up, its him who pays for it. Who pays for the losses in foreign trade and the losses which are caused by the fact that the whole of production is moving in completely the wrong direction? How can I believe that in five years' time it won't be even worse? I can't believe it, because all sorts of writers and a certain Smrkovský are mixed up in it all. Why don't people speak for us too, and why did Šik just talk to a closed group of functionaries, and as usual leave us in ignorance?'

Instead of exclamations about democracy, workers need to know what it'll be like when they have shorter working hours. People who work in offices will look forward to it. But those who do piecework will earn less.

The old Social Democrat: 'Less time, less money! What do you expect?'

The intelligentsia, without whose plans and ideas the workers cannot produce anything, has failed. Pay attention to this, it's an original idea:

'We could only put our suggestions in a working-class way. People who have studied should have translated them for themselves into a language which would have made it possible for them to be put into practice, and it was their duty to arrange it so that they didn't get at the workers.' By 'they' he meant the professional revolutionaries.

The general impression of most of the people I talked to was 'this is a defeat for the workers'. And because they are tired of talking, which they are not used to, tired of the disturbing disclosures which the papers keep on making of the constant destruction of other small certainties, and of the absence of an up-to-the-minute, comprehensible programme, some of them, I don't know how many, end up thinking this simple thought: 'If only the people up there would shut themselves up somewhere, come to an agreement, and tell us in a straightforward way what will be happening from tomorrow onwards, and not subject the people to all those bad jokes!'

These are people who have for years been deprived of their natural leaders, who have forgotten what solidarity meant in the trade unions, and who have lost, in their membership of the Communist Party, any independent political judgement. Everything that has been said about power choosing the obedient and weak and being hard on the proud and on the honest also applies among the workers. They have lost the same things as we have lost. Moreover, they made the mistake of thinking that they were in control. In the shake-up that they are now going through, they can become the political prey of whoever comes along first, calls a big meeting, and instead of all these discussions, says quite simply what's going to happen from tomorrow. Who's it going to be?...

The Doubrava technicians Our voice joins the discussion[6]

Literární Listy, 18 April 1968

On 5 March 1968, the daily of the North Moravian Regional Committee of the Communist Party of Czechoslovakia[7] published Ivan Sviták's reply to *Literární Listy*'s public enquiry entitled 'Where from with whom and where to'. He replied as follows:

From totalitarian dictatorship to an open society, to the liquidation of the monopoly of power and an effective control of the power élite by a free press and public opinion. From a society and a culture bureaucratically directed by 'the cut-throats of the official line' (Wright Mills) to the realization of basic civil rights at least as extensive as those of bourgeois-democratic Czechoslovakia. With the working class movement, but without its apparatchiks; with the vast majority of the people, but without mindless collaborators, and with the intelligentsia as the leading force. The intellectuals of this country must claim their right to the leadership of an open socialist society which is progressing towards democracy and humanism, if the reinstatement of the editorial board of a literary newspaper isn't to become yet another episode in the monstrous comedy of the collaboration between the unscrupulous and the power-seekers.

Because he is claiming that the intelligentsia should occupy the leading positions in the country and fulfil the most important tasks, we think it our duty to express our point of view, so that people don't get the impression that Ivan Sviták is speaking with the tacit approval of the whole intelligentsia as a social group, for the truth is of course that his words can be interpreted in a number of ways.

6. Doubrava, a mine in the Ostrava-Karvína basin, which was the stronghold of Kolder, one of the conservative group in the leadership.

7. *Nová Svobodá*, the daily of the Party's Regional Committee North Moravia, published in Ostrava, the area in which Doubrava is situated. This daily was the most advanced and daring of the regional papers. Kubíček, the author of the article on the Workers' Committees (see 'An initiative from below'), was one of its staff.

As far as the term 'totalitarian dictatorship' is concerned, we get the impression that it's imprecisely used here. We think it's possible to date the *proletarian* dictatorship from February 1948, but this means something essentially different, in its social and political significance and in its definition of power, from the term 'totalitarian dictatorship', and it also has a different purpose.

We are in the habit of confining the idea of a 'totalitarian dictatorship' to a description of fascist Germany, which is the most outstanding example of this type of government. We do agree that since the time of the tragic trials in Czechoslovakia the proletarian dictatorship did deviate slightly from the route it was supposed to be following. Yet it nevertheless managed to come back to its senses and not become a totalitarian dictatorship, as is proved in no uncertain terms, we consider, by the democratic discussions about the recent past which are being carried on at this very moment.

We agree with Ivan Sviták that it is indeed necessary to destroy the monopoly of power by people and groups of people, that it is necessary to control those who form the power élite by a free press, public discussion and the pressure of public opinion.

But we should examine more carefully the phrase – 'To the realization of basic civil rights at least as extensive as those of bourgeois-democratic Czechoslovakia.' We know very well that the scope of these rights was narrow enough to limit severely the activity of the working-class movement, and its political party, the Communist Party. We can remember 1921, when many repressive measures were taken against the working class and its leaders, and when the communist press was censored. We don't think even Ivan Sviták had a restoration of this state of affairs in mind, but he didn't deny it. Our understanding of this question of civil rights is that we want to take part in a better democracy, which will defend freedom and human rights, not just in the same way that the bourgeois-democratic Republic did, but to a far greater extent, because it will include all the working people. We think that now we have a pretty good chance of achieving this and thus of developing an up-to-date socialist society.

Sviták doesn't explain or enlarge on what he means when he says, 'With the working class movement, but without its apparatchiks,' but this was obviously impossible in such a short statement. Our view of it, however, is as follows: the Party has always had a group of professional politicians, revolutionaries, its secretaries and practical administrators, which Ivan Sviták now proceeds to call apparatchiks. The Party's political life cannot be conducted without a group which concerns itself with political activity and organizes it professionally. The destruction of this apparat would mean the destruction of the Party. Quite naturally, we couldn't agree with this, because the working class cannot exert its influence in the state and in a socialist democracy merely by defending its economic interests. It must inevitably have its own political organization which has to pursue a policy beneficial to it – a policy which guarantees the cooperation between the country's various classes and social groups, and encourages the rapid progress of the scientific–technological revolution, so that every member of society can develop his personality to its full extent and benefit from man's high level of social and cultural achievement . . .

At the moment, however, we think it's necessary to revitalize the Party's apparat, and that there are people in it who, either because of their views or their personal failings, don't belong there. We consider that what is essential is a radical change in the secretariat's methods of work and a reduction of the size of the apparat. We believe that it's necessary to make sure that it is the elected organs which make the majority of the decisions, that it's necessary to make the election of Party members to the apparat more democratic and finally that the apparat should serve the Party and not the Party the apparat.

We are members of the technical intelligentsia and we are determined that our role should be to serve the working class and the rest of the working people in the very best sense of that word. We make up, with them, a single productive organism; many of us know what hard manual labour means from our own experience; most of us were educated after 1945.

As long as Ivan Sviták summons the intelligentsia to the fore and has service to the people in mind as its noblest task, as the best and most humane way of using intelligence and education for the needs of the working people, then we agree with him.

We admit quite openly that Ivan Sviták's statement served us as a pretext for joining in the discussion which is going on among the public. It was republished in our daily regional paper, and that's why we were all able to read it. But it might have been a different kind of statement and there were others which we noted with some trepidation. Ivan Sviták may have every right to reproach us for attributing to him ideas which he didn't in fact put forward. But this is how we understood and interpreted what he said and other similar things by other writers. Ivan Sviták should tell us if we have misinterpreted him, though we don't intend to instigate a continuous polemic. We think there are enough healthy forces in our nation for us to solve all our problems without having to go from one extreme to another. However we firmly demand that the Central Committee of the Communist Party of Czechoslovakia brings its work to a conclusion, for in our opinion it isn't at an end. We are of the opinion that if the work of the revival process isn't completed in the central bodies and then from the top downwards, the victory of the progressive forces won't be convincing and will lose a lot of its attraction.

If we were asked to say which ideas are, for us, the most attractive, then we should declare ourselves in favour of the ideas which can be found in the work by a scientific collective led by Academician Richta entitled 'Civilization at the Crossroads'.[8] We think that 'Civilization at the Crossroads' is the modern Communist manifesto of the young and middle generation. If we don't allow it to fossilize and become dogma, then with it our scientists have provided us with a prospect for the future which is worth working and living for . . .

To come then to a conclusion: we are of the opinion that this far-ranging discussion should progress quickly towards finding the right jobs for the right people. And further, the whole democratic discussion should lead to the political conditions being created

8. Radovan Richta, head of the research team at the Czechoslovak Academy of Sciences which produced the study 'Civilization at the Crossroads' (1967) which was concerned with the impact, effect and implications of the 'Scientific–technological Revolution' on socialism, particularly in Czechoslovakia. It advocated that far more attention be paid to efficiency, modern scientific methods, individuals' initiative, and an outlook going far beyond the narrow sphere of the class struggle. The more theoretical and general character of its recommendations, which in no way questioned the position of the Party, appealed to the cautious and 'technocrat' minded.

for the efficient operation of the new system of management and thus for our Republic's economic progress.

Doubrava, 12 March 1968

Signed by 62 members of the technical intelligentsia of the Doubrava mine at the Ostrava-Karvína coalfield.

Ivan Sviták

Open letter to the workers and technicians of the Doubrava mine in Ostrava

Literární Listy, 18 April 1968

Dear comrades, communists and trade unionists of the Doubrava Mine,

Some technicians from your mine published an extensive reply in *Nová Svobodá* to my answer to the *Literární Listy* public enquiry and invited me to respond. I am replying not only to the technicians but directly to you, the workers, because it is in the alliance between workers and intellectuals that I consider the most important guarantee of the socialist and democratic character of the revival process lies. It lies in you, the working class of the Ostrava region, and not in the signatures which some shifty, conservative apparatchik managed to get together very quickly during the complicated situation which existed in Ostrava at the beginning of March. He wasn't able to stand up for himself and so he had to hide behind the posturing of the so-called democratic voice of the technicians and the intelligentsia of your mine. I agree with the basic direction of the technicians' resolution, that is with the attempt to make the technical intelligentsia display their solidarity with the workers and struggle together for their common interests. At the same time, however, I consider all the three principal questions which were asked in the article to be the wrong ones.

Comrade technicians, don't you now feel, at the end of March, that when you signed the document you were being taken in by a small group of apparatchiks who were afraid of losing their jobs, at the same time as the job of the apparatchik at the head of the state was so conspicuously unstable that he was considering using the Army and the People's Militia[9] for his own ends, those of a bankrupt politician? Why do you bother to argue with ten lines written by an unknown philosopher instead of pushing forward progressive resolutions in support of the revival process? Why don't you publicize the outrageous fact that not far away from you, in the Opava gaol, Rudolf Barák,[10] one of Novotný's victims, is still being held? Why don't you ask yourselves whether the Party leadership is not adopting a peculiar double-dealing position in critical situations? Why do you keep quiet about the fact that a delegate of the Ostrava Regional Party Conference, Karel Zorek (elected once again), is quite openly threatening Alexander Dubček and the intelligentsia with the arms of the Militia? . . .

Technicians and workers, surely you're not in need of the apparatchik to lead you by the hand, to prescribe what you ought to think, and to organize a campaign of signatures in support of the wrong cause. Why don't we all speak for ourselves, and then we'll easily find a common language and the compromised apparat won't be able to hide itself away. Apparatchiks have become accustomed to treating the people, the working class and the intelligentsia like children, as objects to be manipulated. They have been and still are managing our work, our ideas, our confidence and our money badly. They put themselves in the position of people who have the right to make decisions about our lives, who claim to know what we should think, or do, and who know how to

9. The People's Militia consisted of communists at factories who trained and drilled as an armed unit. They were still being organized in February 1948, and did play some part, though not a large one, in the events of that month by dispersing pro-Beneš students. In 1968 their existence as an exclusively Party organization was widely questioned, but Dubček and the new leadership would not yield in any way on the issue. The Militia remained a predominantly conservative body which felt itself threatened by the democratization. It sent an alarmist letter to the Soviet Union, which was used to justify allied fears.

10. Rudolf Barák, Minister of the Interior (1953–61) and Deputy Prime Minister (1959–62), was arrested on Novotný's orders in 1962 on trumped-up charges and sentenced to fifteen years (see Introduction). He was released in 1968.

manage the economy; it's enough to give them authority and then to sign the odd resolution or two. They behave like a worried parent who gives his child anything it wants but in fact want nothing better than for it to be obedient and thrifty. With great magnanimity they give the child a money-box, but when it's full they empty it and buy cod-liver oil with the child's money. These apparatchiks have been giving us cod-liver oil long enough. We know all about them, and we say – 'Enough!'

The term 'totalitarian dictatorship' which I used in the article in *Literární Listy* is a scientific term with a precise meaning. It can't be changed just because the authors of the resolution associate it exclusively with fascism, for the meaning of a scientific term doesn't change according to just anybody's whim, but according to reality itself. A totalitarian dictatorship can be instituted with various aims and in the interest of various social classes, so that it is possible to have a totalitarian dictatorship in Nazi Germany, in fascist Italy, in a Catholic country, such as Franco's Spain, as well as in Communist China or in a People's Democracy. Although every one of these régimes was or is pursuing different aims, its structure is the same, just as coal has been mined in roughly the same way in Nazi Germany, fascist Italy or in the communist countries. The differences lie in the social relations in each of these countries, in the problem of ownership of the coal and of the means of production, but not in the actual process of mining which is almost identical in each case. A totalitarian dictatorship is a *certain type of government*, not a class system characteristic of a state or society; it is the manner in which one class controls another. Similarly, a democracy is a kind of government which emerged independently of the character of social relations under conditions of slavery or in feudal city republics, long before the appearance of capitalists and workers. It was naturally a type of democracy different from today's, but the basic principles, the form of government, were identical. If the authors of the resolution characterize the past twenty years as a *proletarian dictatorship*, they are at odds with the facts, because what is happening at the moment bears witness to the fact that the workers, the intelligentsia and the people were ruled by the apparat. Whether we like to face the fact or not, we have been living for the past twenty years in a totalitarian dictatorship controlled by an ever narrowing circle of people linked directly with the apparatus of the police and the bureaucracy. Executive power, helped by the police and the bureaucracy, that is with the aid of the state or political apparat, is the most vital characteristic of a modern totalitarian dictatorship. It doesn't have much in common with the great democratic idea of a proletarian revolution as Marx and Lenin saw it. While I always fall back on Marxist–Leninist ideas, I can never hide the fact that the distorted pseudo-humanitarian values of the totalitarian dictatorship and its apparatchik-like bureaucracy fill me with the same disgust that the vast majority of the people of this country feel.

The most pressing problem today is to replace totalitarian dictatorship with socialist democracy, which means changing the manner in which power is wielded without abandoning socialist achievements, in particular the social ownership of the means of production. To solve this problem, however, needs a totally different form of government; it requires the real possibility of human and civil rights 'at least as extensive as those of bourgeois-democratic Czechoslovakia'. This point of mine so enraged the authors of the resolution that they suggested that I was asking for the restoration of the First Republic. But the persecution of workers by the police meant that basic civil rights were violated and trampled on, since to fire on orderly demonstrations is always and everywhere a crime, whether it be in a bourgeois republic or a socialist country, in Ostrava during the First Republic or in Poznan in 1956. So if anyone talks of the need for basic civil rights at least as extensive as those defined by the pre-war constitution, it doesn't of course follow that he's asking for police persecution. On the contrary; in the case that concerns us, it means that he's asking for the Ostrava miners to have the right to strike, to demonstrate, the right to elect their own representatives freely, and the right to freedom of assembly for the workers. Why then are the apparatchiks throwing mud at somebody who is asking for the very things that you are going to need in the coming months? Why? For the simple reason that this person is demanding exactly those rights which the apparatchiks deprived you of during the last twenty years, the rights which they won't give back to you of their own accord, because once you've got them, they know that you'll kick them out of their jobs. And the sooner the better.

The authors of the resolution also make no attempt to conceal the fact that they entirely support the interests of these apparatchiks and they maintain quite frankly that the workers' movement cannot do without them. If you abolish the apparat, they think you abolish the Party. They're wrong. The Party is you, the actual people, and not the apparat. The workers' movement, a wonderful and vital force in contemporary history, was founded by miners, metal workers and other workers long before the first apparatchik got into the saddle. The movement grew and expanded through the political struggles of the people and the working class, not as a limp mass manipulated by the apparatus, but as a progressive, decisive, historical force. Every movement creates an apparat, but the crucial question is whether it is you who is controlling the apparat, or the apparat you. And here lies the crux of the matter. Nobody has the intention of disbanding the apparat; that would be senseless and impossible. But those who support the revival process are today asking in no uncertain terms, unlike those who adopt a middle of the road line, for *the abolition of the decisive influence of the bureaucratic apparat on Party and national life.* And this is not a senseless or an impossible demand, but a perfectly reasonable and realizable goal for today's workers' movement. This goal, of course, sends the members of the apparatus completely berserk because it means an end to their power, an end to their privileges and an end to their unlimited control of workers, technicians and the intelligentsia. Your apparatchiks who seem to be exchanging shots with an unknown philosopher in Prague, and do it via the technicians of your mine, are in fact very purposefully firing at you, the workers and miners. They do it in exactly the same way as they've been doing it for the last twenty years, but they're on their beam's end and their gunpowder is getting rather damp. However, they're still dangerous, especially to you, the workers and technicians of industrial enterprises, and it's still very advantageous for unscrupulous, mercenary people to be their allies. A person who wants to be of some use to the workers and technicians must link himself to the workers' movement, without its apparatchiks.

Expressing my full solidarity with the communist revival process, but at the same time expressing my resolute lack of confidence in the apparatchiks of the Doubrava mine in Ostrava, or anywhere else, I send comradely greetings to the miners and technicians of Ostrava.[11]

Yours,

Ivan Sviták

Prague, 29 March 1968

11. Sviták's reply was, to his own surprise, printed by *Nová Svoboda*. The response from the miners was a telegram of congratulations and an invitation to Sviták to attend a meeting at Doubrava. It lasted for eight hours and resulted in a victory for Sviták and later defeat for Kolder in the elections for delegates to the Extraordinary Congress.

Ivan Sviták
The meaning of the revival

Práce, 19 May 1968

The rights of the workers

Civil rights are the same for all citizens of the state, but the demand for these rights to be respected and applied means one thing to the workers and another at the University. The writers who sparkled with jokes at the Congress Palace[12] forget to explain to the workers the elementary matter of what civil rights mean for the basic class in our society, the working class.

They mean something much more important for the workers than the arsenals of the Militia. They mean firstly, the right to strike, secondly, elections of directors by the producers, and thirdly, the defence of the rights of the workers by free trade unions. In a word, they mean an end to the apparatchiks' rule over the working class; they mean the immediate and direct influence of the industrial workers on production and its management. These rights, which the working-class president, Antonín Novotný, never wanted to give them, are the most potent weapons of the working class everywhere in the world, much more important than the machine guns and artillery of the Militia . . .

The basic rights of the working-class movement are just as important as the freedom of the press is for the intellectuals. Today, these demands are separate things, because neither the intellectuals nor the workers have so far fully realized the identity of their interests. That is why the intellectual must quite openly tell the worker today, 'If anyone interferes with your right to strike I shall defend it as resolutely as I am defending freedom of

12. A mass meeting attended by 16–18,000 people, mainly students, on 20 March. It was the high spot of the freedom of speech and public excitement of the period. Writers such as Kohout, Procházka, and Hanzelka cracked jokes and answered questions on any subject, along with more guarded speeches from Goldstücker, Husák, Smrkovský, and others. See also pp. 167–8.

speech for myself.' Similarly, the worker should openly tell the intellectual: 'If anyone interferes with your freedom of speech, I shall strike.' This is the only way to establish socialist democracy and there is no other way . . .

The trade unions

If the working class was satisfied to replace the private owners of industries and factories with state functionaries, then in a socialist society it would have no need of its own organization and the trade union movement. The standard of living does not depend on the sort of managers who are organizing the industrial enterprises. It depends on the productivity of labour, the growth of which must be organized and guaranteed by the growing efficiency of the workers.

For this fact precisely, the basic producers, the workers, must be protected by their own trade union organizations. Without this protection, there will be no guarantee that the growth of the productivity of labour will have any real meaning for the producers themselves and that it will not occur in an unbalanced way, to the disadvantage of the workers. So the trade union movement should defend the interests of the workers no less resolutely against the apparatchiks, the manipulators, technicians and managers, because a change of social ownership is not in itself a guarantee that under social ownership of the means of production the workers will not be exploited just as much, if not more, than before.

The system of bureaucratic despotism liquidated the rights of the working class, just as it did the rights of every citizen in the country . . . At a time when the power structure of Stalinism is disintegrating, there is no more serious and urgent task than the revival of the trade union movement as the movement which defends the basic rights of the workers. Trade unions do not as yet exist as equal partners with the employers, but it can be assumed that after the ideological power monopoly has been abolished, there will be much greater opportunities for the trade union movement to unfold . . .

The trade unions forfeited their basic rights in that, instead of real guarantees and the right to free association, they were offered much bigger rights and freedoms. But these freedoms never materialized however. The liquidation of real rights always takes place on the pretext of extending formal rights; people would not allow their real freedom to be restricted unless this restriction was presented as a temporary sacrifice on the road to greater freedom.

The revival of the trade union movement as a real reflection of the interests of the working class is no easy matter, because the working class itself has changed a great deal. When we use this expression, we have to acknowledge that even the social sciences give a very poor idea of the true nature of the working class, because ideological delusions and personal confusions have overlaid the reality. The working class is considerably differentiated today, both politically and in its social standing and income. The assumption that this class is homogeneous and has a 'moral and political unity' is just as wrong as the assumption that the intelligentsia has a blanket, undifferentiated viewpoint, corresponding to its interests.

The revival of the trade union movement has got under way quite spontaneously in several places, and there has been a spontaneous tendency for the influence of the trade union movement on factory managements to grow, as well as for wage demands and criticisms to be voiced. And the first signs of open support for basic civil rights can be seen. The fact that at the Dukla Mine in Ostrava, for probably the first time in the history of socialism in Czechoslovakia, the director was elected to office by the staff is one of the most important things to happen in the past few months.[13]

Similarly, the establishment of workers' committees in defence of the freedom of the press in the Ostrava district is one of the most positive signs of a new phase in the development of the democratization movement, in which a common front of workers and the middle classes – the intelligentsia – based on their political interests, is beginning to form. This is the alliance between manual and mental workers which is the only possible guarantee of true democracy in a socialist society.

13. The Dukla mine was the scene of the first dismissal (at the end of March) of a manager by the workers themselves. This was welcomed by most, including *Rudé Právo*, but provoked Kolder into saying, 'The street will not choose managers'. The old manager's deputy was elected by the workers at the end of April.

What About the Workers?

The working class's trade union movement has essentially the same interest in destroying the power structure of Stalinism as the writers', the scientists' and the artists' movements. As the citizens, workers and the intelligentsia rid themselves of their inhibitions, which have been built up by the old régime of fear, a deeper awareness grows that any attack on the freedom of the press would be also an attack on the standard of living of the workers, and vice versa. The stronger this awareness of identity of interests between the workers and the intelligentsia becomes, the more irreversible will become the progress towards socialist democracy.

Ladislav Anděl
The intelligentsia and the working class

Literární Listy, 28 March 1968, a letter from Ladislav Anděl, member of the Works Committee of the Mír Printing House, Prague

On 8 March, *Práce* carried an article by Comrade Matějka entitled 'How we see the Trade Unions and the current situation'. I was exasperated by the first paragraph. I quote:

In my opinion the Central Committee should lay down some line before the Party's action programme is worked out, so that this anarchic democracy should at least be brought within reasonable bounds. Some writers and some members of the intelligentsia are making a direct attack on the working class and time is on their side at the moment. I'm afraid that they may begin, in their confusion, to make suggestions other than those that are strictly necessary, and in this way strengthen their positions.

As I'm a worker and a member of the Works Committee, I hope you'll allow me to make an analysis of this paragraph.

So the Central Committee should lay down some kind of line! Haven't there already been enough of them? I was under the impression that a line had already been laid down by the fact that we have all, together and with no intention of reversing the process, decided to finish building socialism, and that any other question can be freely discussed, since there can never be too much democracy or freedom. No one has the right to give freedom as a prize or to take it away, and discussion of course is just about methods and not about aims.

With his demand for a regulation of what he calls 'anarchic' democracy, Comrade Matějka is surely showing that he is afraid of a reactionary about-turn. Doesn't he fail to see the situation clearly? In the past twenty years our working class has matured a great deal politically. Today it knows exactly what it wants. This knowledge has been paid for dearly in the past, which makes it all the more precious. If today socialism can be understood in its real meaning, giving freedom and democracy, then we are definitely in favour of socialism. The handful of people who, even today, still have a vested interest in setting the clock back, has been thinned out over the past twenty years, and still further decreased in size during the present events. To underestimate people's desire for socialism is basically to show a deep distrust of them, which is foreign to socialism, because without trust in people socialism must remain a Utopian dream.

Recently in particular, I've been systematically following all the most important things in the whole of the daily press, the radio and television. Nowhere, without exception, have I so far found so much as a line, nor heard so much as a word, about writers and intellectuals attacking the working class. I'd like to know when and where it was. On the other hand, I've heard many brave things which openly defended the rights and interests of the working class. At the same time, it's a shame that the working class didn't express its solidarity with the writers at the right time. Their words would surely have carried some weight last October.

What exactly does Comrade Matějka mean by 'time is on their side at the moment'? I think time is at last on the side of freedom and democracy within the framework of socialism, that it's on the side of all our citizens, the working class included, and also of course on Comrade Matějka's side. It's on their side as a result of the pressure of public opinion and decisions made by the progressive part of the Central Committee. If Comrade Matějka still talks about 'disorientation' today he's presumably one of those people who still feel 'disorientated'. Obviously for the whole of twenty years people like this haven't been keeping track of affairs with their own minds and have believed everything they've been told. They will probably have to reconcile themselves to the sad fact that they will stay 'disorientated' for ever.

At last, everybody in Czechoslovakia knows where he wants to go to. The big problem now will be the long drawn-out discussions as to how we go about it!

Even with the greatest effort in the world, I can't understand what, according to Comrade Matějka's interpretation, the writers and part of the intelligentsia want to suggest and what they're asking for. It seems to me it's just what we all want to suggest and what we're all asking for: democracy and freedom. What position is it that they want strengthened? They could, of course, have strengthened their positions a great deal under the old régime, because of their importance to the nation and their capabilities, had they been willing to further their own interests by prostrating themselves in a servile way before the forces which reduced our nation to moral decay and complete passivity. But on the contrary they were willing – and they were among the few who were – to risk their positions in society and certainly not to strengthen them!

These views I am criticizing have deep roots in the past. A certain group among the leadership of the Communist Party of Czechoslovakia has apparently not lived up to its tasks in every respect. They haven't grown out of their workers' overalls and they haven't become what Ernst Fischer called (and he said it a long time ago!) 'the engineers and architects of modern Marxism'. They were just pathetic men who serviced the machinery. They proved unable to develop it and to use their own intelligence to keep abreast of the changing world and our needs. And the fact that they realized this made them jealous of the progressive intelligentsia, and that's really why, perhaps unconsciously, they sowed discord between the intelligentsia and the part of the working class which was rather similar to them and wasn't capable of independent and progressive thinking. So dogmatism and mediocrity won the day!

How can we really define what we mean by the 'working class', both at the moment and in the future? What will the working class consist of when in the distant future the scientific–technological revolution will be complete, when the typical working-class man of today will have become an engineer or a technocrat, i.e., a member of the intelligentsia, which will in fact be composed of the working class itself, or its successor. This fact alone must surely bring the working class and the intelligentsia together today, because in the future this working class will inevitably become the actual intelligentsia. Or are we perhaps, until the end of time, going to judge a man according to his origin rather than by looking at the man he has become through changing social conditions?

The world changes with amazing speed. In the interests of socialism, it's becoming vitally necessary to select new methods of doing everything, especially in the sphere of political ideas and behaviour. I fully support the December and January resolutions of the Central Committee of the Communist Party of Czechoslovakia. My confidence, which was completely shaken, like a great many people's, is quickly growing again.

I consider that the views I have expressed in this letter are absolutely fundamental in clarifying the present relationship between the working class and the intelligentsia, and I would like to put them forward here for discussion.

The workers speak
The search for a common language

Literární Listy, 30 May 1968

VÖRÖS: We're afraid that it's all some kind of story, that it won't last for long, that it's just a change round of positions, a little bit of self-popularization. We still think that there's a lack of real ideas in the declarations and speeches . . .

I've read the Action Programme. There's nothing in it apart from something about small enterprises, and proposals that the general managements should be abolished and somewhat greater authority and independence given to private enterprise. But this isn't an idea which would change anything.

There are two ideologies in the world. Capitalism, by which I mean private enterprise, and socialist enterprise. Unfortunately, I have to say that capitalist enterprise is more profitable than socialist. We talk about how socialism has developed and call it deformed socialism, and that therefore it wasn't socialism at all. But the big question is what it will be. It seems to me as if the people at the top know what they don't want, but don't know what they do want. I should find it very difficult to say how I imagine the basis of the economy and of production, because I'm just not well enough educated. We're really just seeing all the things that happened in 1948 repeat themselves: let's take the enterprises, let's take the government into our own hands, and the rest will somehow happen. But it wasn't true.

KRATOCHVÍL: We often hear that people are concerned because tendencies have appeared which are in favour of returning to capitalism. I don't know what the older people who remember capitalism are thinking, but I personally can't for the life of me imagine how it would be possible to re-establish capitalism in Czechoslovakia . . .

ČECHRÁK: I'd be very interested to learn what the present system of socialist democracy wants to set up, in the production process, as an alternative to the private enterprise which exists in the West. If we want to bring our standard of living into line with that in the West, how can we do this in Czechoslovakia, when the socialist way is declared to be the only way? 'Socialism' is much too generalized a word. When we use it, we may be thinking of the Utopian socialism of the thirties. And when you talk about capitalism, you also mean the same capitalism of the thirties when there were crises. But I think capitalism has changed a great deal in the last thirty years. I'd like to know how socialism will catch up. What can it offer people so as to win their support again? Quite a lot has been wasted in the last thirty years! . . .

VÖRÖS: Whichever way it is, people want certainty. To exchange a certainty of stupidity for uncertainty is a strange bargain . . . I don't care whether I work for Bat'a[14] or for a state enterprise; the decisive factor for me is which place I'm better off in, and where it's better to work . . . You've got to realize that in those twenty years, no one really educated us people at the bottom . . . And until a personality comes along, and takes us along with him, nothing will change . . . It's only a man who is able to deal with the people at the bottom who can, in my opinion, really change the situation. Nothing is really happening, people are allowed to write things. If for instance, when you see that what should now be moving fast, things that should be happening at a fever pitch of activity, go on sleeping just as soundly as ever before, then you despair of finding a way out. They say it's the fault of the economic system. I should think that therefore all kinds of things should be happening in the economic sphere. But it's just the opposite – nothing is happening!

When we don't see for ourselves that our work is better organized, that things are really getting better, it's obvious the people in general will say to themselves, 'We know all about this, we've seen it all before.' We know about different kinds of revival processes, there have been enough reforms during all the years. We can remember at least five of them, even if they weren't as wide-ranging as this one is . . .

14. Bat'a: a large pre-war Czechoslovak shoe manufacturer who symbolized free enterprise capitalism.

Karel Bartošek[15]
Open letter to the workers of Czechoslovakia

Reportér, 8 May 1968

For several weeks now our country has been living through a period which cannot possibly be described as ordinary. And it has not been an easy period. Rulers, both great and small, have had their positions of power challenged, no matter how long and self-assured their reign has been, and a whole series of values which seemed eternal have been challenged too. Thousands of facts have come to light about a whole ocean of wrong-doing and injustice, perpetrated in the name of the workers' revolution, facts which must have shaken every single honest person. For many people, decades of belief in a single faith lie in ruins and their convictions destroyed. And other people are concerned about what everything happening at the moment means, and worried lest the kind of democracy that ended with Munich is being revived.

But for several weeks now we have been living in hope. Hoping for a revolution which would overthrow the Stalinist bureaucratic system without returning the factories and large properties into capitalist ownership. Hoping that these factories and all the values of society should really belong to all of us, and not just to a narrow class of uncontrolled bureaucrats who are hiding themselves behind the façade of the state and the Party.

The emergence of this new revolutionary hope has not been accompanied by a Czech or Slovak Poznan, or by a nationwide public mourning on the streets for the people who were unjustly hanged in the course of our political trials. The struggle against the bureaucratic system has had its first big positive results; whole legions of the corrupted have been forced to give up their jobs, and the country is beginning to learn the truth about its own situ-

15. A historian by profession, he was one of the leading advocates of the immediate establishment of workers' councils, mainly on political grounds.

ation. But all this is only a beginning. A system which prevented man from being liberated in this country can only be negated through deeds and not words; its revolutionary, that is its real, repudiation cannot be carried out by a mere change of personalities. Otherwise the crumbling thrones will remain thrones, from which a new bureaucratic oligarchy will rule us all, even if the members of it have in their pockets the membership cards of several political parties. And then at some time in the future, people will once again be hearing about an ocean of wrong-doing and injustice, created in the name – but against the interests – of socialism.

What can we do to take action against the bureaucratic system of the past? The most important thing is that any action should be yours. Without you, without all the people who work in our factories, either on shop floor or in the engineering or trade departments, and those whose position in society makes them modern technocratic workers, without all of you, it is not possible to really iron out all the inhumanity that has been experienced in Czechoslovakia. Without your activity, the freedom of speech which is necessary, not just in the interests of a few intellectuals, but above all in your own political interests will be just an ornament in a new, 'more enlightened' bureaucratic system, but no one will have any guarantee that it will last.

Many of you are voicing demands about wages and society in general. This is your way of making a concrete historical criticism of the bureaucratic system (this is how Lenin saw this kind of activity on the part of the workers), but it is a very incomplete kind of criticism. Wage and social demands are a reflection of the state of affairs brought about by the bureaucratic system, and fall within the framework of that system: you do not feel that you are the owners of the products of society, but 'state employees'. Why? What real differences are there between your position as 'state employees' and your former position, when the workers were employed by the individual capitalists? Why don't you feel that you are employers and employees at the same time, those 'free producers' which Marx talked about, when after all the means of production belong to the whole of society and above all to you, its majority?

Your answer to these questions can only be in the form of action.

It will not consist principally of organizing the work in the factories, for this can be thought up at any time by any capable local heirs of Bat'a, with or without you. Nor will it consist of thinking about how to organize the job of managing the enterprises, for this can be thought up by any capable state technocrat, with or without you. Activity which would really do something to change your position is the election and the activity of workers' self-management bodies, which would both *with you and through you* administer what is primarily yours. It isn't important whether they are called Workers' Councils or Works Councils, or by any other name. What is important is that *you should elect them immediately and choose the most able and most honest people from your own collectives to work in them*, and not just from among the workers on the shop floor, but also from the technicians and the administrative workers, because they too are 'producers' . . . History has so far not been very kind to Marx's ideas about producers' self-management, and in many countries they have succeeded in doing away with the organs of workers' self-management that once existed. But is this sad fact a good enough reason why the workers of Czechoslovakia should not once again try to realize this idea, especially – and this is immensely important in evaluating our past experiences – since this was a country that was industrially advanced for the first time in its history?

We are aware that the work of these self-management bodies will not be easy and without conflict. But without democracy in the enterprises it is not possible to talk about democracy in society.

It would be unrevolutionary if we were not to find an immediate answer to a question like, 'Who has the right to make a decision as to how to distribute the surplus value created by your labour?' and other similar questions. Is it the state which has this right, that is, its apparatus? Who has the most right to make decisions about the values of a society to which millions contribute their labour? One or several political parties? Whose duty is it to keep a check on the constitutional obligation to work? Parliament and the courts? Whose right is it to undertake the employment of the directors of enterprises which belong to the whole collective? You, the people of the collectives, or the 'state'? Whose right is it and whose duty to make decisions about these and other fundamental matters concerning all of our lives? Individuals or groups of individuals, the regimented apparatuses of perhaps not one, but of several political parties?

Manipulators, in the economic and social fields, will certainly often try to prevent you electing your own organs of self-management. They are afraid of you and will sometimes try to hide their fear by shouting out that 'it could lead to anarchy'. Don't lose heart; they have always done this and in many different places. You only have to think back to the way they liquidated the elements of self-management in our Works Councils in the past. We think there are enough intellectuals who will be able and willing to tell you about the experiences of self-management in the past, and of the experiences of Yugoslavia and elsewhere at the present time.

You have to engage in other political activities at the moment as well. You have to create a trade-union movement which is really revolutionary, and which, in the potential new system of several political parties, would be recognized with the respect that a mass organization of working people in a socialist society merits. You should be helping with the radical revival of the Communist Party, so that it shouldn't any longer be what it is at the moment – a Party of both criminal individuals and honest people who have been and who still are struggling for the true liberation of the producers, and for everybody's liberation.

It is not the time at the moment merely to make gestures and thereby to create the illusion that our activities are deeply political.

The fate of the revolution which was set in motion to put an end to the exploitation of man by man is in your hands. Our future system cannot be dreamed up in the heads of a few 'enlightened socialists' – it must be formed in practice and in activity as well as in theory. This is the only way of really overcoming our past.

In the past, revolutionary papers often used the slogan, 'Freedom which is given stinks'. Genuine freedom is not awarded by legislation or by Action Programmes, but has to be fought for. If we don't set out with the intention of realizing the truth of this today, then we, and our children, will still be waiting for freedom tomorrow. History can wait, but we can't.

So – long live the May of working class activity in the political year of 1968!

Miroslav Jodl
An attempt to see things clearly

Literární Listy, 30 May 1968

The new régime was endowed with an unenviable inheritance, which could perhaps most fittingly be called 'devastation'. Economic, political and moral devastation. Anyone at all who succeeds in looking at the causes and effects as they really are would surely acknowledge that if Dubček and his team declare at the end of a year that they have failed, it will have been because they couldn't develop superhuman powers and not because they were incapable.

The régime wants to fight against the economic devastation by means of the New Economic System. This, like Richta's 'scientific–technological revolution' has been written about so much now that we've got used to the sound of it, and the foreign words don't frighten us any more. But our economy is running basically in the same old way; the necessity for sweeping changes is still talked about all the time. It reminds you of the chorus in the opera . . . all the time telling everybody that something must be done, urging everybody to march forward, but standing still, marking time. What is stopping the New Economic System from advancing? It's only rational after all that it should progress. Perhaps the difficulty lies in the fact that old habits, which permeate even the smallest cell of the economy, have no very great love for rationality.

The economy, like the whole of society, can be managed in one of three ways: ideologically, by common sense and scientifically . . . For twenty years, the state gave full vent to its ideological defilement of economic functions. An ideological approach to the economy leads to a free for all, which is unreal and ineffective, a free for all which inevitably comes up against serious difficulties and which must needs have people's enthusiasm and yet at the same time is inclined only to give orders. And frequently uses force. The result is a deterioration of the whole economy. And our society has paid quite enough for ideological rubbish on the subject of the economy.

What About the Workers?

Twenty years of the management of our economy has led to the loss of a sense of enterprise, activity and initiative. The régime is confronted with the question – will it succeed in creating the conditions for an improvement, on a socialist basis? Will not the existing state of affairs, even with its immobility, its torpor and its production and business monopolies, remain more acceptable to the majority of workers? The existing state of affairs did not usually make it possible to expand the economy, but it did provide a quite considerable feeling of security. Even if it is true that every Czech longs for the average standard of living of the Western market, anyone who was clever made more on the side by his own private initiative.

The last twenty years have left their traces in people's mentalities. They rotted working morale and relationships between people in the production process. More than ever, democracy is identified with wage levelling, and a kind of genial plebianism; more than ever before, relationships of superiority and subordination are not respected. The government has to realize that the transition to the New Economic System will come up against a psychological barrier. An economic opposition can come into existence among the working people in this way, which could then be supported by the old dogmatic policy and opposition of those who have been partly pushed to one side during 1968, but are waiting for the hour of their offensive to come . . .

Certainly, without a visible improvement in the economic situation, the 'men of January' will not succeed in winning the *active* support of the majority of the people. And up until now, there has not even been the first sign of such an improvement.

Ota Šik
Lecture to the Czechoslovak Society of Economics

Rudé Právo, 22 May 1968

Before us lies a complicated process of structural changes, among which is the process of de-levelling (reintroduction of differentiation in wage scales according to qualification, position, and intensity of work). The correct management of this process is very difficult. The workers often ask how the shortcomings in the economy became possible, who will rectify them and will it be done quickly? To this I think it's necessary to reply in no uncertain terms that the enterprises themselves, on their own initiative and of course encouraged by the pressure of really socialist, regulated, market relations, must play the decisive role in the whole process of recovery. And to this end, it's essential to complete the economic system and to give to the enterprises the necessary authority and responsibility . . .

I think that Workers' Councils should be established, and should be set above the enterprise managements. They should be composed, according to the size of the enterprise, of between ten and thirty members. Most of these members should be elected by the workers from among their own ranks, and those elected should of course be people whose characters and specialist knowledge are guarantees to the rest of the workers that they will skilfully and honestly defend their long-term interests.

In larger enterprises and those where the work involves complex technical and market conditions, about 10 to 30 per cent of the Councils should be experts from outside the enterprise. But of course, in my opinion, even these experts should be indirectly elected by the elected council members . . . The management should submit the basic idea and plans behind the economic development of the enterprise to the Workers' Councils; the workers would give their opinion about the proposals from the management, but would not take away from the management the responsibility for the implementation of the decisions. If the council disagreed with certain of the proposals, the management would then submit a second set of proposals, but if the conflict could not be resolved after the second discussion, the management would assume responsibility for the decision.

The Council could set up a body to watch over the work of the management. If they disagreed with the management about some large investment which they thought not really justified, and not promising to give increased efficiency to the enterprise, after analysis of the problem the Council would either reprimand the management or declare no confidence in it. The Council would be able to make extraordinary payments to the management, and make decisions about the appointment and recall of managers. It would also have to make decisions about statutory questions, such as the merging and grouping of enterprises.

This way of organizing the leadership and management of the enterprises would, in my opinion, be one way of realizing the demand for our enterprises to be specialized and modern and of pursuing the long term prosperity of commerce and the long term interests of the workers and the whole of society. It would also be a way to answer the demand for the democratization of the leadership of the enterprises and to increase the responsibility and interest of the workers themselves in the development of their enterprises. Only if the factory workers are given more responsibility and more authority will they be able to overcome their feeling of alienation from the factory and their need to have to ask for everything from someone 'up there' . . .

All this will not be easy. There will be considerable social problems, which our workers should understand lie in intolerable, absolutely uneconomic methods of management and of production. The old leadership maintained these because it was afraid that disclosures would be made about the grave state of the economy, and people would start asking the question, 'And whose fault is it all? . . .'

Today, we have the real interests of the working people at heart. As soon as possible we have to create conditions in which it is only possible for work which is socially useful, highly efficient and whose products are competitive to be carried out in the enterprises and industries. Society will only temporarily and in exceptional cases be able to give relief and aid to individual enterprises . . .

While the old political leadership relied on the most backward thinking among the workers, who themselves got used to living, without any great effort, at the expense of the initiative and the achievements of good workers, the new political leadership wants to get rid of the whole system of protectionism in no uncertain way. Slapdash workmanship, large-scale non-utilization of working time and wastage of the means of production in many areas of industry were all actually encouraged by the old system.

If the wealth of society and of those people whose highly competent and efficient work contributes to the growth of this wealth is to increase, then the prosperity of those who work less than the others and are less productive and less efficient, cannot grow at the same rate.

We have to develop quickly a system of social aid for people who will be temporarily affected by essential structural changes, and by the attempt to make production more efficient. A socialist state cannot economize in this direction . . . but in the economy crucial qualitative changes can no longer be postponed if the younger generation is not going to ask us sooner or later what we did to find solutions to our needs and demands, what we did to try to achieve a standard of living which is taken for granted in the other industrially advanced countries.

Petr Pithart
What matters is the right to self-management

Literární Listy, 1 August 1968

I'm afraid that the threat of another scandal is in the air. There is the danger of one of the ideals of theoretical socialism being spoiled, the ideal of the social self-management of producers. Without being aware of the dangers, we may well introduce this self-management and at the very same moment it will be a failure, as happened in Poland and Hungary twelve years ago . . .

I'm afraid of the fact that people are impatient and also at the same time I'm wondering who stands to profit from the impatience.

The time factor is very important here: it controls what our priorities are and in what order the events occur. An awful lot has been said, and reams of paper have been filled, on the subject of self-management. But personally, I still think that there's a lack of exploration of the most basic and preliminary questions, which have to be asked and solved in a practical way if any effort to establish self-management is to be more than an enthusiastic groping around in the dark . . . Self-management in a political system, where political institutions do not even have the safeguards of the traditional, bourgeois, political democracy, can lead, paradoxically, to the much more effective depoliticization of the people, to their atomization, to their engulfment by problems of daily life – fragmentary problems, rather than more general ones. That leaves the power centre free and gives scope in it to almost anybody.

So we should be careful . . . we should not allow ourselves to be persuaded that self-management is the guarantee of the control of power, that it is in itself a fundamental element of some kind of 'higher democracy'. What we should be paying attention to is precisely the lower storeys of that democracy. Because it's on them that the house in which we live will stand . . .

Can self-management fulfil its purpose as a form of co-management of the enterprises by the producers unless the whole economy functions on a consistent market basis? Without entrepreneurial activity and the state power being decisively separated? In other words, unless the enterprises are economically independent? Probably not. What it can do is to act as a kind of quasi-democratic façade for the present improved command system of management, which we still have with us.

But today, self-management means something else apart from this demanding, and after all difficult, decision-making about strategy, cadre policy, etc, etc . . . Self-management, the Works Councils, can play a more outstandingly political than industrial role in the coming weeks and months. They can be used to replace the silenced trade unions or the discredited and disorientated leadership of the Party's works organizations. They can make demands of the leadership and put awkward questions to it, which can't be done in many places by any other institution. They can get the enterprises moving politically, they can clear the static atmosphere surrounding personal relationships and the taboos there are there. What they can do is to function as worthy partners of the leadership. That would certainly be a worthwhile and even perhaps an irreplaceable function, which would take the 'Prague democratization' into every part of the country. Such Workers' Councils would then fulfil the role of a kind of Action Committee, the same as were established in Czechoslovakia after February 1948 . . . but they would not work out the strategy of the enterprise, because the state economic centre still has that sufficiently in hand . . .

We should, then, hurry rather slowly. The only questions that have to come to a head are the questions posed by the philosophers, economists and theorists of management, and that's quite natural. But the daily concerns of the ordinary man in the street are often incompatible with these problems and seem painfully banal beside them . . .

The worst thing of all would be for the state to legislate about self-management, to make it compulsory. One cannot force anybody to be free, just as you cannot order the people to manage themselves in the factories starting from tomorrow. Just imagine it – 'Manage yourselves, or else . . .'

That would be just another abortive scheme. It would be born of ideology and a quite pointless haste. And I'm afraid that it might be the pre- and post-January conservatives opportunistically taking a firm grip on the flag of progress who would be the fathers of the scheme. Czechoslovak society cannot afford, as far as institutions are concerned, not to plan parenthood carefully.

Josef Smrkovský
Speech given to the Central Committee of the Communist Party, 2 April

Rudé Právo, 4 April 1968

In the past, the policy which we pursued was called 'the workers' policy'. Speeches, resolutions, theoretical articles and our activities were all the time talking about the working class, its leading role, its interests, its policy. And yet we have to ask whether that policy of ours was in the past really in harmony with the interests of the working class.

Was it in the interests of the working class to take part in production, to work, to compete and to bear the burden of all the shortcomings in our industry, and for the fruits of their labour to be partly, indeed largely, transformed into unsaleable supplies or exported, as they are still, for dumping prices? Was it in the interests of the working class to work in bad conditions, on old machines, without adequate safety precautions at work and without adequate social and hygienic facilities? Was it in the interest of the working class for the trade unions to stop being their own specific organizations, to become a part of the state machinery and always to act in unison with the economic management; was it in the interest of the working class when the economic reforms were only carried out in an unconvincing way, when the leading positions were not quickly filled with people who would have been able to put production and marketing on rational economic foundations and apply their expert knowledge to solving the complicated problems which most of our enterprises are up to their ears in?

Every day we hear that the workers are dissatisfied, that they will only have one-third representation in the planned Works Councils. They maintain that this is not big enough. But has anyone taken any notice of their opinions? How have they taken part in controlling the management of enterprises, and of the management itself? Did they have an opportunity to influence the appointment of leading economic officials; was it in the interest of the working class that we showed an incorrigible preference for heavy rather than light industry and that we neglected the development of a technology for the consumer and foodstuffs industries?

I could go on and ask whether it was in the interest of the workers that nothing was done about the transport situation in Prague, that flats were not built and so on . . . The old policy may have been proclaimed in the name of the working class, but it did them precious little good. Today not even our most modern factories are as pleasant to work in as those that the workers in some of the advanced capitalist countries have won for themselves. And our working class has on average a lower standard of living than those few West European countries who were on the same level, if not a slightly lower one, as we were at the end of the War . . .

Oldřich Švestka
Questions about a workers' policy

Rudé Právo, 14 July 1968

... Confidence in the Communist Party has grown significantly; the slogan 'socialism without communists' has lost a lot of its force. The extent to which it will continue to go out of circulation depends on the activity of the Party and its policy. Above all on its attitude towards the workers ... to the life of the workers and their families ...

The most basic attack on socialism in Czechoslovakia at the moment is not an attack on the social ownership of the means of production, but an attack on the working class, on its social position and its role.

At the moment there can hardly be anyone who could any longer have any doubt that the workers will in the end decide the fate of this country, the whole process of democratization and the further development of socialism. Everything that has been achieved so far in the revival process must now be guaranteed ...

The fundamental problem which many people are reproaching the workers for is that they are passive. Why is this? Mainly because the beginnings of the democratization and most of the things that have happened up until now have been carried through without enough attention being paid to the fact that the workers are still the most powerful force in the creation of social values. In spite of the efforts of the most important Party organs, the workers have been pushed out of the democratization, and the better opportunities to enable them to make decisions, which the Action Programme promised them, have not been offered to them yet. They have been and they still are being manipulated, without having any possibility of participating directly in politics. They have often been misinformed, and not taken into account ... Right from the start of the movement it was clear to them that the process which was beginning would affect them above all. And it has to be underlined that from the beginning, most of the workers sympathized with the process and go on sympathizing with it, in spite of the fact that it fails to give them adequate social security.

The political struggle has up until now taken place outside their immediate sphere of influence, and what is more, really clear answers have not been given to most of the fundamental questions. The political struggle taking place has obscured rather than clarified a number of questions. The Action Programme of the Communist Party . . . has created the *conditions* in which freedom and socialist democracy can be established, for the creation of a better controlled political system . . . But because it is vague in those points which are specifically concerned with the workers, it gives them very little.

The working class is at the moment differentiated like the rest of society, but it is on the whole united in its mistrust of words, which are not at present being supported by actual measures. The tendency of the whole class to a 'wait and see attitude' is still very much in evidence.

But there are certain tendencies in the factories which can be seen as being reflective. Neither the differences between the workers, nor the establishing of the committees for the defence of the press can hide this fact. And it is not just the old communist functionaries, the dogmatists who are afraid for their jobs, who are like this . . . The thing is more complicated than this, and should not be oversimplified. The real influence of these local functionaries, who did not enjoy the confidence of the workers in the past or at least only had their formal confidence, lies in the fact that they are now at one with the workers in their fears about their social positions and security.

A great deal has been said in the past few years about the workers and about the achievements of the workers. But if we look at the history of the last twenty years we can see quite clearly that if anyone was the loser in the so-called 'workers' policy', it was above all the working class. Despite the constant declarations that it was the workers who were in power, they were gradually excluded from power by the pressures of a small group of functionaries. Their good will was frequently misused.

The policy of the past, however, did bring them one basic thing, and, generally speaking, that was social security . . .

At the moment, the workers are asking each other, 'Is it our fault that our factory is making a loss? We didn't have any say in its management. Should we in the factory now take the responsibility on ourselves for these losses which we're not to blame for? Who is responsible? Who directed industry? . . . How will workers be retrained when they leave unprofitable production lines? How will this be ensured? Will not the present over-employment really turn into unemployment?' These questions should be answered. The theories of the economists must be turned into clear statements, which everybody can understand, into realities which will convince the people.

And finally, there is once again the question, 'Is the working class conservative?' which has to be asked. It is not. But it cannot be activated just with words about freedom and democracy even if it understands that it is vitally necessary for these ideas to be realized in practice. But the working class wants to come into its own as a creative and valid force in society, as an active and recognized force, as the active instigator and supporter of great values, with the right to manage its own affairs.

The circumspection and caution of the workers has to be seen as an act of intelligence. Ultimately the workers are our most progressive force, and they will decide and ensure that we do not retrogress, that society will not jump out of the frying pan into the fire, but will move confidently forward.

Pavel Machonín[16]
A reply to Oldřich Švestka

Večerní Praha, 15 July 1968

Švestka's evaluation really distorts the revival process. He maintains that the revival and the overwhelming part of its development up until now have been carried on without regard to the fact that the workers are the main force in the creation of the values of society. Workers, he says, have been 'pushed out' of the process by the leading Party organs, they are 'manipulated', 'misinformed', and they have not been taken into account . . .

I can't remember any other group of communists for many years having done such an enormous amount of work for the activation of the factories and the workers as this group has done in the past few months, especially in their preparations for the Fourteenth Extraordinary Congress. I can't remember any other group having made such a concentrated effort to formulate a workers' policy.

I do not remember such really *independent* political activity on the part of communists and trade unionists in the factories as there has been in the past few weeks . . . although I do agree that this is only a beginning. The new spokesmen of the working class do not flatter, they do not keep on saying things about its leading role. And thus they bring out into the open all the more acutely the anti-working class character of the pre-January policy, and put the political alternatives of the moment all the more clearly before the workers: that they can either go back to the old conservative policies or continue on the road of democratic socialism. That is not obscuring the issues, surely?

A lot of misguided voices have been heard during these struggles. There have been attempts to divide communist and non-communist workers, to set the workers against other workers employed by any kind of administrative apparat, generalized attacks on 'technocrats', etc. But when and where, however, has

16. A sociologist and director of the Institute of Marxism–Leninism, Machonín was one of the leaders of the progressive Prague Party organization.

there appeared in Czechoslovakia an attack on the working class, on its social position, on its role in society, the attack Comrade Švestka talks about as a basic attack on socialism? The security which he talks about consists in immobility, in the persistence of inefficient productivity and unjust prices, in egalitarianism, hidden unemployment, in a low rate of technological development, the slow growth of wages . . . And for this social security, the workers – and not just the workers – have paid because the economy is stagnant, the standard of living is in danger, and there is a restriction of civil liberties. This narrowly conceived security is in fact today total insecurity, because it is paralysing the whole of society.

The spokesmen of the revival process, and among them the workers themselves, have defined a new concept of social security, worthy of true socialism – without Comrade Švestka having noticed it. The workers are sober people and they know that it is not in their interests to maintain inefficient production, unjust prices, artificial preference, technical backwardness. They understand that essential changes in all these areas cannot be achieved without there being great difficulties and problems. But they are asking for guarantees that these changes, which in the end will bring positive results in the overall growth of national wealth, in the standard of living, should not be carried out at their expense, against their interests. Where are these guarantees and what do they consist of?

Firstly in our socialist conditions. Democracy should give the workers, who make up 58 per cent of the population, the decisive say in all state affairs, which they have not had up until now.

Secondly freedom of speech. Organization and assembly would enable them to make decisions on the basis of reliable information and to choose allies with whom they agree, and from whom they have been artificially separated, for example from among the ranks of the intelligentsia, agricultural workers, etc.

Thirdly democracy in the trade unions would give them a powerful weapon to defend their own interests . . .

Fourthly the Workers' Councils, whatever the exact nature of their organization, will be a very powerful means of increasing the influence of the workers on the economy . . .

Groping in the wind

Literární Listy, 18 July 1968,
an unsigned article

Four workers came into the editorial office from the Czech Rubber and Plastics Works in Prague's Zahradní město, a little embarrassed and full of apologies. The discussion was a long one and somewhat confused; it jumped back and forth, from conditions in the factory to politics and the economy and then back again to working conditions. In contrast to previous meetings of this sort, the workers came of their own accord: a new element had thus appeared. The fact that they came is in a sense inevitable. Following a period of indifference after January this year, people were very uncertain, then they became interested, and began making resolutions and taking part in the expressions of active solidarity. Now the period of searching is beginning.

These four workers came along to ask for advice about how to join in with the democratization process. 'At the moment in the factory, there's the feeling that a lot of people couldn't care less whether Novotný or Svoboda is president; it's enough for them if, for the time being, they can scrape some money together. They don't even care at what cost to themselves or in what conditions,' complained one of them. And another added: 'We workers still think in the old way a great deal. We believe what we're told, at least we do where I work. Sometimes it's terribly difficult. The factory works three shifts. We often get round finally to reading some of the papers in the tram, if there's any room in it, but we can only watch the television for one week in every three, when we have the morning shift. And it's very difficult for us to make sense of it all: in the end we probably learn most in the changing rooms between shifts, when we exchange information about who has heard what and read what.'

He said it simply and a little sadly. But he said it in spite of twenty years of phrases about the decisive force in the state, about class instinct and automatically inherited 'progressiveness'.

'People talk about Workers' Councils. Give us some advice on how to begin, what actually to do. We haven't got any experience of such things. We can't just call a meeting. We've got no right to do that. We haven't even got a hall which belongs to us.'

The first small steps for them consist in feeling their way, in self-awareness, but this brings new problems, which the functionaries can very rarely give an answer to. That is why the search for answers outside the factories is beginning. And with this, a long-lost feeling of solidarity and the awareness that everything that is happening in the country is somehow interconnected is returning. Small barriers which were kept erected over the years are beginning to be broken down.

It isn't very important that these four workers came along to the offices of *Literární Listy*. What is more important is the motive which led them to do so. Their visit is typical of the fact that we are moving from explaining things and expressing basically passive sympathies to a search for real cooperation.

Ivan Kubíček
An initiative from below, not planned from above

Workers and freedom of speech

Reportér, 28 June 1968

The isolated criticisms of the Czechoslovak press, radio and television in May and at the beginning of June developed into a campaign, in which all the functionaries who, between January and April, had used up all their energies trying to prevent themselves from being either seen or heard, took part.

The beginning of the campaign – a sort of trial run – can be dated back to the Regional Conference of the Communist Party in Ostrava, at which Alois Indra,[17] a secretary of the Central Committee of the Communist Party, was the first Czech politician since January 1968 publicly to accuse the journalists of 'disorientating readers' and of 'inciting nervousness'. The first climax of the campaign thus coincided with the return of our leading politicians from the talks in Moscow, during which a collection of documents was apparently submitted to them by the Russians as evidence of the so-called anti-socialist or anti-Soviet attacks in the Czechoslovak press.

Thus a target, or an outlet for their energies, was at last presented to the functionaries who were worried and had been made nervous either by the development of the revival process as such, or because they had momentarily been given no precise orders. Some of the functionaries in the People's Militia threatened to use guns. And exactly at that moment the first workers' committee for the defence of the freedom of the press came into existence, in the Ostrava Nitrogen Works.

17. Alois Indra, a member of the conservative group in the new leadership. Minister of Transport 1963–67, and a secretary of the Central Committee from April 1968. One of the leading collaborators with the invasion forces, and in the post invasion period in the group 'right' of Husák.

An initiative from below, not planned from above

The declaration of fifteen workers on the second shift, which was published in *Nová Svoboda* on 26 April, included the following passages:

> The suppression of censorship has played a very important part in the rapid development of the political life of Czechoslovakia in the direction of democracy ... But there are more voices, similar to that of Indra in his recent speech, which are saying the democratization process has dangerously invaded the frontiers of the Communist Party of Czechoslovakia ...
>
> All these things are happening in a situation in which censorship has been suspended but not abolished, in which no guarantee of the freedom of the press exists apart from the benign attitude of comrade Dubček and other progressive comrades in the Central Committee of the Communist Party of Czechoslovakia ...
>
> We think therefore that it is extremely urgent just at the moment that workers' committees for the defence of the freedom of the press should be created, as a basic civil right. These workers' committees will go on existing as long as censorship, in the form of the Central Publications Board, is not abolished, as long as the freedom of the press is not explicitly guaranteed by clear laws which would make it possible to prosecute anyone who wished to jeopardize this freedom in any way whatsoever.
>
> The workers' committees for the defence of the freedom of the press would, if the need arose, in a decisive manner use such action as would make it quite plain that the suppression of freedom in Czechoslovakia always occurred against the will of the working class.

This call from the workers at the chemical factory was immediately taken up by the tramworkers in the Borubský Depot, by trade unionists, communists and non-Party people, by most of the members of the Socialist Work Brigades; later by metal workers from Liskovec, large workers' collectives from NHKG in Ostrava and from the Vítkovice Iron Works, and then, at the end of May, this completely new workers' initiative spread from the Ostrava area into Bohemia, to the Nový Bor glass works, the Plzeň Škoda workers and the Prague ship workers. Without any kind of organizational support from the political apparatus, in the course of one month, tens and probably hundreds of voluntary collectives for the defence of freedom of speech have come into existence in this way.

Together, they unite thousands of workers who have grasped the fact that press freedom 'on one's word of honour' can revert at any time to a repetition of post-Bach censorship,[18] which was really damaging to the interests of the workers. The vital interest of every citizen who wants in the future to take part in decision-making and engage in activities really freely, they have discovered, is to be well-informed.

It is very important to look at the exact moment when these workers' press collectives came into existence to understand their full significance. Up until that time democratization had been pushed forward by the intellectuals in particular, and was getting its breath back. The idea of 'those people up there on top' had been challenged between January and April, but had not been undermined. People were exhausted by all the meetings, the resolutions, the analyses, the demolition; the whole of the activity of society – activity which had caused people to *examine things* in detail – had considerably slackened off, as could be seen, for instance, by the attendance at Party meetings.

'What, are the journalists so feeble that they really need someone else to defend them? And is there any censorship any longer?' (Engineer Smetana from the Ostrava Nitrogen Works.)

The workers from the second shift of the Nitrogen Works, in which Engineer Smetana also works, realized much earlier than he did and much better than he, that they were not defending freedom so much for the journalists as for themselves. They realized that to defend the freedom of the press – a newly born and very fragile freedom – is above all to defend the interests of the ordinary man in the street, who reads the newspapers, listens to the radio and watches TV. The workers from the 'press collectives' discovered that in a modern society the freedom of the press and of expression are of fundamental importance, for without them other civil liberties, from the freedom of assembly to the right to strike, can hardly be guaranteed. They were spurred into action as a result of their bitter experience that even the most enlightened power tends to make itself absolute, to make sure that it is itself inviolable, and that no really effective means, or institutional safeguard, for the control of power exists.

Stanislav Vystavěl, from the workers' collective for the defence of the freedom of the press in Kunčice, NHKG, told me: 'We

18. Bach was an Austrian Minister of the Interior (1849–59), whose rule embodied a tought, centralist policy, with strict censorship.

want to see into the government's hand, we want to see whether a fair game is being played. And that can't be done without freedom of the press.'

First impressions in the Nitrogen Factory were really not so happy. It was sufficient for the Chairman of the Works Committee of the Communist Party, V. Šimek, to spread it around the works that it was a criminal who was at the head of this surprising move, and notify those above: 'The so-called workers' committee for the defence of the freedom of the press was founded in the second team by a certain Lumír Balička, who was sentenced in 1966 to sixteen months' corrective custody' (from internal information given to higher authorities).

But of course he did not mention that Lumír Balička had been sentenced for leaving the Republic unauthorized, and prosecuted under the notorious Clause 109, the validity of which the Action Programme had by that time seriously questioned. The young, well-read worker Balička had left the country when a works official had quite arbitrarily made it impossible for him to go to university. It didn't seem to matter that after he has served his sentence an offender is once again a citizen with full rights: it didn't matter that other members of the workers' 'press collective' were non-criminals, communists!

To make sure of their case, security officials came to the Party office of the factory one day in May, and with Chairman Šimek went through the cadre origin, the past and criminal records of all the members of the first workers' committee for the defence of the freedom of the press. Their good work was successful; from out of forty workers in the committee, the inspectors discovered four ex-jailbirds. One was alleged to have stolen unrefined sugar, another had had a ride in someone else's car, etc, etc. The machinery which had lain idle since January was once again put into motion. A report was sent 'upstairs', from the town to the regional headquarters, and from there to the centre in Prague. It all happened completely democratically of course, because information can no longer be 'filtered'! And we know what the result was in the Spanish Hall, at the plenum of the Central Committee . . .

And while I am on the subject of the press and the mass communications media, allow me to express my surprise and to ask what the setting up of a so-called committee for the defence of the press in fact really means. Who's doing it? And why? And against whom? On Sunday, I learned from the television that comrade Indra, a secretary of the Central Committee of the Communist Party, is jeopardizing the freedom of the press. I think this is absolute nonsense and very dangerous.

Why should the Party and some of its representatives want to restrict the freedom of the press once this has been achieved? To encourage the idea that someone is once again preparing to muddle the press is tendentious and engenders confusion and mistrust. It seems to me that what is needed in some places is much more a committee for the defence of the Party, for the defence of the socialist system against the increasingly audacious reactionary attacks.[19]

Serious questions should receive serious answers. The establishment of workers' collectives for the defence of the freedom of the press, since January 1968, has been without any doubt the most significant, completely spontaneous and really *independent* political action on the part of that class of society without whose presence the Communist Party or the successful progress of the democratization is unimaginable. And it seems to be this fact which had made those who support pre-January conditions really angry about the workers' committees.

The political activation of the workers in Czechoslovakia is not intended to restore pre-January conditions . . . but finally to make a clean break with them. The Novotnýites relied on social demagogy, but this cannot have any effect as long as freedom of speech and freedom of the press last.

19. Vilém Nový, in the discussion at the plenum of the Central Committee.

Six
Two Thousand Words

Forward!

Jiří Jirásek *Literární Listy* 20 June 1968

Two Thousand Words

At the heart of the revival process of 1968 lies an unfinished, unculminated dialogue between the Party and the people which was aborted by the invasion. The dialogue might have given an answer to the question: is the Communist Party at all capable of transforming itself from a military, bureaucratic organization into a citizens' Party which respects elementary human rights? Or, as Ivan Sviták asked:

> Does it want to win over millions of people to support its vision of democratic socialism, or is it just interested in keeping a hundred thousand people in their official positions? Do the communists see their Party as the people's political party and the Party of all the different classes in our society, or as a power apparat which must fight tooth and nail to maintain its naked power over the powerless masses?

At the beginning of this dialogue, the progressive representatives of the Party set out in a revolutionarily open and direct manner the intentions of the Party to change the entire structure of the Party's rule. Above all, the approach of the new leadership was declared to be a partnership with the people at large. The confidence which had been completely lost by Novotný was now to be earned by the new policies and new methods: 'People must again put their trust in the effectiveness of our measures ...' (Smrkovský). The chasm between words and deeds, between theories and realities, was to be bridged, and the real unity, not the enforced and artificial iron hand of Novotný, was to be the hallmark of the Dubček régime. This section traces, in approximate chronological order, the development of this dialogue.

Goldstücker and many of the intellectuals were filled, by early March, with the 'blissful awareness' that the right road had at last been found, that Czechoslovakia had the unique opportunity to marry freedom with socialism. 'I don't think any revolution in history ever had such a chance . . . to bring to fruition the legacy with which we have been entrusted. I want to communicate to my readers a sense of the urgency of this task and at the same time to warn them against . . . excessive impatience . . .' (Goldstücker, 'Eppur si muove!'). Most of the people remained very sceptical, and in an opinion poll made in mid February, only about 50 per cent of the people interviewed thought that the January meeting of the Central Committee was 'of great significance'.

As soon as the controls over the expression of opinions were relaxed, a gap began to appear between the ideas of the new leadership and those of the progressive writers and journalists. Kliment's demand for 'free elections, and a dynamic Parliament with an opposition', and Sviták's demand for the transition 'from a totalitarian dictatorship to an open society' were large demands. They were fairly obviously not going to be content with the extent of the democratization under the Dubček leadership. Very early on in the revival process, it was evident that the intellectual critics would challenge the right of the Party to introduce its own interpretation of democracy, at a pace which suited it best.

The progressive section within the Party envisaged a gradual, very controlled process, which could be slowed down or accelerated at will, always taking into account the impact of the reforms on the Soviet Union and the other socialist countries, always restrained and tactful, but giving free reign to the force of public opinion, which many people saw as the only real achievement of the early months of the revival. 'There is only one factor at the present time which justifies hope in the democratization process – the free expression of public opinion,' says Sviták, just as he had regretted at the end of March that 'If we look realistically and critically at the results of the three-month-old process of revival so far, we must come to the conclusion that there have been no structural changes in the mechanisms of totalitarian dictatorship . . .' The Party leadership was in the very delicate position of having created a situation for itself in which there was a constant disparity between the theoretical extent of its plans and the pace at which it was able and willing to realize them, and thus between its own promises and the expectations of more progressive people both inside and outside the Party.

One way in which they might have brought about a reconciliation between these different viewpoints would have been to welcome all criticism, wherever it came from, as a useful inspiration to the Party and state policy. This right of free criticism from within and without the Party was most certainly implied by the Action Programme. But from the beginning, Dubček was so wary of the dangers of the conservatives taking advantage of 'extremes' to take over power once more and attempt to reinstate their discredited régime that he always tempered his support for the upsurge of real public participation with the warning that things 'must not be taken too far'. In a speech given to the Central Committee of the Party on 1 April, Dubček warns that

> it is impossible to bring about fundamental changes fast, in an improvised way and at the same speed which has been happening in recent weeks . . . We should not be afraid of . . . spontaneity, but should learn something from it . . . It is in the interests of the Party and of the whole society that this [democratization] process should take place in relative calm, without any serious upsets. A different kind of transition could put our aims seriously in danger . . .

And in a second speech to the Central Committee made later in May, Dubček, much more worried than before about the upsurge of critical progressive opinion, expresses very grave misgivings about the whole situation in the country:

> . . . anti-communist tendencies have intensified and there are certain elements which are trying to adopt more intense forms of activity. This danger . . . at the moment constitutes the main threat to the further development of the democratization process . . .

Criticism, he warns, could lead 'to a disparagement of the work of communists and of all the people who sincerely helped in the post-war reconstruction . . . We must not allow unsocialist or even anti-revolutionary forces free reign . . .'

With one hand the Party was giving the right of free criticism, but with the other it was trying to define and restrict the sort of criticism it would accept, and the direction in which it should be applied. The difficulties of mounting such a platform are obvious. Dubček's tone of voice, his unveiled threats, are like slogans learnt from the textbook of Novotnýism:

> . . . we shall resolutely and publicly expose all anti-communist tendencies, and isolate those who hold anti-communist views. They are a very great danger to the uninterrupted socialist development and the process of socialist regeneration. The measures of the Central Committee directed against the attacks on the Communist Party are not being taken against, but in the interests of, the furthering of the process of democratization . . .

These were certainly the most cheerless words that had been heard from the new leadership since its assumption of power.

Expressions such as 'consolidation' and the necessity of 'passing from words to deeds' from the leadership provoked commentators to remind them that they had condemned Novotnýite methods and should not give the people any reason to suspect that they contemplated a return to the old ways. Throughout this extremely unstable period, when so many promises had been made and so little seemed to be happening in any concrete way in society, many journalists and critics of the new régime tried to persuade Dubček and the Central Committee of the truth of Dubček's statement in the Action Programme that their 'greatest capital' was the people's confidence, and that this, and not compromise with conservatives at home or abroad, should be their touchstone when they were making policy decisions. And these conservatives, who retained their domination of the apparatus throughout 1968, were the object of most of the practical concern at all stages of the dialogue between the Party and the people. A great deal hinged on the comparatively simple and obvious matter of who had what jobs, who was going to fall from positions of privilege and influence and who was to get the new posts. Outbursts such as Bohuš Chňoupek's were not answered as directly as they could have been in the forum of the Central Committee, and they had therefore to be refuted in the press. In an almost paranoically distorted 'progressive' speech, he had said:

> What has made me uneasy above all is the fact that the current of the democratization process has this time developed outside the Party and has become a public affair, an event unparalleled in the whole of Party history . . . We have to advance quickly and energetically, but while we are progressing, we have to get rid no less energetically of those rightist elements which could put the whole of the process in jeopardy . . .

Jiří Hanák replies to this in *Reportér* that he can't understand how the democratization should be the privilege of only one Party:

> Are we to understand that Party members should somehow carry on their discussion about democracy among themselves and then tell – or perhaps not tell – the rest of the people what they have decided? I'm afraid that [Chňoupek] has to be interpreted in this way, because there's

absolutely nothing in his speech which makes another interpretation possible.

He then voices the familiar complaint of the more progressive elements right through 1968:

> I can't conceal my feeling of fear, however, that the need for opposition, for a really political opposition, is still seen as something completely abnormal by the highest of the powers that be, as a really insolent, preposterous demand and something which should not be discussed any further . . .

This carefulness on the part of the leadership only afforded the conservatives ground on which to build. Statements saying that the new democracy had to be a socialist one were not perhaps harmful in themselves, but their overemphasis and their dogmatic tone of voice provoked retorts from outside the Party that once again the Party was trying to limit and define concepts which should be allowed to find their own definition:

> I don't in any way want to cast aspersions on the characters of these people – in fighting the conservatives they have shown considerable personal courage – but I am convinced that one of the laws of every individual's psychology, independent of personal character, is that men resist the attempt to put limitations on them. They may try to direct, to regulate the wave which has put them where they are. *They may try to regulate democracy.* And this leads once again to people being manipulated . . . The question is what kind of democracy. Bourgeois? Socialist? In my opinion . . . *there is only one kind of democracy.* Simply, democracy.[1]

The people, says Hanák, should be free to choose the leaders they consider best for them.

The Dubček leadership, however, continued to consider such basic rights as irrelevant and to stress the Party's right to control and regulate the revival. The honeymoon between the Party and the people expressed in the festivities and the down-to-earth goodwill of the May Day celebrations were contradicted and shattered by such a forthright statement of concern as the Dubček speech at the end of May which we have already mentioned. Dubček refused to take an open stand against the conservatives, and was still urging that the now fable-like 'honest and honourable

1. Alexander Kramer, 'What Kind of Democracy?', *Student*, 3 April 1968.

officials' had to be defended against 'unjustified attacks', although great progress was made towards an administrative and personnel reform by the decision to hold an Extraordinary Party Congress in September, a decision that was probably also partly responsible for determining the date of the invasion. Dubček attacked both the extremes in the process, both right-wing and conservative, and declared them to be a great danger to further progress, but the amount of attention that Dubček devoted to the right-wing 'attacks' showed that his preferred course of action was a tendency to pacify the conservatives. Old terms which had not been heard in the official press since January were revived: enemy espionage was again encountered, emigré circles were plotting, as of course were 'the remnants of the defeated bourgeoisie'. More consistent were Dubček's pleas for a gradual consolidation process, which reasserted the Party's determination to continue to do everything at the pace it set and not to be influenced by outside pressures. 'We cannot allow the existing political power structure to be destroyed before we have gradually and deliberately replaced it with a new one.'

To tell the truth, no one really wanted any such destruction; everybody was much too aware of the realities of the situation. As Antonín Liehm and later Vaculík himself pointed out, 'too many words, too much talking' had taken place, and the time had come for some positive plans for the transition to a new system, such as the elections to the National Assembly suggested by Liehm.

> In the deluge of talking, speeches, declarations, manifestos and resolutions, our route and destination are becoming more and more confused . . . in the programme and in the actual resolutions, and in the amount of talking, there is too much of the old routine . . . too many old ideas, and you can't quite make out whether they have real political content or whether they are just . . . jargon.

What people need, says Liehm, is positive proof they can really trust their leaders to carry out their earlier promises. They still need 'the calming, reassuring feeling that there is no longer any game being played with them'. The reappearance of the old bogies of anti-communism and anti-socialism could do nothing to provide that essential reassurance:

In a country like Czechoslovakia, professional anti-communists can of course be found, but above all, there will be millions of people who have come to the conclusion, simply on the basis of their own experience, that the communists have not made a good job of governing the country. They may even perhaps think that they are incapable of governing it, for the reasons that they are much too ready to justify everything they do . . . and because, like everyone else, they are not able to resist the temptations of power . . .

With only three of the conservatives voluntarily stepping down at the May plenum of the Party, and the conservative attacks increasing, the timid and compromising responses of the Dubček leadership were felt as a danger in themselves. The revival seemed to be clamping shut once again, and the fear that many progressives had expressed right from the beginning of the year about the lack of guarantees seemed to be fully justified.

Ludvík Vaculík's Two Thousand Words, which was published on 26 June in *Literární Listy*, *Práce*, *Mladá Fronta* and *Zemědělské Noviny* was the culminating point of the advice, the fears and criticism, which had been offered by Party and non-Party people to the new leadership since the beginning of May.

This declaration and appeal, supported in spirit by the vast majority of the population, divides into two parts. In the first, Vaculík included a general retrospective survey and a practical call to the people to act of their own accord to do what the Party leadership had failed to do, to get rid of the conservatives by relying on the support of the Czechoslovak people, a force which Dubček and the Action Programme had constantly declared their readiness to depend on. Characteristically, Vaculík began with a few home truths. No gratitude was due to the Party for opening the revival process since this was 'only a part of the debt which the Party as a whole owes to the non-communists, whom it has kept in a position of inequality'. His analysis of the past was as devastating as it had been in June 1967 at the Writers' Congress, even if it seemed less out of the ordinary and daring in June 1968.

The main task of the Two Thousand Words was to direct attention to the paramount necessity of driving out the conservatives, which should be done by all legal means available, including strikes and demonstrations. The conservatives, says Vaculík 'are still defending themselves against changes, and they still carry a lot of weight. They still have means of power in their hands, especially in the Districts and in the small communities . . .' He continues:

> Don't let's kid ourselves that these [progressive] ideas are now winning the day because truth has a force and strength. The fact that they are now winning is much more because of the weakness of the old leadership, which apparently had to be weakened beforehand by twenty years of unopposed rule during which no one interrupted it. Obviously, all the faults hidden in the very foundations and ideology of this system had to mature before they could be seen properly developed.

Vaculík urged the people to break out of the old stereotypes of organization and activity, and to set up, in a very simple fashion, their own committees and commissions and their own information networks.

> Let's give up this impossible demand that someone above us must always provide us with the only possible interpretation of things, one simple conclusion. Every single one of us will have to be responsible for arriving at his own conclusions . . . We do not mean to cause anarchy and a state of general instability. Let's not quarrel among ourselves; let's give up spiteful politics.

Such spontaneity has always been intolerable to Communist Parties whose official policy is to encourage the initiative of the people. In the tense international situation, and with the middle-of-the-road, compromise policy of the leadership, the rejection of the Two Thousand Words by the Praesidium was only to be expected. The good intentions of the signatories were not questioned, but their methods, especially the practical 'call to action' were declared to constitute an 'attack on the new policy of the Party . . .' which

> opens the way for the activation of anti-communist tendencies and plays into the hands of extremist forces which could provoke chaos and a situation fraught with conflict. It is an attack on the present leadership of the Communist Party and the state, which it is hoped will be provoked into using force against the appearance of disruptive anti-socialist forces.

In the National Assembly, General Kodaj made his only contribution to the political development of the revival process by declaring that the Two Thousand Words was an open call to counter-revolution, and insisting that the whole affair should be handed over to the Prosecutor General, while even Smrkovský gave way to the prevalent feeling and called the Words a 'tragedy', although he later retracted this statement and called them just 'romantic'. The government made a more reasonable criticism on the grounds that the timing had been wrong and some of the phrasing unsuitable, but the statement of the Praesidium, and conservative attempts to take advantage of the situation, provoked a huge wave of popular support for the article and its contents. Workers, scientists, farmers, students, housewives and writers all sent in their resolutions and letters declaring their unequivocal support for the Two Thousand Words (see the resolution of the Cultural and Artistic Unions for example), and their opposition to the standpoint of the Praesidium. At no point perhaps in 1968, was the gap between the Party and the people so wide.

The declaration and the hugely differing reactions showed that there was a credibility gap and a loss of contact and confidence between the Party and the people. The attention of Dubček and the other politicians had been absorbed for too long with political and diplomatic concerns, and the concern with the state of public opinion which had characterized the earlier stages of the revival process had fallen far into the background. The leaders had displayed their inability to tolerate, or to get in the habit of tolerating, the public expression of a viewpoint different from their own, which is precisely what they had asked for and hoped for in March. 'The fact that different people have different ideas . . . about the most fundamental problems of political strategy and tactics, should be seen not as a tragedy and a tremendously significant thing, but as a completely normal part of life' (Selucký).

This failure, which was a remarkable one in the light of earlier statements, in spite of the fact that the circumstances were politically and internationally very difficult in June, induced some commentators, of whom Sviták was one, to wonder whether the Party was at all capable of the transition to real democracy. He pleaded for an early Party Congress to make important administrative decisions, and underlines the fact that:

> the leadership of the Communist Party cannot again and again go on overlooking the fact that a programme of democratization cannot be put into practice or developed by using neo-Stalinist methods and that

only newly and quickly elected representatives of the *people, not just of the Party*, can lead the nation out of its crisis. Repeated threats of violence can only end in tragedy . . .

For the great majority of the people, however, the foreign crisis of mid July soon overshadowed this crisis of the internal development of the democratization, which would probably have continued at its July pitch until the special Congress had resolved the more pressing cadre problems. And the increasingly pessimistic nature of the once so young and joyful reformist leadership's policies were hidden beneath the surge of national solidarity which greeted the threats of outside intervention.

Eduard Goldstücker
Eppur si muove!

Literární Listy, 1 March 1968
(the first issue of the resurrected paper
of the Writers' Union)

There are very few moments in life when a man feels the liberating awareness that a real hope exists of fulfilling every decent person's wish to live once more in harmony with his society. There are few moments in life when hope, buried by disappointments and covered with the ashes of grief, comes again to the surface, saying, with a sigh of relief, 'In spite of everything, the truth prevails!'

At just such a valuable moment, and thanks to it, the weekly periodical of the Union of Czechoslovak Writers is being resurrected. With every resurrection goes a peculiar sort of curiosity which we carry in the innermost depths of our personality, and the people who look on expect some kind of revelation. If their hopes go unfulfilled, they will turn away in disillusion. What, in our case, is the revelation? The game of chance, which we cannot escape as long as we live, has pointed its finger at me and asked me to say something, and although I have always felt the magic power of language, I am filled on this occasion with a consciousness of its weakness. I'm not trying to speak for anyone else; that's why I'm writing in the first person singular, and please, reader, forgive me for it.

Since the 5th of January this year I have had the feeling that all of us, in this country, which is statistically so small, but so full of experience and purpose, who desperately want to realize the ideals of socialism, i.e., human brotherhood and freedom, have been full of the blissful awareness that we have come back from being lost in a maze onto the right path. I feel that now it is worth devoting all our strength to the pioneering – and therefore difficult – work of progressing forward in this direction a step farther than any of our predecessors has managed to do. I wish that my words could arouse in your minds, my readers, an appreciation of the uniqueness of this moment. It is a chance given to us once again by history, after the whirlwind of anger has passed, to attempt for the first time to join socialism and freedom, which belong inextricably together, in a real marriage.

I don't think any revolution in history ever had such a chance and that what has now become our lot will put us, the heirs to this country, through a great trial of strength, so that we will be able to show whether we are able to bring to fruition the legacy with which we have been entrusted. I want to communicate to my readers a sense of the urgency of this task and at the same time to warn them against the excessive impatience which arises quite naturally from an awareness of how short our life is, and which often leads us to be much more annoyed with how slowly the wheels of fate are turning rather than to be thankful for their turning so surely.

I would like to give my readers a little germ of hope and to tell them that it doesn't spring from naïvety or flippancy, but that it knows the anguish of doubts, years of self-examination, life and the world, that it has been fertilized with grief and watered by the tears of disappointment. Such a germ I would like to offer them, and in spite of everything, and today's world of uncertainty and scepticism, I shall ask them not to be afraid to nurture this little germ of sober hope with the warmth of their own thoughts, and not to think it inappropriate to remember with me the words of an old revolutionary song about beloved freedom: 'Liberté, liberté chérie.'

Action Programme of the Communist Party of Czechoslovakia (extracts)

Comrades!

We are submitting to you quite frankly all the main ideas by which we have been guided and of which we want you to take notice at the present time. Everyone will realize that the proposals which we have made in this Action Programme are far-reaching and that if they are realized they will profoundly influence the life of this country. We are not fundamentally changing the direction in which we are going. In the spirit of our traditions and the decisions we have made we want to make our country into an advanced socialist society, without any class antagonisms, advanced both economically, technologically and culturally, socially and nationally just, democratically organized, with a highly qualified management, and promising the possibility of a dignified human life, comradely relationships between people and freedom for the development of personality and character.

We want to start building up a new intensely democratic model of a socialist society, which would best suit Czechoslovak conditions. But our experience and our knowledge of Marxism lead us to the conclusion that we cannot realize these aims by using the same old ways, which have been out of date for a long time, or the harsh methods which are always retarding us. We can say with great responsibility that our society has embarked on a difficult period and we can no longer rely on traditional schemes. We cannot squeeze life into patterns, however well-intentioned we may be. It is up to us now to make our way through new conditions, to experiment, to give a new look to socialist development at the same time as relying on creative Marxist thinking and the experience of the international working-class movement . . .

We are not suggesting the measures we have outlined with any intention of making concessions to our ideals – let alone to our opponents. On the contrary, we are convinced that they will help us to rid ourselves of the burden which has for many years given our opponents a great many advantages by restricting, reducing and paralysing the efficiency of the socialist ideal, and the attraction of the socialist example. We want to set new penetrating forces of socialist life in motion in this country to enable them to confront much more effectively other social systems and world outlooks . . .

We will need the confidence, understanding and hard work of everybody who really wants to take part in this great experiment. And the hard work and initiative of every communist, above all, will be needed . . . We want to create such conditions that every honest citizen concerned with the fate of socialism and of our nations can feel that he is the actual architect of this fate, that he is needed, that he is a force to be reckoned with. Therefore the Action Programme should become the programme for the revival of socialist efforts in Czechoslovakia. There is no force which can resist people who know what they want and how they can get it.

Alexander Dubček Speech to the Central Committee of the Communist Party, 1 April

Rudé Právo, 2 April 1968

The markedly socialist and democratic development since the January plenum which was initiated by our Communist Party has been characterized by the unusual activity of our citizens. The process, which is full of conflicts between the new tasks and methods of carrying out our mission and the old approaches and habits, is taking place in the whole Party. Many people have been so astonished by the process that they are expressing their concern about whether the Communist Party is not giving way to pressure, whether we are not surrendering our positions, whether developments are not going ahead too quickly, and whether it will be possible to oppose the wrong and dangerous demands which always come to the surface in such a process . . .

It has to be said . . . that the Central Committee of the Communist Party at the January plenum and at the District Conferences could not regulate the actual course of events in the last three months, their intensity and complexity . . . within a preconceived framework. You members of the Central Committee know how we set out in January, how the Party leadership opened the doors for the process and placed itself at the head of a development and could not have had any specific step by step plan of action to direct these events with. On the contrary, the special character of the whole process was that its tempo and its nature were determined by the creative and spontaneous activity of the broad masses with the communists at their head, and that they expressed agreement with the conclusions of the Central Committee without being manipulated or commanded from above in any way.

We should not be afraid of this spontaneity, but should learn something from it. We should use it and apply the principle that we will solve problems in good time and with the people. The majority of communists and of the people welcomes such an approach . . .

What is the main problem at the moment? I would say that the main problem is to intensify, to consolidate the process, to get down to putting it into practice. Up until now the necessary personnel changes have been the centre of attention, but another more positive stage is appearing. It is impossible to arrive at our basic ends just by a change-about of people. It is equally impossible to bring about fundamental changes fast, in an improvised way and at the same speed as in recent weeks, which neither we nor the public can keep up for very long.

In the period which is now beginning, it will be important to start creating a system of guarantees and stimuli for a natural process . . . not in a drastic and aggressive way, but in a businesslike and democratic way . . .

Above all it will be a matter of articulating in laws all the positive features of the revival process already under way, of passing laws which will guarantee freedom of speech and expression, the freedom of the press and the right of assembly. These will have the same protection as socialism and the inviolability of our statehood and our socialist achievements, which are a part of our political system, permanently protected by the law . . .

No democracy, and therefore not even our socialist democracy, can live for long only on the free expression of different viewpoints, on the fact that criticism is allowed. This is of the greatest importance, especially when we can see that free and healthy criticism is removing old barriers from the path of social progress. But in order to live and govern our society democratically after all such barriers have been removed, we have to have a well-thought-out and well-functioning system of institutions, organs and organizations working in a new and efficient way, through which new policies will be carried out and which will be under the permanent democratic control of the citizens . . . The meaning and the purpose of the democratization process is quite plain: to create a more perfect type of socialist democracy fitting Czechoslovak conditions. And it is in the interests of the Party and of the whole society that this process should take place in relative calm, without any serious upsets. A different kind of transition could put our aims seriously in danger and could ruin the historical opportunity opening before us for the development of socialism.

Bohuš Chňoupek
Speech to the Central Committee of the Communist Party, 6 April

Rudé Právo, 7 April 1968

What has made me uneasy above all is the fact that the current of the democratization process has this time developed outside the Party and has become a public affair, an event unparalleled in the whole of Party history. I am uneasy because attacks have been quite openly published, or organized by certain groups, against comrades who in January showed personal courage in their unambiguous support of the progressive line; because the first anti-Soviet extremist views have appeared; because other political parties have begun to activate themselves energetically. Moreover, people are challenging the communists, throwing down the gauntlet, saying, 'If you want to speak frankly and above all democratically, you have to allow a confrontation between your ideas and the ideas of the non-communists who make up four fifths of the nation.' And I am made uneasy by the statement we can all read for ourselves from workers in Gottwaldov, saying that if the 'Central Committee is not able to prevent extremist acts, the workers will use methods similar to those employed by the students'.

I think a situation like this is fraught with dangers. My own personal view about the consequences of the January plenum was that the development of activity within the Party would lead to an energetic attack on all the mistakes that have been made in the past. We might resolve cadre questions, but the Party would continue to stand at the head of this political activity, and would always be one step ahead. I felt it would not make decisions under pressure but would establish the tone and the rhythm of a healthy, progressive process, regulating and controlling it all the time in the right direction. It would not even for one moment tolerate attacks from the right and would of course not give an inch to them when they occurred.

Things have calmed down quite a lot since Comrade Novotný resigned. I still think that if functionaries who for decades gave of their best to the Party and honestly fulfilled their duties in the lower echelons of Party work are subjected to the personal tragedy of being dismissed; if works' managers are being dismissed in an uncontrolled way; if demands are appearing – as is stated in official information for members of the Central Committee – for the restoration of the pre-February situation which allowed the employment of up to fifty employees by private enterprise; if members of the State Security are becoming members of the People's Party; if members of the editorial boards of youth papers are joining the Socialist Party; if a West German bourgeois journalist was allowed to attend the Party Conference – and I must admit that this is what has most shaken me; if a kind of race vendetta has begun; if the Czechoslovak Union of Youth has disintegrated; if editorial boards are 'making themselves independent'; if the slogan 'National Committees without Communists!' is circulating in the countryside, and if we have problems about the elections, even then, in spite of all this, there is still no need to abandon ourselves to pessimism or panic, and it is still possible to agree with Comrade Smrkovský, when he says that up until now there has been no really conspicuous attempt to overthrow socialism . . .

Marxism states that revolution does not retrogress. Every country, once won for communism, must remain communist. It is not beyond the bounds of probability, however, that the conflicts within the present process will go on intensifying, that the 'cannibalization of Communists' will continue, and that the situation could become much more difficult to control. We have therefore to unite all our forces into a central progressive stream, to reconstruct the supreme organs of the Party, the government, and the central administrative bodies, to reinforce confidence in the Party and really put it at the head of the revival process. Yes, the way back is impossible, and I don't think that anybody wants it.

Two Thousand Words

We have to advance quickly and energetically, but while we are progressing, we have to get rid no less energetically of those rightest elements which could put the whole of the process in jeopardy . . .

Jiří Hanák
What did Comrade Chňoupek mean?

Reportér, 17 April 1968

... I can't conceal my feeling of fear, however, that the need for opposition, for a really political opposition, is still seen as something completely abnormal by the highest of the powers that be, as a really insolent, preposterous demand and something which should just not be discussed any further. And this feeling was confirmed once again when I read the contributions to the discussion at the meeting of the Central Committee of the Communist Party, especially that of Comrade Chňoupek.

Comrade Chňoupek, for instance, is disturbed by the fact 'that the current of the democratization process has this time developed outside the Party and has become a public affair'. Should we understand from this that a democratization should again be the privilege only of the Party, an internal Party matter which just does not concern four fifths of the people of Czechoslovakia? Are we to understand that Party members should somehow carry on their discussion about democracy among themselves and then tell – or perhaps not tell – the rest of the people what they have decided? I'm afraid that he has to be interpreted in this way, because there's absolutely nothing in his speech which makes another interpretation possible.

Comrade Chňoupek is also shocked to find that other political parties 'have begun to activate themselves energetically'. Well, so what? Why should these political parties exist if not for political activity? Or does Comrade Chňoupek think that the Communist Party has been granted a freehold lease on this country? Just the hint of the possibility that it might have to defend its leading role with concrete achievements is enough to raise the hair of every Party member! I have to emphasize that I don't have at my disposal the results of a public opinion poll, but let us just for a moment assume that say eight million inhabitants of this country didn't want to be led by the Communist Party but that they do want to be led, shall we say, by a Prince from the Přemysl Dynasty. What then? Then quite simply the precept that the revolution does not retreat would be introduced, and that every country won for communism must remain communist. In other words – We'll show you what's good for you, whatever happens! The whole idea's absurd.

In my opinion, people know quite well for themselves what's good for them, what they need and where they will find it. I don't think the Party should have to use force or laws to impose its leading role on the people. I don't think that the Party has much to fear in a competition for power; after all, it has got two good trump cards in its hand: the ideals of socialism are the most humane ideals about how a society should be run; also there are no forces in Czechoslovakia demanding that we should go back to the time before February 1948. If the Communist Party permits an opposition, if it permits competition for power, it need not match itself against a class enemy, against a party which represents a different class. But if it permits an opposition, it will have to keep its eye on people who will claim that they can, and will want to, rule better than the communists do. I'm absolutely convinced – and I'm sure you'll agree with me here – that if two ice-cream manufacturers both operate in one small town, you're going to prefer the ice-cream which is tastier and cheaper, which will encourage the second manufacturer to make even better and cheaper ice-cream than his rival. And I have yet to be convinced that these rules are not also valid in the struggle for power.

Complicated questions are involved here, and no one expects them to be solved overnight. But I'm afraid that because of this complexity, one basic fact has been forgotten: that nothing and no one can be a substitute for an effective opposition, except effective opposition itself, not even the activation of the existing political parties, which Comrade Chňoupek is so much afraid of, because the fact is that in twenty years of inactivity, these other parties have lost a great part of their credibility. And freedom of speech or the amateur attempts of so-called independent politicians are not substitutes for an opposition. It would be pitiful if we were to let a team of rigorously trained professionals take the political playing field against a team of enthusiastic but amateur players, and said, 'Look! Democracy!'

Finally, a word of explanation. The author of this article is a communist. He joined the Party years ago without ulterior motives; membership of the Party did not bring him any advantages except redundant meetings whose outcome no one was interested in. Except the 'advantage' that as a Party member he was always right, even if he was wrong. And it is precisely this advantage that I'd like to rid myself of, but not by leaving the Party. I have the impression – perhaps it is a naïve one – that as a communist I would always be able to hold my ground in any argument with somebody who disagreed with me. But I should like it to be an opponent who had the same rights as I have. That is, he should be a political opponent, not just a non-Party member, which is tantamount to saying that he's a good for nothing. And it is this which is really at stake.

Alexander Dubček
Report delivered to the Central Committee of the Communist Party, 29 May

Rudé Právo, 6 June 1968

The most valuable capital for the Party is the fact that after the January plenum it was able to restore confidence in our policy. This is proved by the positive socialist activities of even those people who stood a little to one side of political life in the past, and to whom the January plenum had given new hope and trust in socialism. We realize that their confidence in the Party will depend in the future on whether we will be able to reinforce it with concrete activity.

The contradictions and conflicts which quite naturally appear in the present process, and which quite often become almost dramatically acute, are not the result or the fault of the policy on which we embarked in January. They are principally the fruit of the long social crisis which had been intensifying over many years, during which a large number of unresolved problems and unsatisfied needs accumulated. The previous policy not only did not react to these problems, but even made them gradually worse with the methods it used, although attention had been drawn to the situation by many people in the Party since the Twelfth Congress, and, more intensely, since the Thirteenth Congress. In January we made it possible for them to be solved . . . The present difficulties originate therefore in the burden of social contradictions, mistakes and deformations which crystallized in the last few years, under conditions of concentrated personal power and in a crisis situation.

Naturally, we are not shirking an analysis of our work since January. We are quite aware of the weaknesses in our work. But it should be taken into account that under the former system of working in the Party, it was impossible for us to prepare a ready-made programme of development in advance, and that we had no other alternative but to shape it, as it were, on the march . . . Developments have made it necessary and continue to make it necessary for us to re-examine and reassess things which have been formed and accumulated over many years, even decades, and which have remained unresolved, and to defend them in a public discussion.

The many years of the administrative régime and administrative working methods have also paralysed the capacity of the Party to act, and the Party as a whole was not able to react quickly enough to the rapid changes in the political conditions of its work, to the necessity of carrying on an open battle for the people's confidence. Many Party organizations were pushed into adopting defensive attitudes because of the exposure of the deformations of the fifties. The wave of fundamental criticism and the exposure of the deformations of the past have even disturbed certain sections of the state and economic apparatus.

If we were not to get these developments under control, to give them a purposeful leadership within the system, then things would become hardly supportable for the present political power structure, and conflict would be the result.

The past few weeks have also seen the emergence of certain other phenomena which we are watching with a certain amount of anxiety, since they could hold up the regeneration process. We had already commented on them at the April plenary meeting.

Since that time, however, the situation has changed in that anti-communist tendencies have intensified and there are certain elements which are trying to adopt more intense forms of activity. This danger, which at the moment constitutes the main threat to the further development of the democratization process, has been appreciated by a large number of Party members, and is being appreciated by a growing number of progressive members of the general public . . .

Comrades, what are the characteristics of these negative features in our development? Firstly, there is a biased attack, which is changing and intensifying all the time, on the Party, trying to discredit the Party as a whole . . . I am not referring to the quite justified criticism of the various deformations which is being advanced by people with honest views, or to the justifiable criticism of individuals, but to those attempts at discrediting the whole Party which, seen objectively, tend to suggest that the Party has no right to play a leading role in Czechoslovakia. Even if this is a temporary, biased reaction of a certain section of public opinion to the shortcomings of the past, we cannot ignore the danger that these tendencies and manifestations could be abused.

If this stream of unobjective criticism were to grow and if it were to remain unanswered, it could lead to a disparagement of the work of communists and of all the people who sincerely helped in the post-war reconstruction, the socialist revolutionary changes, the establishment of cooperatives, nationalization and the February events . . .

We must realize that such bias could have very harmful results. We have no reason to allow ourselves to be provoked into changing the political course adopted in January this year. But we must not allow unsocialist or even anti-revolutionary forces free rein . . .

The Socialist Republic has only been in existence for twenty-three years. Among us still live the remnants of the former exploiting classes and their political representatives. Old ideological influences and those who believe in them still survive. We live in a divided world in which the class struggle has not been resolved. These facts do not determine the character of our social development, but they do exist, however, and we should not fail to take them into account, especially in the present time of intense social process.

It is for this reason that we must follow very closely the political and ideological activization of the remnants of the defeated bourgeoisie, of bankrupt pre-February right-wing politicians and so on. We can see how, here and there, they are trying to create ideological and political conditions for their activity. Attempts are also being made to create a legal basis for their activities in certain organizations which are now in the process of emerging, especially in K 231, which also includes people who were quite rightly sentenced for anti-state activities.

Hostile emigré circles are also showing an increased interest in Czechoslovakia. There has been an intensification of the interest of enemy espionage services in what has recently been happening in Czechoslovakia. Various enemy news agencies are spreading false information, half-truths and conjectures, by which they are trying to disrupt relations between the socialist countries, the unity of the Party, and to disorientate Party members and the general public.

It is true that, for the time being, the internal anti-communist forces are showing restraint. They are even ready to maintain that they support the regeneration process. And in this respect they are using the tactic of achieving their ends by degrees. If we consider what a profound contradiction there is between their ends and the real interests of society, we can quite rightly say that these extremist, marginal forces cannot by themselves seriously threaten our Party and socialism. The real danger from this direction, however, lies in the fact that they are trying to create a base for themselves in the atmosphere of anti-communism and anti-Sovietism, by supporting various fundamental and destructive tendencies which would threaten the structure of our society. We have to realize that in the present period of the struggle between the two antagonistic class ideologies, anti-Sovietism is the great fashion among the various kinds of anti-communism.

We must naturally differentiate and distinguish between individual tendencies, between disorientation and deliberate intention. But at the same time, we should demand and make sure that no propaganda be made for, or support given to, the activities of organizations which do not have legal authorization. We need to pass the Act on the Right of Assembly as quickly as possible, so that we may put an end to this present period, when various organizations without legal basis, without a commitment towards the state and the principles of the National Front, are organizing themselves.

Through our policy, we must try to overcome people's doubts and mistrust, try to persuade as many and as varied a section of socialist and democratically minded people as possible to work with us, and we must not allow sectarianism and a commanding attitude in our relations with them. But at the same time, we shall resolutely and publicly expose all anti-communist tendencies, and isolate those who hold anti-communist views. They are a very great danger to the uninterrupted socialist development and the process of socialist regeneration. The measures of the Central Committee directed against the attacks on the Communist Party are not being taken against, but in the interests of, the furthering of the process of democratization . . .

We shall use the Party's full authority to defend honest and honourable members and Party officials, members of National Committees and the state apparatus, who are not infrequently exposed to unjustified attacks . . .

As well as fears about the right-wing danger, fears have also been expressed about the conservative forces in the Party, that we could return to the state of affairs that existed before January 1968. The danger here lies in the conventional ways of thinking which survive, and in the persistence of bureaucratic methods and habits.

Although people who are conservative say that they recognize the rightness of the new policy, they have not yet discarded their old ways of thinking. They are evaluating the development of society in such a way as to encourage nervousness and mistrust in the policy of the leadership, and immediately think of the most unfavourable way to describe every departure from the old routine and anything which shows initiative or originality. Some of them even are elaborating ways of opposing the Party's policy. I can call to mind for example attempts which have been made to distribute slanderous leaflets among Party members and the general public, leaflets which slandered the Party and tried to bring about a rift between the Party and the workers, between Party members and the leadership as well as within the leadership.

Such views and attitudes naturally threaten the capacity of the Party to act, and could discredit the Party in the eyes of many people who are optimistically hoping that the new Party policy will eliminate the old dogmatic and sectarian methods. We have therefore to take resolute action against these activities. Any attempt to revive dogmatism and pre-January conditions in general, even in the name of fighting anti-communism, would greatly damage the Party and its policy, and would objectively play into the hands of anti-communist tendencies.

It is clear, from all that I have said, that our present development is made up of intertwining aspects which vary greatly in character. We have therefore to elaborate a well-thought-out, courageous and sound policy which must take all these different aspects into account . . .

Report to the Central Committee of the Party, 29 May

If I were to sum up the developments since the January plenum, I would say that the most essential fact is that we have entered a new phase of social progress. The present polarization of views in the Party and in society reflects the contradictions which are arising out of the need to manage this transition. Immediately after January we had to create new bodies to fight against dogmatism, to elaborate and popularize the new policy; this policy is now beginning to be tested in practice. If we are to succeed, we must consolidate the democratization process, define clear aims . . . to bring about consolidation and not a weakening of socialism. An uncontrolled process would give scope for the growth of extremist tendencies . . . which could endanger the development of socialism in Czechoslovakia. This would not just be a defeat for the progressive forces of the Party, but also a disappointment for the international workers' movement. We have assumed a responsibility from which we will not retreat . . .

Zdeněk Mlynář
Speech to the Central Committee of the Communist Party, 5 June

Rudé Právo, 6 June 1968

After January developments began in Czechoslovakia which were positive both from the point of view of the interests of our people and the needs of socialism. But, as early as the April plenum, I stated clearly and explicitly that these developments had started late in Czechoslovakia, that in my opinion the main political mistake of the old leadership was precisely the fact that it did not begin the necessary reforms in time and on its own initiative, but all the time showed itself more and more prepared to smother any possibility of them appearing . . . and that the present conflicts had been provoked by Comrade Novotný's policy of autumn last year. And I think that developments since the April plenum show very plainly that it was this delay that has been the fundamental cause of all the difficulties in the present very grave situation.

The fundamental feature of our present situation in my opinion is that too many problems and conflicts accumulated in the past, and that there is too much discontent (most of it legitimate) in all the classes and in every section of our society. Discontent which was 'kept quiet' for years. And at the same time no one, neither the Party nor the state, nor the entire National Front, can really solve the whole complex of these problems as quickly as people from every part of society would like.

Thus a situation is created in which, instead of the reform of the old system, a conflict could arise aimed not at the transformation of the political system, but at its destruction. A political system is of course a system of power . . . Conflicts could arise which in the end take on the nature of power conflicts. That would be a setback: we would lose in no uncertain terms the historical opportunity to develop socialism in Czechoslovakia in such a way and at such a rate as suits our own conditions . . .

Speech to the Central Committee of the Party, 5 June

The dispute as to whether today the main danger lies in the formation of rightist, anti-communist forces, or in the conservatives who would like to regress to pre-January conditions, is in its way an important one . . . but I do not think it is right to put it in the first place, before the issue as to whether or not a conflict could come into being in this country capable of growing into a threat to socialist power itself.

I do agree, however, with those speeches which have drawn attention to the fact that to exaggerate the danger from the right plays into the hands of the conservative forces . . . An attempt to return to pre-January conditions would equally pose the threat of a conflict, and it would mean going against the opinion of the majority of people.

What does public opinion show? Quite a lot can be learnt from the survey of the Institute for Public Opinion Research at the Czechoslovak Academy of Sciences, the results of which were published in *Rudé Právo* . . . If we take all the figures together, the outlook for our policy looks rather good, because about half of the population sees the present developments favourably, and has confidence in an improvement in certain specific questions. At the same time, the other half still really expresses, in one way or another, a certain amount of discontent and does not feel that its interests and needs are being responded to. And this does not of course mean that this second half is in any way an anti-socialist force. It would be sheer nonsense to come to this conclusion. But it does mean that in certain conditions these dissatisfied people could be won over by the political demagogy of the numerically small anti-communist right.

I think therefore that if we express concern about this, we are not diehard conservatives, but responsible politicians. Of course leftist reactions to the dangers of the influence of anti-socialism could separate us from the thinking of many people, for, as the above mentioned survey shows, the overwhelming majority of people, over 70 per cent, think that anti-socialist forces cannot make an attempt to upset the situation in Czechoslovakia.

Antonín Liehm
Seriously now, let's be specific

Literární Listy, 13 June 1968

What's going to happen, do you think? Where does the greatest danger lie? How will things turn out? Does anybody really have any idea how Czechoslovakia will look two years from now? Just a glimmer . . . ?

People are asking themselves these questions every day. Some of the questions are related to foreign affairs, but most of them concern us, they are domestic problems. Because in the deluge of talking, speeches, declarations, manifestos and resolutions, our route and our destination are becoming more and more confused. And at the same time, everyone knows, even people who want answers the most, that there are no quick and easy answers, that there are no slogans which can be used to sum everything up and solve all the problems. So there appear to be too many words, too much talking.

Both in the programme and in the actual resolutions, and in the amount of talking, there is too much of the old routine, there are too many old ideas, and you can't quite make out whether they have real political content or whether they are just being voiced to pay lip service, using the right jargon. And if they do have a real political meaning, then what exactly is it? Once again, people are not discussing the actual content of words, but spending their time guessing at their meanings.

Because they're not in the habit of believing, they go on being mistrustful, and so many of the words that are being used sound so familiar, so well-known, that they only encourage the mistrust even more. Included here are the calls to purposeful work, to make use of the information media, and the appeal to look forward now that we've started to discuss the main issues . . . but where to?

We all know, says the citizen to himself, that even the jargon hasn't changed. At the same time, it is trust that is most needed in this country, the calmly reassuring feeling that there is no longer any game being played with people, that the nation is being talked to as an adult, to whom it is possible to say, pen in hand, 'Let's sit down and we'll work things out together.'

Personally, I think that a great deal has changed. But the jargon least of all. Why? Why do the resolutions and speeches always sound the same, in spite of the fact that they mean something different now, at least something a little different? Why does it always appear as though the leadership of the Party was concerned above all with safeguarding the apparatus, or rather the apparatuses, internal and foreign affairs, rather than with the problems of the majority of Party members and with them the two nations of this country, whose legitimate leader it considers itself? Could it be because for twenty, thirty or forty years it has been thought almost indecent, if not treasonable, to call a spade a spade, and the people who write this down are themselves still not able to do it? Of course, the Central Committee is what it is, and so is the apparatus and its officials. We know who chose them, when and why and according to what criteria. And also for what reason. So in fact, it would be a little naïve to expect its active element suddenly to change character.

Except there is some change: the people who will alone be responsible for the way things develop from the September Congress onwards know full well that neither the people nor the Party can be talked down to in the old way. Do they know to what extent it depends on them whether the Congress sets a completely new tone? Do they appreciate, after all the experiences they have been through, how unimportant it is to have power? Do they realize that if the people, communists and non-communists alike, aren't saying to themselves after the September Congress, 'There now, that's what I call a new language, new people, a new Party ...' then the words about the leading role of the Party and even the threats will all have been completely pointless? Once again people would be completely indifferent and mistrustful and some kind of a catastrophe would be unavoidable. And if they get angry instead of relapsing again into indifference, the result would be just the same. Do they realize this? Do they know? Are they aware that today everything can still be stage-managed, everything can still be fixed, everything can still be prepared, especially now that the summer and the holidays are here? Do they know that all the arranging will be useless if there is still too much hot air, too many wrong people, and too many old habits which still refuse to be dislodged?

The leading role

Let's look for example at the so-called leading role of the Party. It is talked about as though it were something which could not be questioned, as though there were some moral and political right involved. Yet, at the same time, even the people who use the expression know very well that at this moment there is nothing in this country which is being challenged so strongly, which has become so much divested of any moral or political rights, as this idea. There is nothing either strange or incomprehensible about this fact.

The economic decline of Czechoslovakia for the twenty years following February 1948 is something every little child knows about, and there have been so many wounds to scar the moral character of these twenty years that one is almost afraid to start making comparisons with the past. Responsibility for everything that happened in this country during these years lies with the Party. For absolutely everything. All the results. And all the communists with it, although some are more to blame than others. Most of all the ones who were not personally responsible for anything, but just drifted along with the tide, forming the necessary mass base. Obviously there is not a normal, tolerably healthy nation in the world which, after such an experience, would not have doubts about the moral and political right – drummed home *ad nauseam* – of the Communist Party, and which is unfortunately not made any more convincing by the claim that it is 'the communists themselves who began the fight against the deformations . . .' Who, for God's sake, was supposed to begin this fight in a system of rule by one party; who else had the possibility, the opportunity, of guiding and leading the fight to its successful conclusion; who if not those in whom all the power and control of power was concentrated – the communists and the leading bodies of the Communist Party? No, these are just not good arguments and they do not arouse confidence.

But there are other arguments which are more cogent, political

Seriously now, let's be specific and honest. Most important of all, the Communist Party still has all power in its hands, just as it had before January 1968. Whether a peaceful, gradual democratization occurs in Czechoslovakia depends on the Communist Party and on its internal development. The Communist Party will never hand over its power to anyone of its own accord. Perhaps some people think that it would be possible to take power from it by force? Rubbish! At that moment the Czechoslovak experiment in democratic socialism would be drenched in blood and the country pushed back ten years or more. You only have to look at the map to realize this, or think about the world's basic political situation. A person who doesn't know and understand this is either an idiot or a provocateur . . .

There is a second argument, which can be found in a resolution of the Central Committee: 'The Party is the main guarantee of good relations between Czechoslovakia and the other socialist countries.' We know this is true, and everyone should also realize that without these good relations there would not at this moment be any democratic development in our country.

The leading role of the Communist Party at this stage of our political development is therefore an objective necessity which is neither good nor bad, but simply a historical fact which has to be taken into account. In this fact, however, lies the great opportunity. For very few movements with so much chalked up against their account get the opportunity – as a result of a whole series of different circumstances – of proving to themselves and to other people that they are capable of rising again from the ashes. The Communist Party of Czechoslovakia has received this opportunity from history because of the circumstances mentioned above. And the way in which it resolves the opportunity will be decisive for itself and for the country. If we don't make full use of it, I don't think the Czechs and Slovaks will try to drive the Party out with force. They will simply turn away again, this time for ever, with a shrug of the shoulders, and only then will things be really bad.

Anti-communism

Anti-communism is discussed in the same way as the leading role of the Communist Party, as though the people were just a stupid, unthinking herd, without a memory . . .

In more than one leading body of the Party there are still sitting people whom we told for years: 'Let things go on like they are doing, and the time will come when people will no longer make any distinction between Novotný and you, between people who have stood in the way of any kind of progress and those people who at least between 1955 and 1956 tried to make some kind of a break through the barrier of dull routine.' Then they smiled at us ironically, condescendingly, and declared that we were naïve. Today they are pretending to be surprised, as if they didn't understand why this is all happening. Czechoslovakia is a country where the communists have been in power for twenty years, where they have had the opportunity to turn into a practical reality ideas which elsewhere remain theoretical and hypothetical, in which they were given the opportunity to realize the great humanist ideals of Marx and Lenin. In a country like Czechoslovakia, professional anti-communists can of course be found, but above all, there will be millions of people who have come to the conclusion, simply on the basis of their own experience, that the communists have not made a good job of governing the country. They may even perhaps think that they are incapable of governing it for the reasons that they are much too ready to justify everything that they do and to make compromises on personal and national issues, and because, like everyone else, they are not able to resist the temptations of power, with the added disadvantage that for many different reasons they entrust the control of power to far too small a number of quite incredibly incompetent people. Are these people anti-communist in the sense in which the word is generally used? After all, they are not crying out for exploitation to begin again, and they don't want to start exterminating other countries or anything like that. They just think that the communists have not made a very good job of things and that somebody else might be able to do it better. People who think like this are speaking out in the open at the moment, and my feeling is that the word 'anti-communism' is being used as a kind of way of escaping from a state of emergency in which it is not quite safe to throw around that rather vague label, 'anti-socialist forces'. What can be done about 'anti-communists' of this sort, who I'm sure make up an absolute majority among Czechoslovak anti-communists? Rather than wagging a threatening finger at them, thereby encouraging the only possible reaction – that they will shrug their shoulders, say, 'Go jump in a lake!' and retreat into their own thoughts – it would probably be more sensible to explain to them that the dividing line in this country is not between communists and non-communists (a thing that everyone who doesn't want to spend the rest of his life eaten up with hate and bitterness should understand), but in quite a different place. There are just as many dividing lines, barriers and boundaries between communists as between non-communists. Only an insignificant number of communists really govern the country (even if, I know they are members of the ruling Party and even if there are first and second class citizens); we should explain that the Communist Party, incidentally like any party which is in power alone for twenty years and has well over a million members in such a small country as Czechoslovakia, is inevitably made up of a coalition of many widely different interests, and that in a quarter of a century it has become so firmly rooted in the country that it cannot simply be obliterated and trampled upon. It would be a good idea to explain to them that the Party doesn't need to defend the communists who can and will still be useful to society – and I think there are many people of this sort – because they will defend themselves in their work, in their indispensability, in the mere fact of their existence. And they should also understand that communists who cannot defend themselves in this way, and who are in need of the crutches of the Party to help them keep their heads above water, will no longer ever be accepted without question by society, and that they will be much more of a disadvantage than a benefit to the Party. This will all be part of a long process. So too, will be the attempt to resurrect the Party as a political movement, the leading role of which people will no longer be able to have any doubts about, being more concerned with its deeply democratic and humanistic character. This process needs a lot of time and a great deal of patience on both sides. But if people who have every right to be sceptical and negative in their attitude towards the communists are just blackened with the label 'anti-communist', it means that the movement is deprived of any hope of success even before it has got off the ground.

The period of transition

On the one hand, its leading role in Czechoslovakia is not a moral and political right for the Communist Party, but a historical fact and a vital factor in the present situation, and, on the other hand, the process of national reconciliation and thus of the transition to democratic forms is a long-term process. If we accept these two facts – and I think that the population and the political leadership can recognize them as points of departure – then it will be necessary to come to some agreement at last as to how this leading role will be carried out and what limitations it will have, and how, at least in its first phases, the process of the gradual transition to socialist democracy should appear.

Obviously there won't be much argument about the fact that at the moment no one knows exactly what this democracy should be like. In this respect, we need only point out the differences between those people who think that any opposition or opposition party is automatically an anti-socialist one (an idea which is so obviously nonsensical that one almost refuses to engage in a discussion about it), and those for whom the creation of an opposition party is the only thing that matters at the moment and for whom any other alternative is a backsliding into Stalinism. There's nothing especially strange about this. For several reasons.

For one thing, after thirty years almost without public opinion and with a very short supply of information, people simply do not know what the political map of the country looks like, who represents whom, what is what, and who is who. It will take a long time, perhaps years, before we find out even approximately. Secondly, because in the last twenty years there have been such huge changes in the social structure of Czechoslovakia that it would be quite impossible to apply any of the social mechanisms which function elsewhere, and simply graft them on . . . And thirdly, there is the question of whether it would be at all worth while to graft on to Czechoslovak conditions any of the well known mechanisms, whether that would be possible, and whether, within the framework of the democratic development in our country, there will not also be born a new mechanism whose existence at the moment we are very far from being aware of.

Naturally, we cannot go on for ever prolonging the provisional state of affairs, when the old system is dead and no new one has yet been born . . . One fact which is very closely connected with the other facts I have mentioned is that the only organism within whose framework the Communist Party, as the main source of power, is willing to share any power at all is the National Front . . . Because politics is the art of the possible, because if we are trying to achieve a peaceful evolution to democracy it is necessary to proceed from the existing institutions, the National Front is evidently the form that can guarantee the really right course of the transition period on the way to a new type of socialist democracy. Not, of course, the National Front as we know it at the moment, but one which has been expanded to include all those really representative groups which have been formed and are being formed . . . Such a National Front is not, of course, an end in itself, but merely a means for the process of democratization . . . providing it with a constitutional framework and enabling it to find its bearings and to choose its path onwards calmly and sensibly . . .

The National Front then, in a new and enlarged form, will undoubtedly become the main force in the transitional period . . . It will not become this automatically via a decision of the Communist Party. It can only do so on the basis of a mandate which will be given to it by the two nations of this country. If we imagine, as we have often been told in the last few weeks, that the mandate from February 1948 is still valid, this is just a political naïvety. This mandate ran out a long time ago . . . A force which could bear the responsibility for the execution of a social revolution must be willing to stand before the people again and ask for its mandate to be renewed. The National Front then will have to ask for the mandate, and it should do so in the form of a referendum, in the form of a question put in a concrete form, to which the people would answer yes or no. And the mandate should be at the same time a kind of agreement with the nation, a contract which would bind both parties temporarily to carry out certain measures and would set a time limit after which both parties would again decide whether and in what form the mandate should be prolonged or revised.

A new enlarged National Front should ask the country for its agreement to the National Front's arranging elections to a

Constituent National Assembly. These would be held within the National Front, and the voters would be able to choose from a large list of candidates, representing all the component parts of the National Front. Elections such as these to a Constituent National Assembly are the only ones which can be carried out in the country in the near future, if the development towards democracy is to be calm and uninterrupted . . . By the time the mandate of the Constituent Assembly had elapsed, several things would naturally have become clear. For instance, to what extent the Communist Party was capable of renewing its democratic and humanistic standing in the country, what other political groups were representative and viable within the Czechoslovak socialist community, and how they should relate to each other. The experiences of the transitional period and the political profile of the country at the end of it would then be anchored in a new constitution, the approval of which would also end the validity of the mandate entrusted to the enlarged National Front. The constitution would be submitted to the country in a further referendum and after its eventual acceptance, political life would flourish in a new framework about the nature of which I dare not at the moment hazard a guess . . .

This then is a rough outline of the period of transition, into which we shall be entering in September this year. At this date the Extraordinary Fourteenth Congress of the Communist Party will bring to an end the amorphous, fundamental period which started in January 1968. From September onwards, it will not be possible to govern the country without a firmly established time schedule, and without its confirmation by the Czechoslovak people. Without this, new conflicts will arise, and the situation will gradually become more and more difficult to resolve; we will simply set out on a different road leading once again to the completely open dictatorship of the Party and its apparatus . . .

Ludvík Vaculík
Two thousand words to workers, farmers, scientists, artists and everyone

Literární Listy, 27 June 1968

The life of this nation was first of all threatened by the war. Then still more bad times followed, together with events which threatened the spiritual health and character of the nation. Most of the people of Czechoslovakia optimistically accepted the socialist programme, but its direction got into the wrong people's hands. It would not have mattered so much that they did not possess enough experience as statesmen, have enough practical knowledge or intellectual training, if they had at least had more common sense and humanity, if they had been able to listen to other people's opinions, and if they had allowed themselves to be replaced as time passed by more capable people.

After the war people had great confidence in the Communist Party, but it gradually preferred to have official positions instead of the people's trust, until it had only official positions and nothing else. This has to be said: communists among us know that it's true, and their disappointment about the results is just as great as that of others. The incorrect line of the leadership turned the Party from a political party and ideological grouping into a power organization which became very attractive to power-hungry egotists, reproachful cowards and people with bad consciences. When they came into the Party, its character and behaviour began to be affected. Its internal organization was such that good people, who might have maintained its development for it to have fitted into the modern world, could not wield any influence at all without shameful incidents occurring. Many communists opposed this decline, but not in one single case did they have any success in preventing what happened.

The conditions in the Communist Party were the model for and the cause of an identical situation in the state. Because the Party became linked with the state it lost the advantage of being able to keep its distance from the executive power. There was no criticism of the activity of the state and economic organizations. Parliament forgot how to debate: the government forgot how to govern and the directors how to direct. Elections had no significance and the laws lost their weight. We could not trust representatives on any committee, and even if we did, we could not ask them to do anything, because they could accomplish nothing. What was still worse was that we could hardly trust each other any more. There was a decline of individual and communal honour. You didn't get anywhere by being honest and it was useless expecting ability to be appreciated. Most people, therefore, lost interest in public affairs; they worried only about themselves and about their money. Moreover, as a result of these bad conditions, now one cannot even rely on money. Relationships between people were harmed, and they didn't enjoy working any more. To sum up, the country reached a point where its spiritual health and character were both threatened.

We are all of us together responsible for the present state of affairs, and the communists among us are more responsible than others. But the main responsibility rests with those who were part of, or the agents of, uncontrolled power. The power of a determined group was conveyed, with the help of the Party apparatus, from Prague to every district and community. This apparatus decided what one might or might not do: it directed the cooperatives for the cooperative workers, the factories for the workers and the National Committees for the citizens.[2] No organizations actually belonged to their members, not even the communist ones.

These rulers' greatest guilt, and the worst deception they perpetrated, was to make out that their arbitrary rule was the will of the workers. If we were to continue to believe this deception, we would have now to blame the workers for the decline of our economy, for the crimes committed against innocent people, for the introduction of the censorship which made it impossible for all this to be written about. The workers would now have to be

2. National Committees are the units of local administration elected on a National Front basis at city, town, district and regional level.

blamed for the wrong investments, for the losses in trade, for the shortage of flats. Of course, no sensible person believes in such guilt on the part of the workers. We all know, and especially every worker knows, that in actual fact the workers made no decisions about anything. Someone else controlled the voting of the workers' representatives. While many workers had the impression that they were in control, a specially educated group of Party officials and officials of the state apparatus ruled. In fact, they took the place of the overthrown class and themselves became the new aristocracy.

In all fairness, we should say that some of them were aware of what was going on a long time ago. We can recognize these people now by the fact that they are redressing wrongs, correcting mistakes, returning the power of making decisions to the Party members and the citizens and limiting the authority and the number of the apparatchiks. They are with us in opposing the backward, obsolete views among the Party membership. But many officials are still defending themselves against changes, and they still carry a lot of weight. They still have means of power in their hands, especially in the districts and in the small communities, where they may use these instruments secretly and without any risk to themselves.

Since the beginning of the year, we have been taking part in the revival process of democratization. It began in the Communist Party. Even non-communists, who until recently expected no good to come from it, recognize this fact. We should add, however, that the process could not have begun anywhere else. After all, only the communists could for twenty years lead anything like a full political life, only the communists were in a position to know what was happening and where, only the opposition within the Communist Party were privileged enough to be in contact with the enemy. The initiative and efforts of democratic communists are therefore only a part of the debt which the Party as a whole owes to non-communists, whom it has kept in a position of inequality. No thanks, therefore, is due to the Communist Party, although it should probably be acknowledged that it is honestly trying to use this last opportunity to save its own and the nation's honour.

The revival process hasn't come up with anything very new. It is producing ideas and suggestions many of which are older than the errors of our socialism, and others which came up to the surface after being in existence underground for a long time. They should have come out into the open a long time ago, but they were suppressed. Don't let's kid ourselves that these ideas are now winning the day because truth has a force and strength. The fact that they are now winning is much more because of the weakness of the old leadership, which apparently had to be weakened beforehand by twenty years of unopposed rule during which no one interrupted it. Obviously, all the faults hidden in the very foundations and ideology of this system had to mature before they could be seen properly developed.

Let us not, therefore, underestimate the significance of criticism from the ranks of writers and students. The source of social changes lies in the economy. The right word carries significance only if it is said in conditions which have already been duly prepared. And by duly prepared conditions in our country we have to understand our general poverty and the complete disintegration of the old system of rule, in which politicians of a certain type quite calmly compromised themselves, but at our expense. So you can see that truth is not victorious here, truth is what remains when everything else has gone to pot. We have no reason to be patting ourselves on the back, but there is reason to be a little more optimistic.

We turn to you in this optimistic moment because it is still being threatened. It took several months for many of us to believe that we really could speak out, and many people still do not believe it. But nevertheless, we have spoken out, and such a huge number of things have come out into the open that somehow we must complete our aim of humanizing this régime. If we don't, the revenge of the old forces would be cruel. So we are turning now mainly to those who have been waiting. This moment will be a decisive one for many years to come.

The summer is approaching, with its holidays, when, as is our habit, we shall want to drop everything and relax. We can be quite sure however that our dear adversaries will not indulge in any summer recreations, that they will mobilize all their people, and that even now they are trying to arrange for a calm Christmas! So let us be careful about what happens, let's try to understand it and respond to it. Let's give up this impossible demand that someone above us must always provide us with the only possible interpretation of things, one simple conclusion. Every single one of us will have to be responsible for arriving at his own conclusions. Commonly accepted conclusions can only be arrived at by discussions, and this requires the freedom of expression which is actually our only democratic achievement of the last year.

In the future, we shall have to display personal initiative and determination of our own.

Above all, we shall have to oppose the view, should it arise, that it is possible to conduct some sort of a democratic revival without the communists or possibly against them. This would be both unjust and unreasonable. The communists have well-constructed organizations and we should support the progressive wing within them. They have experienced officials and, last but not least, they also have in their hands the decisive levers and buttons. Their Action Programme has been presented to the public. It is a programme for the initial adjustment of the greatest inequalities, and no one else has any similarly concrete programme. We must demand that local Action Programmes be submitted to the public in each district and each community. By doing so, we shall have suddenly taken very ordinary and long-expected steps in the right direction. The Czechoslovak Communist Party is preparing for the Congress which will elect a new Central Committee. Let us demand that it should be better than the present one. If the Communist Party now says that in the future it wants to base its leading position on the confidence of the citizens and not on force, then we should believe what it says as long as we can believe in the people it is sending as delegates to the district and regional conferences.[3]

Fears have recently been expressed that the democratization process has come to a halt. This feeling is partly caused by the fatigue brought on by the worrying times, and partly because the times of surprising revelations, resignations from high places and intoxicating speeches of a quite unprecedented bravery, are now

3. Two Thousand Words was published just before the extraordinary Party district conferences which elected delegates to the extraordinary regional conferences which in turn chose delegates to the September Fourteenth Congress.

past. The conflict of forces, however, has merely become hidden to a certain extent. The fight is now being waged about the content and form of laws, over the kind of practical steps that can be taken. And we must also give the new people, the ministers, prosecutors, chairmen and secretaries, time to work. They have the right to this time so that they can either prove their worth or their worthlessness. One cannot expect any more of the central political organs than this. They have, after all, shown that they are responsible enough.

The practical quality of the future democracy depends on what becomes of the enterprises, and what will happen in them. In spite of all our discussions, it is the economists who control things. We have to find good managers and back them up. It is true that, in comparison with the developed countries, we are all badly paid, and some are worse off than others.

We can demand more money – but although it can be printed, it will be worth less. We should instead demand that directors and chairman explain to us the nature and extent of the capital they want for production, to whom they want to sell their products and for how much, what profit they can expect to make, and the percentage of this profit that is to be invested in the modernization of production and the percentage to be shared out.

Under quite superficially boring headlines, a very fierce struggle is going on in the press about democracy and who leads the country. Workers can intervene in this struggle by means of the people they elect to enterprise administrations and councils. As employees, they can do what is best for themselves by electing as their representatives on trade union organs their natural leaders, capable and honest people, no matter what their party affiliation is.

If at the moment we cannot expect any more from the central political organs, we must achieve more in the districts and smaller communities. We should demand the resignation of people who have misused their power, who have damaged public property, or who have acted in a dishonest or brutal way. We have to find ways and means to persuade them to resign, through public criticism, for instance, through resolutions, demonstrations, demonstration work brigades, collections for retirement gifts for them, strikes, and picketing their houses. We must however, reject improper or illegal methods since these might be used as weapons against Alexander Dubček.

We must so strongly condemn the writing of insulting letters that if some official still receives one, then we shall know that he has written it to himself. Let us revive the activity of the National Front. Let us demand that the meetings of the National Committees should be held in public. And let us set up special citizens' committees and commissions to deal with subjects that nobody is yet interested in. It's quite simple, a few people get together, elect a chairman, keep regular minutes, publish their findings, demand a solution and do not allow themselves to be intimidated.

We must turn the district and local press, which has degenerated into a mouthpiece for official views, into a platform for all the positive political forces. Let us demand that editorial councils composed of members from the National Front be set up, and let us found other newspapers. Let us establish committees for the defence of the freedom of the press. Let us organize our own monitoring services at meetings. If we hear strange news, let's check on it ourselves, and let's send delegations to the people concerned, and if need be publish their replies. Let us support the security organs when they prosecute real criminal activity. We do not mean to cause anarchy and a state of general instability. Let's not quarrel amongst ourselves; let's give up spiteful politics. And let's show up informers.

The recent apprehension is the result of the possibility that foreign forces may intervene in our internal development. Face to face with these superior forces, the only thing we can do is to hold our own and not indulge in any provocation. We can assure our government – with weapons if need be – as long as it does what we give it a mandate to do, and we must assure our allies that we will observe our alliance, friendship and trade agreements. But excited accusations and ungrounded suspicions will make our government's position much more difficult and cannot be of any help to us. After all, we can ensure equal relations only by improving our internal situation and by carrying the process of revival so far that one day at elections we will be able to elect statesmen who will have enough courage, honour and political talent to establish and maintain such relations. This, of course, is the problem of the government of every small country in the world.

This spring, as after the war, we have been given a great chance. We have once again the opportunity to take a firm grip on a common cause, which has the working title of socialism, and to give it a form which will much better suit the once good reputation that we had and the relatively good opinion that we once had of ourselves. The spring has now come to an end and it will never return. By winter we will know everything.

And so we come to the end of our statement to workers, farmers, officials, artists, scholars, scientists, technicians, everybody. It was written at the suggestion of the scientists.

The standpoint of the Praesidium of the Communist Party on the Two Thousand Words

Rudé Právo, 29 June 1968, a statement issued after a special meeting on 27 June

Quite apart from the intentions which the authors of this declaration and those who gave their assent to it by signing it had – and we have no reason to think that they had bad intentions – the publication of this statement is an act which, because of the consequences which might result, could impede, or even jeopardize the further development of the Action Programme of the Communist Party, the policy of the National Front and the government of our republic.

The declaration does not contain any new ideas, any ideas which are not already to be found in either the Action Programme, or in the programme declaration of the government, or in the declarations of the principal sections of the National Front . . . At the same time, the Two Thousand Words is full of expressions of mistrust in the policy of the leadership of the Communist Party, the National Front and the supreme state organs . . .

If the recommendation to 'speed up the course of the democratization' which is contained in the statement were to be followed, the result – quite contrary to the intentions of the people who signed it – would put the policy of the Communist Party, the National Front and the socialist state seriously in danger. The statement includes a call and an incitement to attack Party and state functionaries in the districts and communities, to develop methods of using pressure such as strikes, demonstrations, the picketing of the houses of individuals, to the setting up of new organizations outside the structure of the National Front and the state, the people's own civil committees and commissions. The directions which are given quite explicitly – 'a few people get together . . . demand a solution and do not allow themselves to be intimidated' – are directions as to how to disorganize state and social organizations . . . If the people who signed the declaration think, as they say several times in the text, that their attitude will be helping the development of our political life, then they are quite mistaken. The Praesidium of the Central Committee appeals to them to reconsider their standpoint and to realize that the only effective way in which to support the new policy of the Party is by actively working for the implementation of the Action Programme.

The Praesidium of the Central Committee sees the publication of this declaration on the eve of the meeting of the district conferences of the Party to elect delegates to the Fourteenth Extraordinary Congress of the Communist Party as an attack on the new policy of the Party. The political platform on which the declaration is based opens the way for the activation of anti-communist tendencies and plays into the hands of extremist forces which could provoke chaos and a situation fraught with conflict. It is an attack on the present leadership of the Communist Party and the state, which it is hoped will be provoked into using force against the appearance of disruptive anti-socialist forces. And thus the new policy of the Party would be discredited and the purpose of the Action Programme destroyed.

We believe that the motive behind this declaration was an attempt by the signatories to make a contribution with their personal commitment to the successful course of the revival process. But the manner which they chose to support the aims of the revival process unfortunately gives encouragement to diametrically opposed tendencies.

The standpoint of the various artists' unions on the Two Thousand Words

Literární Listy, 27 June 1968

The standpoint of representatives of the artistic and creative unions, the Union of Czechoslovak Writers, the Union of Czech Architects, the Union of Theatre Artists, the Union of Film and Television Artists, the Union of Journalists, the Union of Composers, and the Union of Visual Artists, on the publication of the Two Thousand Words

The progressive forces of society, which, as the developments since January have shown, have won the support of the majority of people in this country, are trying to make sure that conflicts should be resolved and viewpoints aired in the full view of the greatest number of people. Opposed to them are those forces which can be proved to be responsible for the political, economic and moral mistakes of the past years. These forces, which were thrust into the background during the first four months of 1968, are reforming themselves . . . using administrative and power means, and hiding themselves away from the public eye. They deal in this way with the fate of the country without having to defend their deeds and their activities in public, or in an exchange of opinions. They use illegal presses, anonymous threats, demagogy, half-truths, and distortion, to communicate with the public. The people who are the representatives of these forces retain many decisive positions in the Party and state organs. They put up a stout resistance to the legalizing of the freedom of the press for the reason that they did not have enough arguments which they would have been able to defend publicly.

And so the Two Thousand Words has become for them an excuse to encourage hysteria and nervousness, to bring psychological and political pressure to bear on the forces in the Communist Party, and in other parts of society, which have been trying for a long time to bring about a moral, political and economic revival. The conservative forces are trying to disintegrate the unity of the progressive forces.

We are convinced that an atmosphere of hysteria and nervousness is fertile ground for violence. And violence has always been in the past, and could still be in the future, the last card left in the hands of the people who have shown in the past their lack of ability to lead this society to democracy and socialism. It could renew the old monopoly of power. It is not surprising therefore that they are trying to provoke an atmosphere of hysteria. We have good reason to be sure that had not the Two Thousand Words been published, the conservatives would have found another pretext.

An open letter to the Praesidium of the Central Committee of the Communist Party of Czechoslovakia, the National Assembly, and the Central Committee of the National Front

Práce, 29 June 1968

We read with concern in yesterday's papers the report on the response to the Two Thousand Words.

(1) We are surprised by the declaration of General Kodaj, deputy of the National Assembly, and by that of Josef Smrkovský, in connection with the Two Thousand Words. We have no reservations about the contents and the wording of this statement and we identify ourselves fully with it. We do not agree with Deputy Kodaj's opinion that this is an instigation or a call to counter-revolution, and we do not agree with Josef Smrkovský's categorical view that it is a tragic occurrence with wide implications . . .[4] We think that it is a contribution to the successful development of the whole of the democratization process. And we would therefore appreciate it if the Central Committee, the National Assembly, and the Central Committee of the National Front also saw the significance of it . . .

(2) May we take this opportunity to remind Comrade Smrkovský about some of the speeches which he made after January this year, which do not differ substantially in their content from the Two Thousand Words. Why then does he think differently today? Why the transformation?

4. Smrkovský was chairman of the National Assembly. His first reaction to the Two Thousand Words, when the matter was raised at the Assembly plenum, was to call it a 'tragedy'. In the face of severe criticism and events, he moderated this opinion in an article entitled One Thousand Words (*Práce*, 5 July 1968).

(3) We are surprised and annoyed that the Central Committee declared that the Two Thousand Words was a dangerous attack on the new leadership of the Party and the state. We cannot agree with this, because we did not find anything in this statement which might be dangerous either for the new leadership of the Party or for the state.

(4) Although we did not sign the statement, we fully support the contents, and think that it is our civic duty to sign it. And we feel sure that hundreds more of the workers not only from our factory, but from the whole of the Republic will do the same.

Libeň, Prague

The chairman of the shop committe of the Trade Unions,
the chairman of the works committee of the Trade Unions,
the committee for the protection of freedom of
speech, of the press and of assembly;
the Czech shipyards, National Enterprise.[5]

5. Libeň, a district of Prague generally considered conservative. A group of Libeň communists, headed by Jodas, circulated a 'manifesto' early on in the period, attacking the new leadership.

Radoslav Selucký
What sort of politics?

Práce, 10 July 1968

The apparently becalmed surface of our political life has been disturbed once again, this time by the Two Thousand Words. The whole affair, it seems, has already been settled; it has ceased to be an affair and can now be seen as a quite normal event of political life conducted out in the open, rather than behind closed doors. General Kodaj's hysterical reaction, the rashness of the reply of the Chairman of the National Assembly, and the activity of the political corpses sitting talking and voting in our Parliament, were all put in their place by the intelligent and really statesmanlike declaration of Premier Černík . . .[6]

The Two Thousand Words once again raised the issue which I consider is crucial at this moment: whether we are going to return to the cabinet politics of the past, or whether we shall succeed in maintaining an open political dialogue not just up until the Congress in September, but all through the next stage of our development . . .

No politician in power welcomes statements made in public which take a stand against him, and none of us likes being criticized for our actions or our ideas. But the fact that different people have different ideas not only about, for example, children's allowances, but about the most fundamental problems of political strategy and tactics, should be seen not as a tragedy and a tremendously significant thing, but as a completely normal part of life. The ordinary Czechoslovak had for twenty years got used to the fact that, whether or not he liked and approved of this or that idea held by a functionary in a position of power, he did not have

6. General Kodaj (a Slovak army commander) interrupted the course of debate on social legislation in the National Assembly to demand that the Two Thousand Words be discussed. He declared the article to be a call to counter-revolution and wanted the whole matter referred to the Prosecutor General. Černík's statement on behalf of the government was appreciably milder in tone than that of the Party Praesidium.

the chance to argue with him in public and put his own viewpoint forward, nor did he have the right to oppose him. If we are really serious about democratization, if we are serious about democracy, then politicians will once more have to accustom themselves to having their every act evaluated, judged, accepted or rejected, praised or criticized, in public. Politicians will have to get used to having to defend their opinions and their activity in front of the public, to winning their positions and maintaining them not by means of power, but with the strength and the attractiveness of their political ideas and the success of their activities . . .

I have read the Two Thousand Words very carefully and I could not find anything in it which could damage the vital interests of the Republic and anything that would put the future development in danger. Of course, I would be the first person to admit that everyone has the right to take issue with the ways in which some of the ideas were expressed in the statement, but to start talking about prosecuting people with whom they disagree, and to say that the opinions of some very respected fellow citizens are a call to counter-revolution, is a somewhat misjudged reaction on the part of people who call themselves politicians.

Thank God that we have at last seen that it is possible to have open politics, that there can be a public confrontation of different opinions. Except, of course, that the old system of cabinet politics is too strong to be overcome in the course of just a few weeks, especially by people who could do almost anything else except engage in closed-door politics . . . To make the jump from the manipulation of the people to an open political system is not easy and not even the most starry-eyed optimist imagines that it will fall out of the sky into our laps. I don't think the public should budge an inch from the principle that it is not just the object but the subject of politics, that it has the right to have its say in everything that concerns it, that it has the right to exercise control over not only just the government, but also over its representatives in Parliament, that it has the right to demand that the preparation of important matters should be done not behind closed doors but in the glare of publicity in the press, on the radio and television, and discussed in the organizations of the National Front. This demand agrees entirely with the Action Programme of the Communist Party, and was supported only three months ago by many of the people who are now holding important political positions. Everything which concerns the fate of Czechoslovakia is a public affair, and every single member of the public has the right to express his opinion about it.

Ivan Sviták
What words can do

Literární Listy, 18 July 1968

The Communist Party faces a crucial dilemma in the game which has just been begun. Does it want to win over millions of people to support its vision of democratic socialism, or is it just interested in keeping a hundred thousand people in their official positions? Do the communists see their Party as the people's political party and the party of all the different classes in our society, or as a power apparatus which must fight tooth and nail to maintain its naked power over the powerless masses? Almost everything depends on this question of questions, the future of the nation and whether freedom will exist.

The Communist Party still has a chance, if it chooses the first alternative and allows its mandate to lead the people of Czechoslovakia to be confirmed, to win in proper, secret and free elections. A Party responsible for a victorious democratization process would certainly win such elections, while a Party which found itself responsible for an abortive democratization process would never be able to allow them to take place. And this alternative terrifies politicians like Indra, Kolder and Švestka, although it can inspire the best brains of this country to support the progressive wing.[7]

But is the Communist Party at all capable of transforming itself from a military, bureaucratic organization into a citizens' party which respects elementary human rights? This is such an import-

7. Indra, Kolder, Švestka: all conservative members of the new leadership. For Alois Indra see Note 17 to 'What about the workers?' Immediately after the Praesidium decision on the Two Thousand Words, he sent a telex to all local Party branches which exaggerated the leadership's criticism of the article. This attempt to disorientate the Party membership was exposed in time to neutralize its effect. Drahomír Kolder was a member of the Praesidium since 1963 and retained this position throughout the reform period. Although a conservative, he was one of the leaders of the anti-Novotný group in the Praesidium, but once this goal had been achieved showed his predominantly anti-progressive side. Appointed secretary to the Central Committee in April.

ant question that its significance extends outside our state frontiers. It is the most fundamental question confronting all the working class and socialist movements in the world today, and on it depends peace and the settlement of disputes not just in Europe but all over the world.

In other words: is the Communist Party still at all capable of making decisions about national and state questions in line with the basic rules of European politics, which have been applied since the French Revolution, that is, to ask the people's will before acting and to respect the sovereignty of the people as the basis of state power, superior to personalities and all institutions, not excepting the Communist Party? If it is not, then it must give up its intention of preparing constitutional and other basic changes in the structure of the old power system, and on the contrary ask the people what the basic rules of the democratic game are, so that they have a chance to vote for their real representatives.

This problem, however, can't possibly be solved unless the conservative forces of the old bureaucratic apparat are suppressed, unless a people's movement with progressive communists at its head is formed. If the progressives themselves don't understand this crucial problem, then they may still be able to isolate left and right wing extremists, in the way that leading politicians are frequently suggesting at the moment, and also they may be able to provide a reasonable standard of living within a few years, but the problem will nevertheless hit them once more in a destructive, ruthless and unintelligible way. They would get the same reward for their efforts as the instigators of the Polish October. History is without mercy, like nature.

The path of the Communist Party of Czechoslovakia to power and towards the leading role in this country can only lead through a properly elected parliament; today any other way has already been compromised, and is seen as a swindle. The painstaking efforts of 'centrist' politicians to settle matters of state policy and questions of the national interest without consulting the people, to make decisions in advance within the Party and then submit them for approval in a formal procedure which is without any real meaning, is a totally confused political method which is doomed to failure. It is fatal because it relies on the acquiescence of defeated politicians, who are supposed to resign. The people who envisage this Utopian scheme don't, of course, take into account the fact that so far no power élite in history has ever voluntarily committed suicide in order to open the field for its opponents.

The leadership of the Communist Party cannot again and again go on overlooking the fact that a programme of democratization cannot be put into practice or developed by using neo-Stalinist methods and that only newly and quickly elected representatives of the *people, not just of the Party*, can lead the nation out of its crisis. Repeated threats of violence can only end in tragedy. The progressives are making a tragic mistake in trying to find a solution to problems of state politics without honestly elected representatives of the people, and as time passes they will either have to put this mistake right or else they will become neo-Stalinists.

The conservative wing of the Communist Party today willingly allows itself to be labelled 'centrist', although its members ought perhaps more accurately to be called the 'orphans' of Antonín Novotný. These Novotnýites without Novotný would be glad to put an end to the revival process which they hate from the bottom of their hearts. None of them ever fought for anything more than the change in the leading function of first secretary of the Czechoslovak Communist Party and they never tried to hide their open animosity towards the idea of basic structural changes.

The 'progressive' wing cannot play a game of closed-door politics and factional fighting with these people in Prague Castle, because of course they would lose. The 'progressive' leaders have to realize that their strength lies in their supporters or otherwise they would move towards the 'centre'.

An Extraordinary Party Congress should therefore make decisions which might perhaps mean that the Communist Party would be completely transformed and a break made with the Stalinists and neo-Stalinist technocrats. Let us hope that a non-violent, reasonable solution will be found, but it seems unlikely that the 'orphans' will give up without a struggle. It would be an illusion to imagine that they will. For this reason, to bring these conflicts and conflicting situations out into the open, as will happen during the summer, is not and will not be an expression of the personal intentions and desires of the 'extremists', as some of the leading representatives of the other two factions are now suggesting, trying to forget the alphabet of Marxism. On the contrary, it will be a revelation and a reflection of real conflicts which exist in social relations and between different groups of the population.

Elections as an expression of the secret will of the electors, if such elections should take place, will cleanse the Communist Party of its obsession with the idea that the future of the state and of socialism depends on the Party alone. This unjustified obsession with the importance of one's own party, ideology or personality is as old as the hills and is repeated over and over again in a monotonous way when the power of the older group is waning and it sees its decline as the end of the world. Living parties, ideologies and personalities survive because they are usually protected and ruled by their obsessions.

This obsession with their own indispensability is the only thing that interests some politicians. They act from a defeatist fear that without the apparatus of violence, Communist policy collapses. In this respect they are similar to Novotný. To tell the truth, Novotný was no worse than they are, perhaps even a little better. But 'centrist' neo-Stalinists make a big mistake if they associate the future of socialism with a repressive apparatus. The opposite is the truth: the more the limits of freedom are extended by the Communist Party, the more firmly will the strength of socialism be anchored not only in the apparatuses, but in people themselves.

The 'centrists' have behind them a great potential strength, that is the interest of the present bureaucratic, technocratic élite in maintaining the existing state of affairs. Today it's quite obvious that this country has been governed by ideological and political invalids and that more than half of them are still in their places in Parliament, in the National Front, the central bodies of the Communist Party and the state apparatus. Recent developments have opened up new possibilities, whereby communists would be able to proceed along with non-communists and win elections with a programme which is acceptable to the vast majority of people. Of course, a new type of candidate will have to be put forward, whom non-Party members will also feel able to vote for with a clear conscience. The writer Ludvík Vaculík and the authors of the Two Thousand Words are just as able to win the support of non-Party members as it would be impossible for the Indras and the Kolders to do so. And if these new people are not experienced in politics, it doesn't matter. Even if they wanted to, with their intelligence they are not capable of making so many crude mistakes as the professional politicians of our recent history have made. The victory of socialist democracy is more important than the existing structures, customs and habits. If communists are capable of leading – and at this time they have shown once more that they are – then let them lead. But if on the other hand, professional politicians are capable only of putting more and more new obstacles in the way of democratization, then they had better get out.

Truth can act as a provocation if it is told after many years of government by lies because truth is itself provoked by lies. Truth is merciless, inconsiderate and cruel, like the X-rays which reveal a cancer. A doctor must be tactful to his patient and has to hide the truth from a fatally ill patient because it's his duty as a human being. But he himself should not be satisfied with lies or half-truths, because the only chance of curing a malignant process is to know that it exists and at what stage of development it's at, whether it's in the process of growing or not.

Power is provoked by the truth because merely the outlining of the facts about the existing state of affairs is taken by the power élite as a personal challenge, and not because someone sets out intentionally to provoke it. In every social order and under every political régime fundamental truths have been ridiculed and persecuted as high treason, and in spite of changing circumstances, truth finally prevailed, or at least 'was left behind when everything else had been squandered'. Truth provokes power because truth is stronger than power.

An old political maxim claims that one cannot sit on the point of a bayonet. Modern totalitarian dictatorships have demonstrated that it is indeed possible to sit on the point of a bayonet, because today's fakirs of power have really solid, metal hindquarters. They can sit down, but they are balanced in a very precarious way because the truth is always liable to tear the bayonet from under them. And this is exactly what we have to succeed in doing this summer, because otherwise we'd have another generation sitting on us for yet another twenty years.

Seven
Semily Revisited

Ludvík Vaculík
The process in Semily

Literární Listy, 19 March 1969

People have been talking to me for six months now as if I ought to know and report to them about What Happened Next in Semily. But I lost touch with that little place afterwards. I don't have any relatives there and I hardly know anybody, so why should I have been interested in it? There's no other connection between me and Semily apart from the fact that I once went there, just as there's no direct connection between me and the so-called revival process of last spring and summer apart from the fact that I lived and worked through it. How disappointed were the really enthusiastic people to whom I had to apologize because I honestly didn't have any excellent plans of my own for the revival process! Because I wasn't a member of some revered association of noble-minded and clever people, people with good sources of information and influential contacts on both sides! How disappointed they were that in my case it was merely a way in which I made use spontaneously of my sudden freedom! A lot of foreign journalists seemed to be puzzled by this as well. They kept on coming to see me to ask me something and then they were left wondering. After all, I hadn't said to them, 'Come on, I know something interesting and I'll tell you all about it.' The secret police must be disappointed in me as well: like those other naïve people, they too need to see quite clearly an intelligence, an organization, something palpable that can be locked up, behind every spontaneous activity.

No fear! I refuse to adopt the right moral attitudes and ideological role for you, dear admirers of masculine courage, and as for you, my dear informers, I refuse to be made into a hero so that my friends would laugh at me even more. In August I was afraid and I admired people, I gave myself into the hands of fate and of different people, I listened to a lot of advice and offers and I stayed here not because I was brave, but because I don't like moving. I have a conservative disposition, and now that I'm here, to make an occasion of it, for myself, personally, I think to myself with great humility, 'You know what they can do with their tanks . . .!'

And why didn't I write the article? Perhaps I didn't write it because I didn't know anything definite, and also because a certain amount of silence is also a real part of writing, and then I had other interests and worries as well. So I didn't take much interest in Semily, because I've no connections there. I told myself that it was probably just the same there as everywhere else. And why did I finally go there? Because when I had made quite enough song and dance about not kowtowing to what other people wanted me to do, it occurred to me that I had my own, purely personal reasons for going there to have a look, to find out what was new. No one invited me there this time, and so no one expected me either. When I got to Semily on 13 February 1969, I looked for Mr Hádek, commercial photographer, considering that he was the only person I knew. But I could hardly recognize even him, because since 21 August he had been growing a beard.

'How are things here, then, Mr Hádek?'

'It's gone completely dead here. Our Chairman Mr Putůrek is still carrying on quite happily, people got scared, and all those disreputable 'new men' crept out of their holes again. They didn't give us permission for our Youth Club. Loskot's gone and the District Committee of the Communist Party's got a new leading secretary; his name's Stěhulka – seems a decent bloke – but on the other hand, look here! – the leading secretary before Loskot was Grösser – ask my dad about him, he could tell you a thing or two! and now he's the Czech Minister of the Interior, what do you think of that? Oh, by the way, do you know if a private individual has the right to put up his own notice-board?'

'I don't know, I've never given it a thought. Why do you ask?'

'I want to be sure about it, because the Council confiscated mine, though they had only given an order to confiscate the open letter that I had put on it . . .'

'What open letter?'

'An open letter to Mr Putůrek in fact, asking when he would finally carry out his promise to resign, because we thought the revival process should carry on quite normally.'

'Hang on a minute! How did the court case turn out? Mr

Putůrek was suing you for that resolution that time, wasn't he?'

'Well, he won and lost. The district court ordered us to make a public apology and to pay the costs of the case, but the regional court reversed it. We had no right to say that he shouldn't have been given a state award, or to demand his departure from public life, because that covers too many things. After all, a members' meeting is also political life. But they recognized that we could demand that he should leave his job and that an investigation should be made into his activity. A decent court!'

'That was after August?'

'That wasn't right until December.'

'I'm glad you had an experience like that.'

'But wait until you hear what happened with the notice-board. We put it up in front of the house here and put that open letter on it. Then we got the order to take it down. But before I could even do it, the town clerk, Mr Holubec, took the whole notice-board away. I went along there, and had words with him, and then went to see Hypšman, the secretary. They reported me and I got a summons to the VB, which referred to a clause in the law – the crime of assaulting a state body or a member of a social institution. The trouble was they'd got the number of the clause wrong because I looked it up in the criminal code. So I stayed in bed that day. The police came right into my bedroom looking for me. I told them I would much rather they left, two of them, and they obliged and I went to have a wash, taking my time, while they hung about in the corridor. I had my breakfast and then I went out and they took me along to the VB. There they took down all the details and fined me two hundred crowns.'

'And besides that you had the court case?'

'No, I didn't, because the district prosecutor dismissed it. Listen why, it makes a good story: because Holubec, the town clerk, who I was supposed to have assaulted, was only supposed to remove the letter according to the order, but in fact he took the whole board away, which means that he went beyond the bounds of the decision, in other words he had no right to do it, and Hypšman, the secretary, who I was also supposed to have assaulted, wasn't within his rights at that time either, according to paragraph 156/2, seeing that it wasn't him who had made the decision, but

Holubec. So the crime came to nothing, and I was only found guilty of a breach of the social peace, according to paragraph 19, letter A, law 36/61.'

'Hm. A decent prosecutor,' I remarked.

'Except that they've got the board there still. Do you think they have to give it back to me?'

'I should think they would have to. But why did they refuse permission for the Youth Club?'

'Because we refused to join the National Front.'

'Well, it's not surprising then! Surely you made a mistake there?'

'You'll probably think differently when I've shown you something.'

It was a notice put out by the District Committee of the National Front in Semily concerning the activity of political parties in May 1968. It contained a survey of the newly constituted organizations of the People's Party, with the number of members and a list of 'activists', with their names and addresses. It said that the task of the National Front was to watch over and make reports about the activity of its member organizations – there was nothing surprising about that. But what the notice was really getting at only became apparent when you came to a sentence like this: 'As far as the Czech Socialist Party is concerned, its activity is minimal, but all the more dangerous for that reason . . .' And this was last May, when they were right in the middle of making a big effort in the National Front to revive the idea of it being a partnership again!

'All the same, I still think you made a mistake,' I said. 'How can you possibly work if you don't have an organization? Or is being dragged from court to court and arguing with the cops good enough for you? It may be thrilling, but it's not political activity.'

'Surely you don't think there's anybody here who still goes in for politics, do you? There wasn't a thing happening here, either on the 28th of October, or on the 17th of November. And when Jan Palach died, then it was only us who held a ceremony, but otherwise . . . what do you think? Everybody was afraid. It looks to me as if the fifties are back again.'

'But you were only ten then.'

'I know, but I've heard about it from older people and from my father as well. Hang on a tick, I'll just have a look to see if he's back yet, in case you're interested in that Grösser . . .'

'Don't worry, I'm not interested in Grösser. But you mentioned some disreputable "new men" . . .'

He almost shouted. 'What a fantastic opportunity! Tomorrow they're having an evening of friendship with the Russians! Except that you won't be able to get in. It's by invitation only, and reserved for strictly "reliable" people.'

I winced. I had a feeling that that evening of friendship would be extremely interesting to me.

People were peacefully walking about the square in Semily, in just the same way as they had in the spring, unbothered by the frost. You can't walk for very long here, everything's all in one place, close at hand, all the shops and the offices. People sauntered chatting to each other, now and again half-hidden by the high piles of swept-up snow. Workmen and chauffeurs were standing in the self-service having a snack, and nobody took any notice of me when I went in to have some soup. Not even Captain Tůma, a plain-clothes policeman, knew me: of course I didn't know him either, so neither of us knew who to watch out for. He couldn't have known who I was, because otherwise he would have seen that I was only killing time there until the evening, just to amuse myself, and Major Špáta would never have got the almost superstitious report that he did when he returned from his holiday after the incident was over. Major Špáta, chief of the local VB department, told me later: 'When I got back from holiday, I was informed that you had been behind it all here.'

'But surely you didn't believe that?' I expostulated.

'I didn't say definitely, but I'm sure you were the leading light in the whole affair.'

When the tiny square grew suddenly empty and quiet in the light of the lamps, this meant that they were all in front of their televisions. Except that on 14 February, they had a bad picture here and could hear Russian voices coming over the air. That's why a few people went out into an eleven-degree frost to see if anything was happening. There was a crowd gathering in front of the cinema.

I was worried. I had an invitation card, but I didn't know whether they would have a checking procedure. I saw that Mr

Hádek was also getting ready to set off, with a roll of white paper under his arm.

'Don't do anything drastic, will you, just when I'm here,' I told him.

'Only what's within the bounds of the law,' he promised me willingly.

The people attending the meeting, who were nearly all old, preferred to carry on standing hesitantly at some distance away from the cinema, rather than to face a hostile reception there. 'You haven't got much sense left either, have you, granny,' a voice called – and they laughed. Once inside the cinema, my fears were confirmed: Comrades Stínilová and Kochánková had lists of names. If the worst came to the worst I was resolved to say who I was and claim admittance with my press card. But my short, embarrassed excuse succeeded. Both women interpreted my coming all the way from Prague in their own private way, so much so that they allowed me to go upstairs. Nobody was sitting down there yet; food and drink were set out on the tables, and people, mostly old and nearly all of them in uniform, stood around chatting. Every so often somebody else would come in and shake hands with everybody, including me. My neighbour, whom I didn't know, was stretching his back.

'I thought I wouldn't get here. I was out fishing and fell over, and it's really painful.'

'You still go fishing here at this time of year, then?'

'Of course not. It was way back before Christmas. And it still gives me trouble.'

More comrades arrived, apparently from a long way away, because judging from the length of time they took to greet people, they hadn't seen them for a long time.

'What are you up to these days, old soldier!'

'What's happening to the resistance at the moment then?'

It seemed to me that I really was without a single friend here, so I turned to my neighbour:

'I hear that fish sleep in winter. Do you think it's true?'

'Well, they don't sleep exactly, they're sort of motionless . . .'

From outside there came the sound of whistling, an air of

anticipation filled the hall, and we all took our seats. I sat as far back as possible, near the window, below which you could hear people calling to each other, and the Soviet guests took their places among us. Opposite me there were two free places, and after a while two VB men came and sat in them, a lieutenant and a second lieutenant. Next to me there was an old civilian with a good-natured, softish face, while behind me at the next table was the Chairman of the District National Committee. Outside they chanted: 'Franta, don't go into the cinema, there's a stupid meeting there.' It didn't have much effect, people didn't pay any attention in the hall.

Smiles and epaulettes inside. Wives sitting quietly next to their husbands. Hushed conversation.

'There's a big happening in Semily, and a strange smell coming out of the cinema!'

The lieutenant opposite me shook his head in disgust. 'It's terrible what one little bastard like that can do.'

The civilian visitor looked shocked. 'Can't you see to them?' he asked.

'We could, but not at the moment.'

'I'd beat that photographer up, but you know what that would lead to, don't you? We've got democracy now you know.' He shrugged his shoulders. We could hear an insulting slogan being shouted outside: 'Every sod in the cinema is hugging the Russians.' Both VB officers turned around angrily, and the elder one asked me in exasperation,

'I ask you, is that polite?'

'No, it's rather vulgar,' I said. He opened a bottle of beer, poured some into his glass and offered some to me. I thanked him, but refused; it didn't feel right when they hadn't invited me.

'That little brat, that bastard,' they both thundered. 'We should lie in wait for him and throw him into the Jizera from the bridge,' they raved on, 'or pour petrol over him and let him burn like that idiot in Prague.'

One of the civilians asked whether there might not be some trouble. 'Don't worry,' the lieutenant said, 'there are lads there from other places. Just wait and see if they dare to do anything. We've got things under control.' He pulled the end of his truncheon out from under his coat.

The guests of honour arrived and sat at the Chairman's table: the Commander of the Soviet garrison at Turnov called Belousov, an employee of the Soviet Embassy Solovyev, a member of the Central Committee of the Czechoslovak–Soviet Friendship Society, Dr Barák, and a member of the Central Committee of the Communist Party, Colonel-General Rytíř. We stood up and applauded. 'Long live the Soviet Army!' we cried.

'The élite's at the pictures today,' from outside. 'They're guzzling sausages.'

A peculiar, complex, feeling. I was at an assembly of people, who had not invited me and among whom I didn't belong, while outside, some demonstrators whose slogans I couldn't agree with were protesting.

The evening of friendship with the Soviet Army was a decent sort of affair. An ordinary celebration such as have been the custom in Bohemia for a number of years. It took you back to the time when you were younger, and more foolish. Imagine, dear colleagues from my youth, that you're sitting at a ceremonial meeting once again, where you just clap, and there's nothing to worry about, nothing can happen, and there won't be any changes which might disturb the calm . . . when a rowdy demonstration in the street interrupts things, provoking in you a feeling almost of being threatened. Are we in Czechoslovakia? My God, is the last fruitful achievement of the whole of last year's revival process going to be the excitement of this brawl which is brewing?

The chairman welcomed the guests and said that the evening had been arranged in line with the November resolution of the plenum of the Central Committee of the Communist Party. He handed over to General Rytíř. The General spoke for a very long time and occasionally he made such big pauses that we at the back kept on craning our necks to see if he was still there. He must have been tired. The assembled company listened to him in silence, but it wasn't always an attentive silence, but much more a disciplined one. I bet they didn't all understand what he said, but the opposition out there in the street somehow made them attach more importance to it. I didn't dare to take notes, so as not to be different from anyone else. So consider the following summary as more of a record of what I remember than what was actually said:

'We are accustomed to celebrate this occasion in a somewhat different manner. This escort outside . . . Yes, our country has been through a tragic period, which it will take a long time to put right. Where did this tragedy begin? The post-January policy was supposed to remove deformations, but instead it caused new mistakes to accumulate. The Party's Action Programme, which was intended to be a programme for further reconstruction, did not anticipate the situation which developed after it had been adopted. The leadership put the whole Party on the defensive, because it made incomprehensible mistakes. It abandoned some of its positions to forces which had already been removed once before: what did it expect from spies and subversives, who had finished serving their terms, from criminal priests and representatives of the defeated classes who banded together in the K231 Club? What kind of socialist enthusiasm did they expect from committed non-Party members?

'It's true that the Novotný régime was a bad one which was incapable of rectifying its mistakes by itself. Because it wasn't founded on knowledge of how things developed and on a supply of information, but on a system of complete misinformation. It was characterized by voluntarism and the undervaluing of the intelligentsia. Scientists looked for and formulated a solution, but then the Party leadership wouldn't hear of it. After January, however, there was no improvement. A group of economists led by Šik was given scope to work out a solution, but instead of suggesting a definite solution they just appealed to people's moods. What is the slogan about socialism with a human face if it isn't an appeal to people's emotions?

'The intelligentsia developed its own separate programme. In *Literární Listy*, a philosophy of existentialism and individualistic humanism was propagated. There was a censorship which got excited by cartoons of the head of the state, but which ignored the philosophers. Some of the highest representatives of the Party even began to flirt with that philosophy; it took their fancy. The intellectuals took full advantage of this. Learned men intervened in politics, the most famous example of this was the Two Thousand Words. In August, we asked ourselves the question – how did such a tragedy occur? All of us were inclined to blame the Soviets at that time. After an interval, it becomes more and more obvious that the fault lay with the Party leadership itself: it was not in control of the situation, it had abandoned its class standpoints; it had succumbed to ideas about some other kind of socialism. It was also admitted and we heard that an 'underestimation of the political implications of circumstances abroad' had occurred. I ask you, when a politician 'underestimates the political implications of the circumstances abroad' is he still a politician? The point of departure is the Moscow protocols. But these are still not being carried out, there is still nothing concrete being done here. That is why I respect Kriegel, who refused to sign them, while those who did sign are not fulfilling them. [Applause.]

'The press, radio, and television were controlled by a group of people whom no one could shift. They all spoke in unison. What do you think – does such a communion of souls exist between them, or is somebody organizing it? I don't believe in such a unity.'

And so on – I don't remember anything else from General Rytíř's speech. But for any distortion of the contents I'll be able to apologize after looking at the original text.

The leading secretary of the District Committee of the Communist Party in Semily, Comrade Stěhulka, also spoke. Today is a double celebration for him, because it's his birthday. He's forty-one. He remembers how some time ago General Rytíř here ticked him off for some reason or another. As for his attitude to the Soviet Army, it's one of friendship in his case, because firstly he's a communist and secondly an officer in the Czechoslovak Army, which has temporarily lent him to the District Committee of the Party in order to perform a function. Mistakes had happened, here in Semily as well: for example, the meetings which everybody knows about.

In some organizations things are not at all clear, for instance, in Technolen. It's unthinkable that any primary organizations should have a view different from the Central Committee over important matters. His first task he considers to be that of working for the unification of views among communists. And the rest I've forgotten.

In the Czech speeches there was no talk of gratitude for the troops coming in August, and the Soviet speakers likewise didn't even touch on the topic. About counter-revolution, if I'm not mistaken, there wasn't a word. Brief outline of the Soviet speeches of greeting: October, the Red Army, the fist of the working class, the struggle against intervention, the war against fascism, the liberation of Czechoslovakia in 1945, the common bloodshed, and why we are here – because of the imperialist threat. The speeches lasted over two hours, and then a free choice in entertainment was announced, a small Soviet music ensemble began to play, people rose from the tables, strolled about and socialized. I couldn't control in advance what might happen to me from then on, and also I wanted to make some notes afterwards, so I got up and left. The security check inside the entrance didn't even notice me. The crowd in the dark outside let me through into the street with the words: 'What's this, another worker? Be careful we don't take your glasses off you comrade!'

I was writing when Mr Hádek junior came in, frozen through, and we exchanged experiences for about fifteen minutes.

'It doesn't look at all good to me, Mr Hádek. It creates quite a bad impression.'

'I calmed them down, but you can't keep people under control as easily as all that.'

'You know that this régime could get much worse within a few years and that's when there'll be a need for brave people, and then you'll not be interested any longer, you'll have had your fling.'

'Were you tactful when you were young?'

'No, I wasn't, but my anger lasted longer than yours. You remind me of a short-distance runner, but this one may prove a fairly long run. And anyway, oughtn't you to work harder at your photography?'

'If everyone just looks after his own personal affairs, then it'll soon be like in the fifties again.'

'But you were only ten then!'

'It doesn't matter at all. After all, I've had the time to reflect about it.'

'So you're doing this, if I don't misunderstand you, because you want to improve conditions. But at the same time you are well aware that they have already improved, you rely on this fact, provoke and annoy the police, and then you count on the law being on your side!'

And I gave him a warning. I told him that they were making preparations to get him, and that he shouldn't go out alone and mustn't let himself fall into their hands. I didn't tell him what I had actually heard at the meeting. Originally I didn't even intend to put it in the paper, because I didn't want to take advantage of the fact that I'd got into a meeting which wasn't supposed to be for me. But three quarters of an hour after our conversation, Mr Hádek came back with bloodshot eyes, a cut lip, a swollen face and a caustic sense of humour:

'I thought you'd be pleased to hear that you were right.'

'I came back from my shift after ten in the evening,' says Jiří Urban, who works for Technometra, and is being treated in hospital for a broken nose. 'Two civilians came out of the cinema and the people watching laughed at them. One of them was carrying a paper box. Just for a laugh I threw something into it. Suddenly two men came and dragged me inside . . . they pinioned my arms and the civilian who was carrying the box held me by the neck. VB member Comrade Zámečník rushed up to me and hit me twice in the face, and all of a sudden I felt a third blow . . . then the civilian holding me by the neck hit me. He kept on asking me whether I knew who it was I had dared to do such a thing to. It had been Captain Tůma. I was kept in a room in the cinema until 11.45 and during that time I watched the police, in uniform and in civvies, prepare themselves to disperse the citizens. Later I saw Hádek being dragged inside by the legs, and then they held him up under his armpits and dragged him to the stairs. I even heard shouts from an army officer as well: 'We'll give you democracy!' and things like 'Kill him!' Some plain-clothes policeman in a brown suit came in from outside in the square and threw some papers into the waste-paper basket with the words – 'I'll give you democracy!' I looked into the basket, where there was a photograph of Dubček and one of Jan Palach . . .'

Arne Vaněk, a boilerman, with his arm in a sling: 'I was going past and I noticed a crowd of people. I stood there for a while and they were behind glass and I said to them, "Come and talk to us," and I added some rude words. That was when the plain-clothes men suddenly appeared and one of them squirted tear-gas at me. I turned my back and they kept on hitting me on the back, until

I had fallen down. I hadn't touched anybody, I'd kept my hands in my pockets on purpose. I didn't hear anybody tell us to go away the whole time I was there.'

Citizen Paroulek, a teacher: 'Captain Tůma in civvies was carrying a box. Somebody gave it a tap and straight away he shouted, "Who was that?" He knocked somebody into the door and then they dragged him inside. After that four policemen got hold of Hádek, Gottwald, Sedlák, Jirásko and Seibt. When he evaded them they squirted some gas at him. They dragged him into the cinema and Captain Láska in plain clothes kicked at him from behind on the way. Rokos was there and his comment was, "It's terrible, I'm going." And VB auxiliary Štěpán Ouhrabka said to us, "I should get out of here if I were you, lads, there'll be even worse yet."'

Miloš Hujer: 'Before midnight, a few plain-clothes men rushed out of the cinema, thugs the lot of them, and began to let fly left right and centre with their fists. There was no resistance at all on our part, it was terrible. And after they'd finished, they must have felt they'd gone too far, because Captain Láska came up to us, to me and Honza Chlumů, who's lying in hospital, and what he said was this: "We're just security men; be grateful you got into our hands, if you'd got into *their* hands" – he meant the Russians – "you would have come off much worse." When I retorted that the Russians had protected Hádek, they didn't say a thing.'

That night, though, Mr Hádek described his experiences to me, which are so terrible that they can hardly be put into words. He telephoned from the hospital while I was writing this to tell me that I shouldn't write about his battle with the VB so as not to jeopardize an objective investigation. And so I'll take up the story only at the point where it's practically over, due to a peculiar turn of events.

'When I came to, I was in great pain, because some big man was dragging me to the stairs by my hair. They dragged me upstairs into the hall, which they threw me into saying things like "Here's the chief counter-revolutionary!" The cinema manager, Mr Doubek, shouted out, "Beat him up, kill him!" He even mauled me himself, but while he was shouting a smaller man hit me on the nose; he had a camera round his neck in a case. One of them pulled my hair and somebody else shouted, "Pull out his hair!" Then somebody shouted in Russian: "Nyebyitye yevo, pizdy!" And the Russians made a circle round me, so that nobody could touch me any more.'

When he had finished this description he asked me, 'Can you translate exactly what "pizda" is?' I translated it for him, more or less accurately.

I had gone to Semily to have a look at what circumstances and the mood there were like, not knowing of course what was going on. But I don't know if I would be able to identify so many of the different aspects and moods there if this brawl hadn't taken place. After all, even the people of Semily themselves probably wouldn't have known what sort of mood they were in without it. Now they know more about themselves. All the important factories and organizations protested in an exemplary fashion about what went on. Most people are of the opinion that it was caused by an over-reaction to pent-up emotions on the part of the authorities, who last year had to like the 'Spring' with all its bungling and confused Semily meetings. The view is taken – and the District Committee of the National Front thinks so too – that responsibility for the choice of the time and place for the friendship meeting lay with the Czechoslovak-Soviet Friendship Society, and the hope is expressed that in future none of the members of the National Front will be so extremely obstinate. This is the opportunity for more members of the public to become aware of the fact that as long as the Soviet soldiers are here somebody will also have to have dealings with them, particularly when an explicit condition of their withdrawal is the stipulation that these dealings must be friendly. But let's take into account not only what *has* to be done, but also the fact that there are people who are convinced that it *should* be. Have they the right to their convictions? Yes, just like anybody else. And what about the police? Both sides should take care to observe the regulations. The public, apart from the usual protests via the official channels, also chose methods prompted by sheer ingenuity. Some organizations transferred their dance, which had been planned for the cinema, to somewhere else: the football players of Semily Sparks said that they would not play while Mr Doubek, the cinema manager, was on the team's committee, and so he resigned, expressing the hope that he might perhaps still be allowed to watch the football . . .

I should have to be very concerned if the relevant investigating and prosecuting apparatus was really so crude and corrupt as to thrust onto the table of its chief in Prague a note saying that in Semily it was all stage-managed by . . . a certain comrade, and so I'll leave aside my personal anxiety on this matter. I shall however relieve myself of a somewhat more general worry of mine: what is the real importance, the meaning or even the specific intention of the happenings which I've just described? Did things just get out of hand here or was it a deliberate attempt to precipitate us on the road leading to the terror of the Black Hundreds? There are several of us asking this question, when we abandon our somewhat Springy ideas about democracy and socialism, and when we want to support the government with its programme of economic revival and its guarantees of civil rights, on the condition that it shows a firm hand when it is dealing with people other than ourselves.

I spoke to a group of employees and officials from the Technometra factory. They wanted to know whether Hádek's methods weren't harming the positions of those progressive people who have different and more mature ideas about how to make their views felt more effectively. Briefly what they said was this: 'Whatever Hádek may really be like, they've made a hero out of him.' But the trouble is that the incident diverts attention for a time from the political and economic problems, which need to be solved if things are going to improve. Whoever chose such a method of suppressing a demonstration was acting against the decision to ask the people to work and to be orderly and calm. The disturbing things for them, in their position, they say, are, for instance, the fact that Comrade Beneš continues to be chairman of the District Committee of the Communist Party, the way that primary organization number one behaves, and also such speeches as the one made by Vilém Nový on television. Before the public feels secure and legally protected again, the incident must be investigated quite objectively, and the necessary measures taken against those who behaved in such a brutal way . . . What is interesting and makes you respect them, is the fact that people in Semily don't see all VB members as flowers from the same garden. They do distinguish between good and bad and would be capable of appreciating it if the Minister of the Interior sanctioned the sacking of the worst and in that way showed a bit of discreet favouritism to his town, a weakness for which we would surely be able to excuse him.

A year ago it was just the Youth Club which was in the limelight, and now there are a whole mass of people in the game. They operate more obscurely, but theirs is a more serious game. If only the young people would also realize that this change has come about, and channel their sheer obstinacy into more subtle channels, so that the thug with the truncheon would only be able to stand helplessly. Today each event poses a new question. Whoever finds a suitable answer first will be successful. In Semily's Papcel factory, the Trade Union committee asked the Director to explain his part in that 'evening of friendship'. He explained it something like this: he wanted to encourage the influence of moderation in case the 'friendship' was to become an extremist action of the well-known variety. The committee didn't accept his explanation, and I heard the report about this – which was communicated to me with great pleasure – in two minds. Should a director have to answer to people for where he goes? There are two answers to this, according to how we interpret the present moment. Are they revolutionary times? Or are they times of stabilization, and if so, whose stabilization? Do the workers feel that their director is taking opportunities to work against them? Would they have dared to question him if several people – including three who had to stay in hospital – hadn't been beaten up that evening? I think if the result of it all is that certain VB and STB members were apparently justified in treating the demonstrators as they did, then the Trade Union committee is quite right to make such demands. Force against force. But if the police are punished because they shouldn't have behaved in that way, then it seems to me the Director had every right to fraternize with whoever he chooses, the same as we ourselves have. There are laws in force, and they give us all equal opportunities. And so the local Military Prosecutor's Office will tell us what kind of times these are we are living in . . .

People are demanding an objective investigation into the incident. But a mere report should be objective as well, even though it is written with a purpose. I am trying to be objective by not hiding the inconsistencies of the affair from myself, and the intention lies in the fact that I clearly sympathize with the revival process in

Semily. But objectivity is not easily achieved. I've hardly managed to speak to anyone who belongs to the 'opposition' in Semily. Two old people, communists and members of the Czechoslovak–Soviet Friendship Society, granted me an interview, but at the end they said they didn't want me to use it and that I shouldn't mention their names. Major Špáta, the district VB chief, would also only speak to me on the condition that I treated it as confidential information, because the only person qualified to make announcements is – so he said – the press spokesman of the Ministry of the Interior.

I thought it would be interesting and perhaps appropriate if I was to make myself known to Comrade Stínilová, since I hadn't introduced myself to her at the entrance to the cinema. Although she respected open enemies – as she put it – she couldn't see any point in our talking, and that's why our conversation lasted only the few minutes it took to get from the Secretariat of the Czechoslovak–Soviet Friendship Society to her front door. But she asked me first who's flat I was just coming from: I answered her by asking her why she asked. She wanted to know why I had chosen Semily: I said it interested me as a type. I asked her if she thought I had had a share in the recent events: she replied that she hadn't said that. I asked her what she thought about them herself: she said that her view could not interest me because she had no official position in Semily. I objected that surely she was a member of the committee of the primary organization which had arranged that evening of 'friendship': she replied by asking me whether I had come to have her thrown out. I said that I had not. Then she said that she loved the Soviet Union, just as some people love West Germany, or America. I said I didn't love West Germany, or America, or the Soviet Union, because powers are powers, they don't inspire love. She had arrived home. We said good-bye.

But the Chairman of the local Council, Petr Putůrek, did receive me. I could no longer bear to have my image of him dependent on what Hádek had told me about him. I intended to take a tape-recorder to the interview, but then I decided against it. The Chairman started by asking me if I minded if he switched on his tape-recorder. So I helped him to switch it on, and I can quote almost word for word from the half-hour interview.

'How would you describe Hádek and the people of his kind?' I asked.

'As ultra right-wingers, to judge by the insults which were hurled at the participants of the friendship evening. Talk like that disrupts normalization and order.'

'Under pressure from the public you said in the summer that you would resign. After August you changed your mind. Has your attitude to the public therefore changed?'

'First about your article at the time. I don't consider it unobjective, as far as the description of the meeting is concerned, but of course it was a one-sided view. Just like today, you had the job of coming here and having the problems of Semily explained to you. When young Hádek began his hunger strike, the city committee of the National Front met and the comrades and friends put such pressure on me that I agreed to resign if it would be accepted by the plenum of the National Committee. On the 8th of August it met, with twenty-nine out of a total of forty-four deputies attending. Eighteen were for my resignation, but the majority needed is however twenty-three. At the next meeting on the 3rd of October, out of thirty deputies present there were only nine votes for my resignation.'

'You have publicly expressed the view that Semily was selected as the object of counter-revolutionary plans – in connection with the Two Thousand Words. I feel no need to contradict this – but I'd like to ask you why you think so.'

'The Two Thousand Words are at variance with our Party. In place of National Committees which are not fulfilling their functions, citizens' committees were to be elected. This was a challenge, an attempt to make changes.'

'This is the first time I've met with this particular misunderstanding of my text . . .' I said, and there followed a discussion in which the Chairman rejected my assertion that I hadn't written the Two Thousand Words as part of some plan, but purely as an individual. He said:

'I don't believe it, because people who'd signed the Two Thousand Words came out here. It so happens that Dr Teissig and Burian were here with me, and they have often been seen going to see the Hádeks . . .', to which I had no reply, because it was only later that I found out that these two names are not among the signatures and that not even the Hádeks know them.

'How can any view make itself heard,' I asked him, 'when the person who holds it isn't able to give voice to it?'

'But we aren't against different views. I'm all for socialist democracy. But as soon as someone attacks the Communist Party, its ideas or the Soviet Union, that's the end of democracy.'

'O.K. But part of the Action Programme was concerned with asserting the leading role of the Party in some other way than by using power. How would you assert it if moral authority – which is gained by putting policies into practice,' I added to make it clearer, '– and ideological leadership were not enough, and if – don't let's speak of the nation – if the inhabitants of a certain community aren't able to express their confidence in the communists?'

'Here I would make a distinction. If it was a case of one community, of one district, it would be because of our own mistakes that we had disqualified ourselves. But when it's a matter of the state, conflicts can arise and through the influence of the West, the Party and socialism can be threatened. And then an armed power has to come on the scene.'

But the so-called January policy, which everyone still identifies themselves with for fear of a complete collapse, invigorated the Communist Party and the nation precisely because it saw the necessity for the majority of people, as individuals, to agree voluntarily with socialism, thereby winning a reprieve for it and returning to it its human face. Those of you, comrades, who don't recognize this, but instead carry a truncheon under your coat, don't go on saying the word post-January, but without any more ado, just give orders for that month to be called by some foreign word.